A New
History of India
for Children

Books by Rudrangshu Mukherjee

Awadh in Revolt, 1857–58: A Study of Popular Resistance (1984)
The Penguin Gandhi Reader [editor] (1993)
Trade and Politics in the Indian Ocean World: Essays in Honour of Ashin Das Gupta [co-editor] (1997)
Spectre of Violence: The 1857 Kanpur Massacres (1998)
The Art of Bengal, 1955–75: A Vision Defined [editor] (2002)
Mangal Pandey: Brave Martyr or Accidental Hero? (2005)
India: Then and Now [co-author] (2005)
Great Speeches of Modern India [editor] (2007)
Dateline 1857: Revolt Against the Raj (2008)
A Century of Trust: A Centenary History of Tata Steel (2008)
New Delhi: The Making of a Capital [co-author] (2009)
Indian Persuasions: Fifty Years of Seminar, Selected Writings [editor] (2009)
Remembered Childhood: Essays in Honour of Andre Beteille [co-editor] (2009)
The Year of Blood: Essays on the Revolt of 1857 (2014)
Nehru & Bose: Parallel Lives (2014)
Twilight Falls on Liberalism (2018)
Collected Writings of Manmohan Singh [editor of Vol. 5] (2018)
Jawaharlal Nehru: A Short Introduction (2019)
A Begum and a Rani: Hazrat Mahal and Lakshmibai in 1857 (2021)
Tagore & Gandhi: Walking Alone, Walking Together (2021)
The Best of Tagore [editor] (2023)

Books by Shobita Punja

An Illustrated Guide to Museums of India (1990)
Divine Ecstasy: The Story of Khajuraho (1992)
Khajuraho: The First Thousand Years (1992)
Great Monuments of India, Bhutan, Nepal, Pakistan and Shri Lanka (1994)
Listen to the Animals: Famous Animals [co-author] (1994)
Stories about This and That (1994)
Great Monuments of the Indian Subcontinent (1995)
Khajuraho: An Introduction to the Erotic Temples (1995)
Daughters of the Ocean: Discovering the Goddess Within (1996)
This Is India (1996)
Banaras: Our World in Colour (2000)

Books by Toby Sinclair

India: Continent of Contrasts (1991)
Fur Trade in Kathmandu: Implications for India [co-author] (1992)
Odyssey Guide to India (1998)
For the Leopard: A Tribute to Sri Lanka's Leopard [contributing editor] (2003)

A New History of India for Children

FROM ITS ORIGINS TO THE
TWENTY-FIRST CENTURY

∽

RUDRANGSHU MUKHERJEE
SHOBITA PUNJA
TOBY SINCLAIR

ALEPH

ALEPH BOOK COMPANY
An independent publishing firm
promoted by *Rupa Publications India*

First published in India in 2025
by Aleph Book Company
7/16 Ansari Road, Daryaganj
New Delhi 110 002

Copyright © Rudrangshu Mukherjee, Samiha Mishra, and Toby Sinclair 2025

The Acknowledgements on pp. 291 constitute an extension of the copyright page.

All rights reserved.

The authors have asserted their moral rights.

The views and opinions expressed in this book are those of the authors and the facts are as reported by them, which have been verified to the extent possible, and the publisher is not in any way liable for the same. The publisher has used its best endeavours to ensure that URLs for external websites referred to in this book are correct and active at the time of going to press. However, the publisher has no responsibility for the websites and can make no guarantee that a site will remain live or that the content is or will remain appropriate.

No part of this publication may be reproduced, transmitted, or stored in a retrieval system, in any form or by any means, without permission in writing from Aleph Book Company.

ISBN: 978-81-969061-2-2

1 3 5 7 9 10 8 6 4 2

Printed in India.

This book is sold subject to the condition that it shall not, by way of trade or otherwise, be lent, resold, hired out, or otherwise circulated without the publisher's prior consent in any form of binding or cover other than that in which it is published.

Where the mind is without fear and the head is held high;
Where knowledge is free;
Where the world has not been broken up into fragments
by narrow domestic walls;
Where words come out from the depth of truth;
Where tireless striving stretches its arms towards perfection;
Where the clear stream of reason has not lost its way into
the dreary desert sand of dead habit;
Where the mind is led forward by thee into ever-widening
thought and action—
Into that heaven of freedom, my Father, let my country awake.

—Rabindranath Tagore, *Gitanjali*, 1910

Ammonite fossils, the Himalaya

CONTENTS

Authors' Note		ix
Timeline		xi
Chapter 1:	Making of the Indian Landscape	1
Chapter 2:	Human Beginnings	14
Chapter 3:	Harappan Culture	25
Chapter 4:	Society and Ideas in the Age of the Vedas	43
Chapter 5:	Before Empires and the Age of Mahavira and the Buddha	49
Chapter 6:	The First Empire and Ashoka	65
Chapter 7:	Between Empires	79
Chapter 8:	The Gupta Age and Beyond	89
Chapter 9:	The Delhi Sultanate	113
Chapter 10:	Regional Kingdoms	128
Chapter 11:	The Great Mughals	142
Chapter 12:	Influence of Islam	158
Chapter 13:	Century of Transition	163
Chapter 14:	The Arrival of European Trading Companies and British Conquests	174
Chapter 15:	India and the World	186
Chapter 16:	The Northeast Up to the Coming of British Rule	197
Chapter 17:	Consolidation of British Rule	207
Chapter 18:	Indian Response and Resistance	217
Chapter 19:	Rise of Indian Nationalism	229
Chapter 20:	Independence and Partition	262
Chapter 21:	Independent India	273
Acknowledgements		291
Index		293

AUTHORS' NOTE

This book has origins in friendship. Shobita, Toby, and I have been friends for nearly fifty years. Another old friend, David Davidar, persuaded the three of us to write the book, *A New History of India* which was published in 2023. That book remains in print and if sales figures are any indication, it is being bought and read. While we were in the process of writing that book, Shobita and David in a separate conversation, agreed that the book could have a slightly different version for children to read and learn about the history and culture of India. Shobita, given her expertise, had agreed to prepare such a version. But she was overcome by illness and her tragic and untimely death robbed the book of her invaluable contribution. To honour her the two of us decided to recast the book for children. We are well aware that Shobita would have done it differently.

Shobita, this book is for you as much as it is for children whose company you enjoyed and to whose education you had a lifelong commitment.

As the previous paragraph indicates, this book is intended for children. We believe that it is necessary for children to know about India's past. This book presents India's past through words, images, and maps. We have attempted to present facts and our interpretation of them as lucidly as possible but that does not mean we have simplified and evaded the complex issues. There are aspects of the past that are unknown, unclear, complicated, and debatable. We want our young readers to be conscious of the issues to which there are no clear and definite answers. Most of all, we would like our readers to be excited and curious about India's past and to ask their own questions about India's past. Shobita wanted the learning of India's history and culture to be fun and attractive. We hope that this book meets both those aims.

RUDRANGSHU MUKHERJEE
TOBY SINCLAIR
22 March, 2025.

Timeline

- ABOUT 4.5 BILLION YEARS AGO: the Earth is formed. With a bedrock over 3.5 billion years old, India is one of the oldest land masses in the world.
- MORE THAN 2.5 BILLION YEARS AGO: geographical features, such as the Aravalli Range, Asia's oldest hill range, begin to take shape on what becomes the Indian land mass.
- 1 BILLION YEARS AGO: the great Vindhya Ranges, a collection of ranges that today run from east to west and separate the Gangetic plain from the Deccan in the south, slowly take form.
- ABOUT 400 MILLION YEARS AGO: a great variety of ammonites evolve and live in the open seas.
- ABOUT 280–230 MILLION YEARS AGO: India is part of the supercontinent Pangaea. As the great forests of Pangaea fell 250 million years ago and were covered by sediment, they were compacted to create vast coal deposits in the area of Bihar, Odisha, and West Bengal.
- ABOUT 220 MILLION YEARS AGO: insects arrive on the scene.
- APPROXIMATELY 210 MILLION YEARS AGO: the first dinosaurs appear in Pangaea and become the most dominant creatures on the planet.
- ABOUT 180 MILLION YEARS AGO: Australia, India, Africa, Antarctica, South America, and Arabia are all joined in a single land mass called Gondwanaland.
- AROUND 150 MILLION YEARS AGO: an island, the Indian Shield, consisting of the Indian subcontinent, together with the Seychelles and Madagascar, slowly begins to separate from the larger land mass of Gondwanaland.
- 90 MILLION YEARS AGO: India separates from Madagascar.
- 66 MILLION YEARS AGO: an enormous comet or asteroid hits the earth, triggering a major extinction event and coinciding with the creation of the Deccan Traps.
- AROUND 55–50 MILLION YEARS AGO: the collision between the Indian plate and Eurasian land mass begins. As the two crash into one another, the Indian plate buckles and is pushed beneath the Eurasian plate. The uplift creates the Himalaya, Karakoram, Hindu Kush, and other great mountain ranges, with deep valleys, gorges, jagged ridges, and mountain passes.
- 1.5 MILLION YEARS AGO: *Homo erectus* discovers fire. This discovery was momentous as its multiple uses had a lasting impact on human history.
- ABOUT 700,000 YEARS AGO: a group of *Homo erectus*, after spreading out from central and eastern Africa to the northern parts of the continent, reach across

Asia right up to Java, and later towards China, while another group go westward to Europe.

• APPROXIMATELY 300,000 YEARS AGO: *Homo sapiens* evolve and later learn to alter their food, behaviour, and needs to the changing environment in the new areas that they explore.

• 70,000 YEARS AGO: *Homo sapiens* migrate from Africa to present-day Yemen before pushing further to reach the Indian subcontinent approximately 65,000 years ago. These migrants from Africa are identified as the First Indians.

• APPROXIMATELY 12,000 YEARS AGO: the last Ice Age begins to recede (it peaked c. 21,000 years ago). The region from the Indus to east of Bengal is wetter and more forested, and is home to rhinoceros and elephants. Tigers probably enter the plains from the east about the same time and spread south across the peninsula.

• 7000 BCE: agriculture emerges in South Asia; the earliest evidence comes from Mehrgarh in Baluchistan.

• c. 4500 BCE: there is great development of multiple human skills including the herding and domestication of animals. Initially goats and sheep are domesticated, and later cattle for milk and other related products around 2500 BCE.

• c. 3000–2500 BCE: the wheel becomes a part of daily life, though it was likely invented earlier.

• 3000–1000 BCE: humans inhabit what is now called the Burzahom site in Kashmir.

• LATE 3000–1750 BCE: the Harappan Civilization comes up and flourishes. Evidence of this was found during excavations in the early 1920s at Mohenjo-daro and Harappa.

• c. 1200–600 BCE: the Vedas are composed.

• c. 599 BCE: Mahavira, the twenty-fourth Tirthankara, is born.

• c. 560 BCE: Gautama Buddha is born as Siddhartha, the son of the chief of the Sakya clan.

• AROUND THE SIXTH CENTURY BCE: urban centres and trade develop; Brahmanical ideas of varna and jati take shape; Jainism and Buddhism emerge.

• SIXTH CENTURY BCE: the university at Taxila is established. It continues to function till the fifth century CE.

• c. 324 BCE: Chandragupta Maurya establishes the Maurya dynasty, which rules large parts of India until 187 BCE.

• c. 272/3 BCE: Ashoka ascends the Mauryan throne.

• c. 260 BCE: Ashoka converts to Buddhism after the bloody conquest of Kalinga.

• 230 BCE: the rule of Simuka, the first of the Satavahanas, begins; the Deccan is ruled by the Satavahanas for nearly 450 years from c. 250 BCE.

• THIRD TO SECOND CENTURY BCE: the Shungas usurp the Mauryan throne, but rule for only about 100 years before they are overthrown by the Kanvas.

• SECOND CENTURY BCE: Ajanta, a horseshoe-shaped cliff (carved out by the Wagora River over millennia) is chosen as the location for a large Buddhist establishment. Buddhist monks work for centuries (until the fifth century CE) at this peaceful site to create chaityas (prayer halls) and viharas (monasteries).

• FIRST CENTURY CE: the foundations of the Kushana empire are laid; the empire reaches its peak under Kanishka who becomes the ruler in 78 CE.

• FIRST CENTURY CE: overseas trade with Southeast Asia increases and a variety of goods from India are exported to that region. Trade with Europe via the Middle East brings Jews and Christians to India's shores. These small trading groups settle in Kerala and Tamil Nadu around this time.

• 52: Saint Thomas, one of the twelve apostles of Jesus Christ, is believed to have arrived in India to spread the Christian faith. He was martyred in 72 CE and buried in Chennai.

• THIRD CENTURY: the Pallava dynasty takes over the deltas of the Krishna and the Godavari rivers.

• AROUND 320: a new centralizing political power emerges. This is the beginning of the Gupta empire, which would decline towards the end of the fifth century CE, in part due to the invasions of the Huns.

• AROUND 544: the Chalukyas come to power in the Deccan. For the next thirty years, the Chalukyas of Badami, the Pallavas of Kanchipuram, and the Pandyas of Madurai remain in conflict over the control of the fertile plains.

• AROUND 499: Ujjain emerges as a centre for the study of astronomy; Aryabhata is the best-known astronomer and mathematician of the age.

• FIFTH TO THE EARLY SEVENTH CENTURY: four kingdoms rule over different parts of North India after the decline of the Gupta empire. Magadha is ruled by a dynasty called the Guptas, not to be linked to the Guptas of the Gupta empire. Kannauj is ruled by the Maukharis, Thanesar (north of Delhi) by the Pushyabhutis, and Valabhi (in Saurashtra) by the Maitrakas.

• SIXTH CENTURY: Ellora in Maharashtra is first carved. A World Heritage Site today, it consists of over thirty-four rock-cut shrines—twelve shrines of the Buddhist Mahayana sect in the south (sixth to eighth centuries CE), seventeen Hindu shrines to the north (sixth to ninth centuries CE), and five Jain shrines (ninth century CE).

• EARLY EIGHTH CENTURY: after an invasion of Arab armies into Persia, there is a migration of Zoroastrians to India. Using their trading contacts with western India, many of them settle to the north of Mumbai and Gujarat.

- NINTH CENTURY: the Pallavas are unable to successfully resist attacks from the Pandyas and their tributaries, the Cholas, who rule the territory south of the Pallava realm. At the end of the first millennium CE, the pre-eminent political presence in South India, especially in Tamil Nadu, is the Chola dynasty.
- AROUND 1000: Mahmud of Ghazni invades northern India.
- TWELFTH CENTURY: Muhammad Ghuri begins raiding Northwest India; he is murdered in 1206. His successors gain ascendancy under Iltutmish (r. 1210–36).
- 1204: Bakhtiyar Khalji, a chieftain under Muhammad Ghuri, invades Bengal. Deltaic Bengal had been ruled by the Pala dynasty (c. 750–1161), the Chandras (c. 825–1035), and the Senas (c. 1097–1223) before this.
- c.1192–1210: Qutb-ud-din Aibak, the first sultan of Delhi, sets about constructing the first stone mosque for prayer in Delhi called Quwwat ul-Islam (Might of Islam). In 1296, Ala-ud-din Khalji would seek to enlarge the Qutb complex and add the domed gateway entrance, Alai Darwaza.
- EARLY THIRTEENTH CENTURY: Kamrup, stretching from the eastern points of the Brahmaputra valley to the river Karatoya, sees the arrival of Turko-Afghans from Bengal. Until the arrival of the British, the Northeast did not have any centralized ruling structure.
- 1320: Khalji's senior lieutenant, Ghazi Malik, names himself Sultan Ghiyas-ud-din Tughluq; Bengal is brought under Delhi's control; the Tughluq dynasty reigns over the Delhi Sultanate until 1413.
- 1338: Shams al-din Ilyas Shah seizes power in Bengal and declares himself independent of the Delhi Sultanate.
- 1340s: the Sangamas rise as the reigning power in Karnataka.
- 1469: Guru Nanak, the founder of Sikhism, and the first of the ten Sikh Gurus, is born.
- 1490s: the Portuguese are the first Europeans to arrive in India, docking in Malabar. Their success in maritime trade would bring the Dutch, the English, and the French to the Indian Ocean.
- 1509: Krishna Deva Raya comes to power and his domination of the Deccan begins.
- 1510: one of the earliest of Portuguese bases is secured by the capture of Goa from the sultan of Bijapur, Ismail Adil Shah, by Afonso de Albuquerque.
- 1525: Babur, the first of the Mughals, wins a decisive battle at Panipat and marches to Delhi to establish his empire.
- 1537: Humayun, Babur's successor, has to live in exile after a defeat at the hands of Sher Shah Sur. Humayun would return fifteen years later to stake his claim.
- 1556: Akbar ascends the throne; the Second Battle of Panipat paves the way for

consolidation of Mughal rule in the Gangetic plain.
- 1600: the English East India Company is formed.
- 1605: Akbar is followed by his son, Jahangir (r. 1605–27), who is followed by Shah Jahan (r. 1628–58) who is credited with the building of the Taj Mahal from 1632 to 1658.
- 1613: Emperor Jahangir allows the English East India Company to establish their first trading post at Surat.
- 1658: Aurangzeb ascends the throne through a bloody war of succession in which he imprisons his father and kills his eldest brother and heir apparent, Dara Shukoh.
- 1664: the French establish the Compagnie Française des Indes Orientales and become a late entrant into the Indian maritime trade. They would set up a major trading settlement in Pondicherry in 1674.
- 1674: the leader of the Marathas, Shivaji, declares his independence from the Mughals and proclaims himself king; he dies six years later.
- LATE SEVENTEENTH TO EIGHTEENTH CENTURY: Delhi and its environs witness a series of peasant revolts.
- 1707: Aurangzeb dies. At this point, the Mughal empire has reached its largest geographical extent.
- 1713: Bengal under Murshid Quli Khan becomes one of the first of the Mughal subahs (provinces) to declare its independence.
- 1756: aggrieved by the East India Company's refusal to pay the nawab his legitimate dues since 1717, Siraj-ud-daulah sacks Calcutta.
- 23 JUNE 1757: Siraj-ud-daulah is defeated in the Battle of Plassey; Mir Jafar is installed as nawab in his place. The British conquest and rule of Bengal after 1757 (Battle of Plassey) and 1765 (Battle of Baksar) would make the East India Company (EIC) the de facto government. It later comes into direct contact with the kingdoms of Manipur, Jaintia, Cachar, and Assam as well as with those tribes who live in the neighbouring hills.
- 1761: Haider Ali takes control of Mysore through a coup.
- 1764: the Company defeats Mir Qasim in the Battle of Baksar.
- 1767: the First Anglo-Mysore War begins. It lasts for two years before a treaty is signed.
- 1770: the EIC's uncontrolled increase in demands for land revenue leads to a devastating famine in Bengal. This eventually leads to the British government intervening in the EIC's handling of its Indian territories.
- 1782: Tipu Sultan ascends the throne of Mysore; his power in South India grows.
- 1799: Tipu Sultan dies defending his capital during the Fourth Anglo-Mysore War.

- 1818: the British defeat Holkar in battle putting an end to Maratha power.
- 1828: Lord William Bentinck arrives in Calcutta as the new governor general of India.
- 1829: the practice of sati is abolished.
- 1839: Ranjit Singh, the ruler of the Sikh empire, dies. With his death the politics of the Punjab are completely altered, ultimately leading to the British occupation of the region.
- 1855: the Hindu Widow Remarriage Act is passed.
- 1857: a series of sepoy mutinies occur in quick succession. This triggers a popular and general uprising across North India.
- NINETEENTH CENTURY: in the second half of the century in western India, Jotirao Phule writes and campaigns for the lower castes against the dominance of the Brahmins and the discrimination practised by them. He and his wife, Savitribai, also become pioneers in the sphere of education for women.
- 1885: after a period of nationalistic fervour among India's Western-educated intelligentsia, the Indian National Congress is formed.
- EARLY TWENTIETH CENTURY: in South India under the Justice Party anti-Brahmanical views are expressed in the public arena.
- 1904: the British announce the partition of Bengal. They are faced with widespread protests; the Swadeshi Movement begins.
- DECEMBER 1906: the Indian Muslim League meets for the first time in Dacca.
- NOVEMBER 1909: Gandhi writes the *Hind Swaraj* while travelling from London to South Africa by ship; it is published in December the same year.
- 1911: the British shift their capital from Calcutta to Delhi; British architects Edwin Lutyens and Herbert Baker are brought in to build the capital of the British empire in India.
- 1913: Rabindranath Tagore wins the Nobel Prize for Literature for his collection of poems, *Gitanjali*, published in London in 1912. He is the first Indian (and Asian) to win the prize.
- FEBRUARY 1919: the Rowlatt Act comes into effect; Gandhi gives a call for an India-wide hartal on 6 April to inaugurate the satyagraha against the Act.
- 8 APRIL 1919: Gandhi is stopped on his way to Punjab leading to protests and, sometimes, violence across the country.
- 13 APRIL 1919: Brigadier-General Reginald Dyer orders troops to shoot unarmed civilians in Jallianwala Bagh, killing many.
- 1920: the non-violent Non-cooperation Movement is launched.
- 1929: in the Congress session held at the end of the year, it is resolved that

Purna Swaraj (complete independence) would be the aim of the Congress.
- 1930: Gandhi launches the Civil Disobedience Movement by manufacturing salt; the Dandi March lasts from 12 March to 6 April.
- 18 APRIL 1930: in Chittagong, under the leadership of Surya Sen, a group of armed revolutionaries take over the local arsenal and issue an Independence Proclamation in the name of the Indian Republican Army.
- 1932: Prime Minister Ramsay MacDonald announces the creation of reserved constituencies for the untouchables. This leads to a stand-off between Ambedkar and Gandhi. To protest against the government's decision, Gandhi begins a 'fast unto death' on 20 September.
- 1930s: Subhas Chandra Bose is outmanoeuvred in the Congress party and resigns. He forms his own party, the Forward Bloc.
- MARCH 1940: the demand for Pakistan as a separate country for Muslims becomes the most important demand of the League, as put forth in the Lahore session of the party presided over by Mohammad Ali Jinnah.
- 1942: the Quit India Movement begins with hartals, strikes, and clashes with the police in Bombay, Delhi, Calcutta, and Patna.
- 1944: with Singapore as his headquarters, Bose forms the Indian National Army (INA) which joins the Japanese forces in attacking Imphal in the summer of 1944.
- APRIL 1944: British and Indian forces stop Japanese troops from entering India from Burma during World War II.
- 1945: the British government decides to hold public trials for the INA prisoners leading to massive protests in Calcutta over 21 and 22 November.
- 1946: Ambedkar becomes the chairman of the committee that would draft the Constitution of India.
- FEBRUARY 1946: Calcutta witnesses another upheaval against the seven years' rigorous imprisonment sentence given to Abdul Rashid of the INA.
- 18 FEBRUARY 1946: low-ranking sailors of the Royal Indian Navy, on the signals training ship *Talwar*, go on hunger strike against bad food and racial insults. The strikes spread on shore and to twenty-two ships moored in the Bombay harbour.
- 16 AUGUST 1946: communal riots break out in Calcutta with Jinnah's call for Direct Action for Pakistan. Communal violence would continue to spread through the country until Partition.
- SEPTEMBER 1946: the Tebhaga Movement, a peasant revolt, begins in Bengal.
- 1946: the new prime minister, Clement Attlee of the Labour Party, announces that Britain would pull out of India by June 1948.
- 18 JULY 1947: the India Independence Act is presented to and passed by the

British parliament and the Crown. It calls for the transfer of power to two central governments, India and Pakistan.

- AUGUST 1947: Sardar Vallabhbhai Patel begins lobbying the rulers of more than 560 princely states in the country to accede to the Indian republic. All but three of the states (Jammu and Kashmir, Junagadh, and Hyderabad) willingly merge into the Indian union by the time of Independence.
- 14 AUGUST 1947: Jawaharlal Nehru delivers his famous 'Tryst with Destiny' speech on the eve of Indian independence.
- 15 AUGUST 1947: India becomes free of British rule.
- 22 OCTOBER 1947: the First Kashmir War (Indo-Pakistani War of 1947–48) is fought over the princely state of Jammu and Kashmir, ruled by Maharaja Hari Singh. A formal ceasefire between the two nations would only be called in January 1949.
- 30 JANUARY 1948: Mahatma Gandhi is shot dead by Nathuram Godse in Birla House, New Delhi.
- 26 JANUARY 1950: the Constitution of India comes into force and India becomes a republic. The Constitution had been adopted by the Constituent Assembly on 26 November 1949.
- 25 OCTOBER 1951: the first general elections are held in India (they would end on 21 February 1952). The Indian National Congress comes to power in a landslide victory.
- 1962: a series of border skirmishes snowball into the Sino-Indian War.
- 1964: Jawaharlal Nehru dies; Lal Bahadur Shastri takes up the role of the country's prime minister.
- 1966: Indira Gandhi takes the reins of the country. She would stay in power for the next eleven years.
- 15 AUGUST 1969: the Indian Space Research Organisation (ISRO), the country's national space agency, is founded by Vikram Sarabhai.
- 1971: Indo-Pak War occurs in the midst of the Bangladesh Liberation War.
- 19 APRIL 1975: Aryabhata, India's first indigenous satellite built by ISRO, is launched into space by the Soviet Union as a part of the latter's Interkosmos programme.
- JUNE 1975: Indira Gandhi declares the Emergency; democracy is suspended in India.
- 1977: Indira Gandhi withdraws the Emergency and calls an election, which she loses, only to return to power in 1980.
- OCTOBER 1984: Indira Gandhi is assassinated by her Sikh bodyguards in retaliation for deploying the Indian Army in the Golden Temple complex. This unleashes a pogrom against the Sikh community in Delhi and its surrounding areas.

- 7 AUGUST 1990: Prime Minister V. P. Singh announces 27 per cent reservations for OBCs in central government services and public sector units, based on the recommendations of the Mandal Commission Report from 1980. This announcement leads to protest from thousands of upper-caste students, some of whom self-immolate. The recommendation for OBC reservations in central government institutions would finally be implemented in 1992; the education quota came into force in 2006.
- 21 MAY 1991: Rajiv Gandhi, Indira Gandhi's son and her successor as prime minister, is assassinated by Tamil militants.
- 24 JULY 1991: then finance minister Manmohan Singh, with the sanction of Prime Minister Narasimha Rao, presents a landmark budget in the Indian Parliament. This would mark the opening up of the Indian economy and usher in a period of liberalization.
- 6 DECEMBER 1992: the Babri Masjid in Ayodhya is demolished by Hindutva volunteers; Rao, as prime minister, takes no steps to prevent the demolition.
- 2 OCTOBER 1994: India rolls out the Pulse Polio Immunization Programme at a time when the country accounts for about 60 per cent of global polio cases. The country would receive the 'Polio-free certification' from WHO two decades later on 27 March 2014.
- 1998: Indian economist Amartya Sen wins the Nobel Prize in Economic Sciences, becoming the first Indian to win in this field.
- MAY 1998: India conducts a series of nuclear bomb test explosions (Pokhran-II tests). On 13 May, Prime Minister Atal Bihari Vajpayee announces India's status as a nuclear state at a press conference.
- MAY 1999: Pakistani soldiers and Kashmiri insurgents breach the Line of Control, leading to an armed conflict with the Indian Army and Air Force. This marks the start of the Kargil War.
- 13 DECEMBER 2001: armed gunmen attack the Indian Parliament. They are later discovered to have been members of the terrorist organizations Lashkar-e-Taiba and Jaish-e-Mohammed.
- FEBRUARY/MARCH 2002: in Godhra, a fire on a train returning from Ayodhya kills fifty-nine Hindu pilgrims and karsevaks. This becomes the trigger for the Gujarat riots wherein about 2,000 people, mostly Muslims, are killed.
- NOVEMBER 2003: Pakistan announces a ceasefire in Kashmir; India reciprocates.
- MAY 2004: Manmohan Singh becomes the prime minister of the country.
- OCTOBER 2008: following approval by the US Congress, President George W. Bush signs into law a nuclear deal with India (signed in 2006), which ends a three-decade ban on US nuclear trade with Delhi.

- NOVEMBER 2008: ten gunmen carry out a terrorist attack over the course of 26–29 November in Mumbai, taking hostages at Nariman House, Oberoi Trident, and Taj Mahal Palace & Tower. The Indian Army is called in to end the siege.
- 16 DECEMBER 2012: a twenty-three-year-old woman is raped on a moving bus by a group of men; she dies due to her injuries days later. Dubbed 'Nirbhaya', her assault galvanizes the country and leads to widespread protests. This would further lead to the creation of new anti-rape laws.
- 2014: Narendra Modi comes to power at the centre; he would return to power for a second term in 2019, and then a third in 2024.
- 18 SEPTEMBER 2016: Jaish-e-Mohammed terrorists attack an Indian Army brigade headquartered near the town of Uri; eleven days later the Indian Army would retaliate by conducting surgical strikes in Pakistan-administered Kashmir.
- 8 NOVEMBER 2016: the Government of India announces the demonetization of certain banknotes and the issuance of new ones. This has detrimental effects on the Indian economy due to, among other reasons, a shortage of cash.
- 6 SEPTEMBER 2018: a five-judge Bench of the Supreme Court partially strikes down Section 377 of the Indian Penal Code; this decriminalizes same-sex relations between consenting adults.
- 14 FEBRUARY 2019: a convoy of Indian security personnel on the Jammu–Srinagar National Highway is attacked by a vehicle-borne suicide bomber in the Pulwama district.
- SEPTEMBER 2019: the Central Vista Redevelopment Project is launched to revamp the Central Vista, New Delhi. The project involves the construction of a new parliament house and secretariat, in addition to major redevelopment of other areas.
- 5 AUGUST 2019: Article 370 of the Constitution, which grants special status to Jammu and Kashmir, is repealed by the Indian government. The provision, created in 1950, gave Jammu and Kashmir greater autonomy in comparison to other Indian states.
- 12 DECEMBER 2019: the Citizenship (Amendment) Act is enacted by the Government of India resulting in protests in certain regions.
- MARCH 2020: the Covid-19 pandemic results in the central government imposing harsh lockdown measures, with little notice or planning. This leads to 60 per cent of the migrant population fleeing cities to return to their home states, unsure of their income in the city.
- SEPTEMBER 2020: the Parliament of India passes three controversial farm acts. They are repealed in 2021 after year-long farmers' protests in Delhi and its surrounding areas, and other parts of the country.

- 27 JANUARY 2022: the union government hands over Air India to the Tata Group, which bids ₹18,000 crore for the airline. The airline was launched by J. R. D. Tata in 1932; Air India was nationalized in 1953.
- 25 JULY 2022: Droupadi Murmu becomes the fifteenth president of India. She is the first person from a tribal community and the second woman in the history of the country to hold this office.
- 15 AUGUST 2022: India celebrates seventy-five years of Independence.

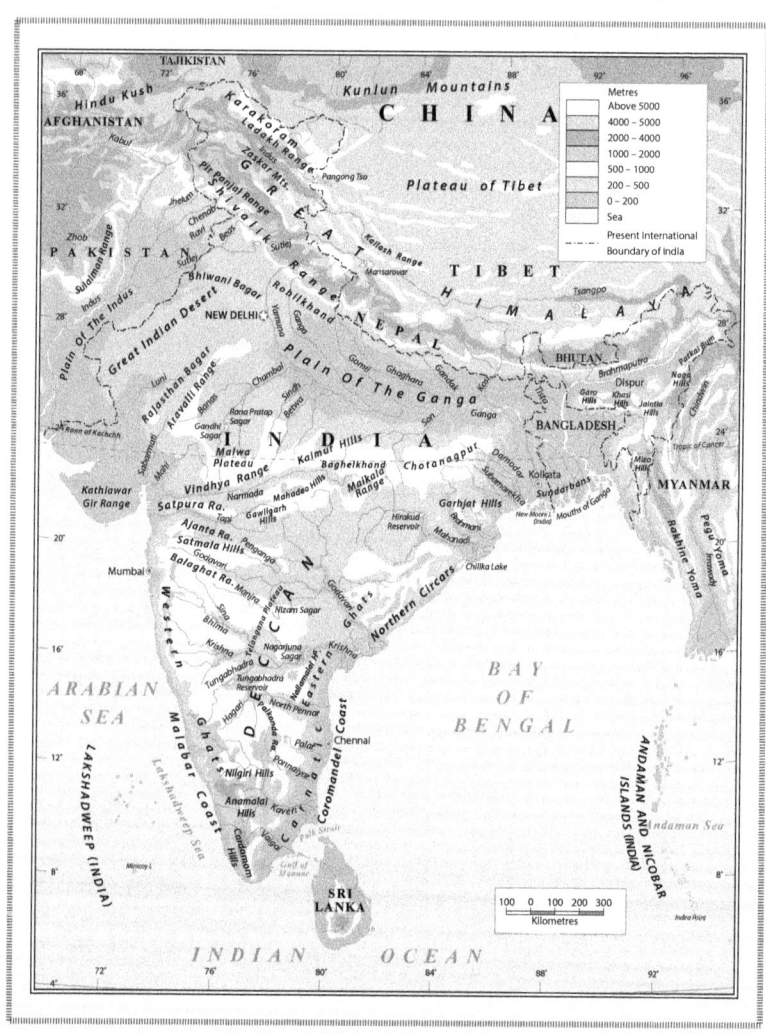

The physical geography of India

Not to scale. This map has been prepared in adherence to the 'Guidelines for acquiring and producing Geospatial Data and Geospatial Data Services including Maps' published vide DST F.No.SM/25/02/2020 (Part-I) dated 15th February, 2021.

· CHAPTER 1 ·

MAKING OF THE INDIAN LANDSCAPE

4.5 billion years ago—10 million years ago

The making of the Indian subcontinent took several billion years, and was punctuated by dramatic events. Some 4.5 billion years ago our planet consisted of a core of molten lava, wrapped inside successive layers of varying rock. On reaching the outer layer it formed a solid mantle with enormous continental plates that moved and floated imperceptibly. Above this mantle the continental and oceanic crust formed—on which all life now exists.

In geological terms, India formed a part of a succession of supercontinents. About 280–230 million years ago it was Pangaea, which later fragmented into plates of varying sizes and shapes that drifted across the earth's surface, forming the various continents that are known today. This phenomenon of the movement of continental plates is called plate tectonics.

By about 180 million years ago, Australia, India, Africa, Antarctica, South America, and Arabia were all joined in a single land mass called Gondwanaland.

On Gondwanaland, the portion of land that was to become India developed distinctive features. With a bedrock over 3.5 billion years old, India is one of the oldest land masses in the world. Bengaluru, the IT capital of India sits on this ancient rock known as the Dharwar Craton.

3.5 billion-year-old gneiss rock, Lalbagh, Bengaluru

The distinctive nature of this ancient rock lies in its strength and suitability for construction. However, ignorance of its ancient past, pressure on land, and development have begun to strip Bengaluru's landscape of this precious resource. The outcrop and hills of Bengaluru are protected by the Geological Survey of India (GSI) as valuable evidence of the antiquity of this land.

Another important feature of this land mass is the Aravalli Range, Asia's oldest hill range, estimated to be more than 2.5 billion years old. Wind and water have slowly eroded these mountains and worn them down to form rounded hills. More recently in geological time, the Aravallis played an important role in dividing the desert of western India from the northern plains. On the northernmost part of the Aravallis are the remains of over sixteen ancient cities of Delhi that were founded at this strategic location.

South of this region are the billion-year-old Vindhya Ranges, a collection of ranges that today run from east to west and separate the Gangetic basin from the Deccan in the south.

Marine fossils, Jaisalmer, Rajasthan

South of the Vindhya Ranges, there appears to have once been a seaway that separated part of Gondwanaland from the land that was to become peninsular India. Some 105 million years ago, the seaway began to disappear as the land moved slowly to fill the gap and fuse with the northern land mass. This sea supported rich marine life, evidence of which is seen today in the fossilized coral reefs on the banks of the Narmada River, the marine mammal fossils encountered in the rocks of Kutch, and the seashell fossils found in the yellow sandstone of the Thar Desert.

As the great forests of Pangaea fell 250 million years ago and were covered by sediment, they were compacted to create vast coal deposits in the area of Bihar, Odisha, and West Bengal. These form 98 per cent of India's coal reserves and provide over 60 per cent of India's energy needs today.

As the land came together and the seaway gradually disappeared, vast quantities of shell creatures from this seaway were crushed and pressed, forming layers of chalk powder that became limestone. In other areas, heat and pressure transformed chalk into solid marble stone to form the multicoloured marble cliffs on the Narmada River, at the very centre of India. Likewise, other deposits of chalk in Rajasthan metamorphosed to form extensive marble deposits in Makrana. It was this fine, high quality white marble from the quarries of Makrana that was used to build the Taj Mahal in Agra in the seventeenth century.

Where once the sea lay and disappeared, river valleys formed, causing the Godavari to move eastward towards the Bay of Bengal, and the Narmada and Tapti to flow in a westerly direction. All these features evolved over 2.5 billion years before the land that was to become India had even taken shape, as it was still a part of the larger land mass.

Around 150 million years ago, an island, the Indian Shield, consisting of the Indian subcontinent, together with the Seychelles and Madagascar, slowly began to separate from the larger land mass of Gondwanaland. As it divided, it left behind what was to become Africa, Antarctica, and Australia. India separated from Madagascar 90 million years ago. As the vast island moved northward, it embarked on one of the longest and fastest journeys undertaken by any land mass on this planet.

Many countries and communities have mythical stories about the origin of their land and people. In India, one myth refers to the 'island' or 'territory' of Jambudvipa floating on an immense ocean. There are paintings and references to this in several Indian literary sources describing India's origin.

The first dinosaurs appeared in Pangaea and became dominant creatures on the planet approximately 210 million years ago. As the supercontinent broke up, many species died out, but dinosaurs thrived and evolved into more species on land, in the sea, and in the air. Giant ferns and other plants grew, died, and were compacted into large deposits that are the fossil fuels exploited today. In 1981, a large hatchery of thirteen different dinosaur species was found at Balasinor in Gujarat and another bed of dinosaur eggs was unearthed near Jabalpur in central India.

Bees and other insects arrived about 220 million years ago and helped the spread of flowers which created a food source for new animals, including small tree- and ground-living mammals.

Sixty-six million years ago a huge comet or asteroid 10 kilometres across, hit the earth, triggering a major extinction. Out of this cataclysmic event only a few creatures survived, such as crocodiles, turtles, and many of the sea creatures. Small mammals that survived gradually evolved into a diverse range of creatures from the tiniest mammal—the pygmy shrew—to the blue whale that is the largest creature ever to live on the planet. Today there are more than 11,000 species of birds that are descendants of the dinosaurs; 1,300 species of birds are found across South Asia. Plants with seeds endured this event. Other species that survive from this period include many amphibians and insect species such as dragonflies that once shared the same landscape as the dinosaurs.

On its journey northward at about the same time as the asteroid hit, the island experienced massive volcanic activity that caused vast eruptions on the land and in the sea. These outflows left their mark, and created what is known as the Deccan Traps (from the Swedish word for 'steps'). This was one of the largest series of lava flows in the earth's history and successive outpourings created layer upon layer or steps of lava, totalling some 2 kilometres in depth. It probably took place over a relatively short period of 1.5 to 4 million years. The cooling and subsequent hardening of the lava flows created the 500,000 square kilometre region that includes the Western Ghats and extends across the Deccan Plateau, retaining its layered form created by the lava. The plateau is rich in mineral wealth and became a fertile agricultural region, still supporting millions of people in the states of Maharashtra, Andhra Pradesh, Telangana, Karnataka, and beyond.

At the same time that the island was moving northward, the northern and central portions of the Western Ghats also experienced severe volcanic disruptions. In contrast, the southern Western Ghats were free of this activity. It is said that the relative peace in this region offered refuge to many species.

As the Indian Shield continued drifting northward it encountered the Tethys Sea that existed between India and the Eurasian land mass. Around 55–50 million years ago, the collision between the Indian plate and Eurasian land mass began. As the two crashed into one another, the Indian plate buckled and was pushed beneath the Eurasian plate. The uplift created the Himalaya, the Karakoram, the Hindu Kush, and other great mountain ranges, with deep valleys, gorges, jagged ridges, and mountain passes.

Chandra River, Himachal Pradesh

This small but significant river flows from the snows of Lahaul in Himachal Pradesh, joins the Chenab River and ultimately merges with the Indus in Pakistan. The five rivers (Sutlej, Beas, Ravi, Chenab, and Jhelum) that flow into the Indus from the north give the region of the Punjab its name (paanch aab; five waters).

Today, the remains of the ancient seabed of the Tethys forms the sparsely populated southern edge of the Tibetan Plateau to the north of the Himalaya. In the high valleys of the Himalaya there is abundant evidence of ancient marine life. Vast quantities of sea creatures are found here. Fossil evidence of the ancient ocean is found in the Zabarwan Hills a few kilometres from Srinagar in Kashmir. In 1956, at the very summit of Mount Everest, a Swiss climber discovered the fossilized remains of a sea lily (crinoid).

Ammonite fossils, the Himalaya

Evidence of marine life from the Tethys Sea is found in fossils embedded in rocks and boulders. A great variety of ammonites evolved about 400 million years ago and lived prolifically in the open seas. They too were wiped out, along with the dinosaurs 66 million years ago. Ammonite fossils can be found in abundance on the banks of Himalayan rivers and in the sandstone of Kutch. The ammonite is considered sacred in India, as a representation of the chakra (disc) of Lord Vishnu, the preserver.

India is today a distinctive part of Asia in the northern hemisphere. The highest mountains in the world form its northern barrier and are shared between India's neighbours—Pakistan, Tibet, Nepal, and Bhutan. Common geographical features created over millions of years are also shared with Bangladesh and Sri Lanka. This story of the creation of the Indian landscape spanning 5 billion years had a significant impact on the climate and the cultural history of the subcontinent.

Enormous mountain ranges stretch from west to east and consist of different landscapes dictated by varying altitudes and rainfall. The lower regions of the Himalaya are well watered with forests and rich agricultural pockets in valleys and on terraced slopes, as found in

Himachal Pradesh, Uttarakhand, Sikkim, and Arunachal Pradesh. Higher regions, with a harsher climate, have a lower diversity of plant and animal species and fewer human settlements. The northern slopes of the Himalaya, the Trans-Himalayan region, have less precipitation making them less hospitable and yet having their own distinctive cultures—as found in Ladakh and northern Himachal Pradesh. The Himalaya have acted as a protective barrier throughout history. There are also a few mountain passes that have linked communities, resulting in cultural exchange and trade for more than 2,000 years. The Himalaya and Karakoram ranges are home to over 10,000 glaciers including the Siachen Glacier, which is one of the largest outside the polar regions. These are rapidly retreating due to the effects of climate change.

The Himalaya are bound on the west and east by two ancient rivers, the Sindhu (Indus) and Brahmaputra (Tsangpo) respectively. Other rivers are fed by melting snow and the monsoon rain.

The name 'India' is derived from the river Indus or Sindhu. The Arabic word 'Hindustan' and other words like 'Hindu' and 'Hinduism' are all associated with the name of this river.

The majority of rivers that feed into the Indus, Ganga, and Brahmaputra flow from sources within the Himalaya. Over many millions of years, these rivers have eroded the Himalaya, bringing vast amounts of rich alluvia into the plains, creating fertile soil that has supported human settlements for the last few millennia. In some parts of the Gangetic basin these deposits are over 2 kilometres deep.

Many of the oldest human habitations in the Indo-Gangetic Plain sustained early agricultural settlements of the Neolithic period and the urban Harappan Culture. Today the Ganga–Brahmaputra basin supports one-tenth of our planet's population. Along the Ganga are some of the most populated cities—Delhi, Kolkata, Kanpur, Lucknow, Patna, and Varanasi. A huge network of irrigation canals brings water to large agricultural areas. Unfortunately, run-off from the fields, waste from cities, and pollutants from industries are threatening both the life and sanctity of the rivers.

The Brahmaputra River, Assam

The source of this river is in south-west Tibet near the sacred Mount Kailash. The river is known as Yarlung Tsangpo here and flows east across southern Tibet and then cuts through the Himalaya in the world's deepest and one of the largest canyons, as it bends around Mount Namcha Barwa (7,782 metres), before entering Arunachal Pradesh and Assam where it becomes the Brahmaputra River.

After the last Ice Age ended about 11,550 years ago, the region from the Indus to the east of Bengal became wetter and forested, and was home to rhinoceros and elephants. Today rhinos are limited to small reserves in the Terai grasslands of the Himalayan foothills and in Assam. Elephants are more widespread. Some northern rivers still support small populations of blind river dolphins and the gharial, a fish-eating crocodilian, and are the winter home for millions of migratory birds from the steppes of Central Asia, Mongolia, and eastern China. Tigers likely entered the plains from the east about 20,000 years ago and spread south across the peninsula.

The Thar Desert is the eastern end of the arid band that stretches from Morocco on the Atlantic coast through Arabia and across the Indus. Nomadic communities, traders, and travellers with camel caravans followed ancient routes across the desert. The Silk Route that linked China to Europe with branches into western India brought trade in precious items of spices and gems, and the cultural exchange of ideas and inventions.

The semi-arid zone is a band that stretches from the foothills of the Himalaya to the Arabian Sea covering the states of Punjab, Haryana, Rajasthan east of the Aravallis, and most of Gujarat. This region receives little benefit from the monsoon rains and was originally grassland—with animals such as the antelope, gazelle, and the Asiatic lion. Today, much of this region is irrigated by canals and wells that serve to make it a rich agricultural region, with wheat, cotton, and groundnut cultivation.

Throughout history this region was also the gateway between West and Central Asia and the subcontinent, facilitating the movement of people and domestic livestock over thousands of years. Indian traders travelled through this semi-arid zone to West Asia carrying goods in both directions. And travellers brought and took Buddhism, Christianity, and Islam to new lands. This was also the cultural crossroads for the exchange of ideas between India and the Greek, Roman, and Persian worlds.

The Western and Eastern Ghats frame the Deccan Plateau and separate it from the sea. The Ghats leave a narrow coastal strip that runs along the coast of the Indian peninsula. The Western Ghats are recognized as an ecological 'hotspot', with some of the world's greatest diversities of amphibians, snakes, mammals, insects, and birds. Many of these species are found nowhere else on the planet. This sanctuary of many diverse species is being threatened by overexploitation and misguided development. The well-watered and moist landscape is an important source of spices, including indigenous pepper and cardamom that were prized in the ancient world and brought great wealth through trade to the subcontinent.

India's coastline from west to east covers 7,500 kilometres, with the Arabian Sea to the west, the Bay of Bengal to the east, and the Indian Ocean in the south. The seas are rich with sea life and provide an abundance of salt. Along this coast are an extraordinary array of both historical and contemporary ports: Dholavira, Lothal, and Surat

Jaisalmer Fort, Rajasthan

This fort was built by the Bhati Rajputs in 1156. Using the local yellow limestone they built palaces, homes, markets, and Hindu and Jain temples within the fort. An ancient water collection system sustained the occupants of the fort during wars, sieges, and drought.

in Gujarat; Mumbai, Mangaluru, and Kochi on the west coast; and Chennai, Visakhapatnam, and Kolkata on the east coast. Two strings of islands: the coral islands and atolls of Lakshadweep are off the Kerala coast to the west, while to the east are the Andaman and Nicobar Islands.

The Andaman and Nicobar Islands form a string of 572 islands to the east of the Bay of Bengal stretching north–south, from about 280 kilometres south of Myanmar to the northern tip of Sumatra. Only thirty-seven of these islands are inhabited. A few islands still have isolated and uncontacted peoples such as the Sentinelese. The original forest cover was predominantly rainforest with indigenous species and a mix of species from the Indian and Malayan regions. Fourteen of the 270 bird species recorded here are not found anywhere else in the world. There are also endemic amphibians and butterflies to be found here.

The coast and seas linked India to the world. Ancient trade routes connected the Red Sea, Arabia, and Africa to the west, and Southeast

Asia, the Spice Islands, and China to the east.

The Northeastern region is bounded by the eastern Himalaya to the north. This region is drained by the massive Brahmaputra River, which provides abundant water. To the east are hill ranges that form the Indo-Burmese border, while to the south are the vast, flat plains of Bangladesh and the Gangetic delta. The annual floods of the Brahmaputra and its tributaries create rich alluvial deposits that support rice-growing areas and, on the lower slopes, tea. The forests and grasslands of the Northeast region are home to the Indian rhinoceros, elephants, and several endemic species. The course of the Brahmaputra is dictated by hills. These isolated hill regions allowed independent communities and cultures to develop.

There are two monsoons: the southwesterly monsoon between May and September, and the northeasterly monsoon between October and January. In summer, intense heat on the plains of northern India and the Tibetan Plateau results in a low-pressure formation. This draws moisture from the cooler high-pressure formations over the Arabian Sea and the Indian Ocean. As these moist clouds move eastward across the sea and reach the barrier of the Western Ghats, the clouds rise and deposit heavy rain on the coastal area, nourishing the rich soil, deciduous forests, and abundant wildlife of the Western Ghats. As the winds continue across the Bay of Bengal they gather additional moisture and reach the eastern Himalaya, and deposit immense amounts of rain that feed the rivers, forests, and paddy fields of Northeast India. The wall created by the Himalaya forces the monsoon clouds to turn to the north-west, and travel over the Gangetic plain. The annual rainfall over the Gangetic plain supports the agriculture that feeds much of the country. By the time the monsoon clouds reach the semi-arid and desert regions of the Northwest, they are depleted and the rainfall is scanty.

The northeastern monsoon between late October and late December draws rain-bearing clouds that travel across the Bay of Bengal bringing rain to the south-east coast of India, to Tamil Nadu, and Andhra Pradesh. These regions are not adequately fed by the

Root Bridge near Cherrapunji, Meghalaya

Mawsynram and Cherrapunji in Meghalaya have been termed the wettest places on the planet. Here traditional building materials do not survive. The living root bridges of the Khasi and Jaintia hills of Meghalaya are made by binding and weaving the aerial roots of a fig tree (*Ficus elastica*). By using the aerial roots of a living tree, the root bridges span a stream or small river, continuing to strengthen each season, and can last for up to 200 years.

southwesterly monsoon.

The monsoons that have watered the subcontinent for millennia are changing in both intensity and predictability, with potentially alarming outcomes for agriculture and thousands of communities of the subcontinent.

The monsoon has also played an important role in trade and the exchange of ideas for many thousands of years, as the monsoon winds helped to push ships across the Arabian Sea from Africa, bringing traders, invaders, pirates, and some settlers who made India their home. These sea trade routes linked India to markets both in the West and the East.

The making of the Indian landscape, its geological diversity that supports varied flora and fauna, enabled the growth of many unique cultures, languages, and identities with their many histories.

· CHAPTER 2 ·

HUMAN BEGINNINGS

700,000 years ago–c. fifth millennium BCE

Research suggests that the hominid or near human-like species originated in Africa and one branch evolved into the species termed *Homo erectus*, which had the ability to stand upright on two feet and walk, leaving the arms and hands free to find fruits, plants, and animals to subsist on. *Homo erectus* gradually began to live in small, interdependent communities, enabling them to exploit better food supplies and protect each other from harsh conditions and predators. Their exploration for food and safer environments over the next million years took them out of Africa. Scholars suggest that these groups of people first spread out from central and eastern Africa to the northern parts of the continent, then about 700,000 years ago they reached across Asia right up to Java, and later towards China, while another group went northward to Europe. The flexible behaviour of the human species enabled *Homo erectus* to adjust to different, often extreme, climates and environments.

It was approximately 300,000 years ago that *Homo sapiens* (Latin for 'thinking man') began to prosper, learning to alter their food, behaviour, and needs to the changing environment in the new areas that they explored. When *Homo sapiens* entered the subcontinent, they shared the landscape with other wild animals in the region including at least two species of elephants and wild horses that went extinct about 30,000–15,000 years ago. With improvements in the flexibility and agility of hand movements and body, and enhanced development of their brains, *Homo sapiens* acquired the capability of imagination and creativity, curiosity, and inventiveness that distinguished them from all other species.

Evidence from bone remains suggests that *Homo erectus*, *Homo sapiens*, and other hominid species evolved simultaneously in different regions of the world. This was an uneven and parallel process. The discovery of fire by *Homo erectus* 1.5 million years ago by accident and then controlled by intent was momentous as its multiple uses had a lasting impact on human history. In India, too, evidence of the early stages of the evolution of human beings is still being explored. Today, genetic sciences are trying to piece together the story of human development to explain where local populations came from and their relationship with others across the planet.

The study of this early period is called 'prehistory' because it is about a time before there were written records or scripts. Any account of the prehistoric lives of early human communities is reconstructed from excavations and archaeological finds of tools, the remains of homes and settlements, together with associated zoological, botanical, and environmental evidence. This scanty information from some parts of the subcontinent provides an uneven record. The evidence is still so sparse that it will be a while before it is possible to stitch together an overall picture of the relationships between humans and their spread across the subcontinent.

Prehistory is divided into several interrelated stages of human development. The Stone Age (when humans used only stone or bone tools) consists of the Palaeolithic (2,000,000 to 10,000 years ago), and the Mesolithic and Neolithic (covering the time from 10,000 to 5,000 years ago); in some places there are also Megalithic sites (5,000 to 3,000 years ago). These were followed by the Chalcolithic era (4,000 to 2,700 years ago), when copper implements were introduced. The dating varies between different sites in the country. It is over this enormous span of time that early human beings made extraordinary advancements, inventions, and ultimately modes of communication and languages that would shape human history.

From studying the remains of settlements of the Palaeolithic era, it is thought that humans lived only in small groups and survived on fruit and edible plants gathered from their surroundings and hunted animals to supplement their diet. Their tools were rocks used as hammers and hand-axes, and roughly cut pebbles fashioned for hunting and food preparation. These early people had a nomadic lifestyle. Most Palaeolithic sites in India would have been at the fringes of forests and jungles where there were better food supplies and sources of water from streams. Across India, several sites have been excavated in the Shivalik and Vindhya ranges, and at several places in Rajasthan, Gujarat, the Delhi Ridge, and around the Narmada and Son rivers, and Hunasagi in northern Karnataka.

Bhimbetka, in Madhya Pradesh, has been studied in detail for more than sixty years and provides a glimpse into the Palaeolithic and Mesolithic periods of human history. At Bhimbetka, the larger stone tools with crude chippings of quartzite rock belong to Palaeolithic times. The finer stone-cut tools made from chalcedony (a type of quartz) date to the Mesolithic, confirming that human communities lived in this area over a long period of time. The hills around Bhimbetka still preserve some of their natural setting and provide information on the natural resources that these early human communities may have found here—a stream that may have provided fish, forests that offered fruits, plants, and jungles with wild animals. They may have encountered the now extinct auroch, the ancestor of India's humped cattle (*Bos indicus*), various deer species, wild boar, nilgai, and smaller creatures. Even at this early stage, relatively small numbers of humans may have had a direct impact on the survival of some animal species.

The colours used in the paintings were derived from natural minerals found nearby; red from ochre (geru), white from limestone, green from chalcedony, black from burnt charcoal or lampblack. Mineral rocks were first powdered and then mixed with water or perhaps a medium made of tree gum or animal fat. The paint was most likely applied on the rock walls using twigs fashioned into brushes or animal fur, perhaps even hair from a squirrel's tail. Most paintings are in monochrome (shades of one colour) and only a few are polychrome (more than one colour).

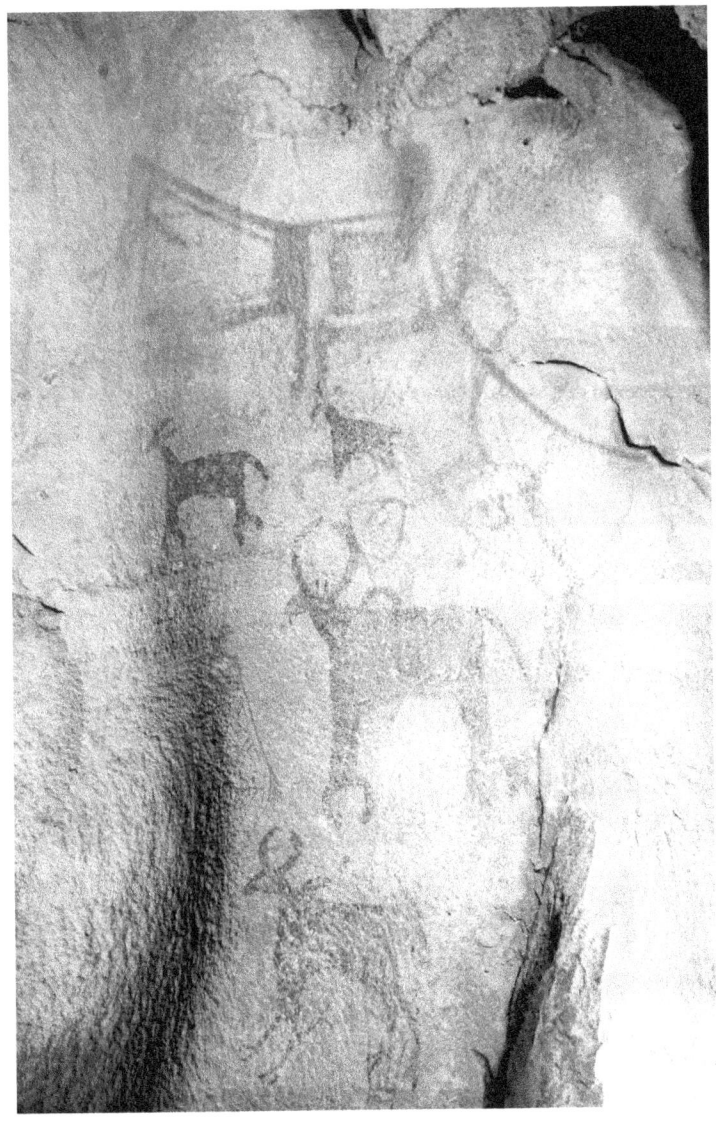

Mesolithic cave paintings in Bhimbetka Caves, Madhya Pradesh

Early prehistoric paintings of animals and birds.

Bhimbetka Caves, Madhya Pradesh

In 1957, while travelling by train to Bhopal, the capital of Madhya Pradesh, Dr V. S. Wakankar noticed some unusual rock formations silhouetted against the sky. He returned with archaeologists and, over the years, they gradually discovered more than 600 prehistoric shelters at Bhimbetka, with some of the oldest known cave paintings in India. Bhimbetka revealed evidence of continuous human habitation from around 10,000 years ago covering the Palaeolithic and Mesolithic phases through to historical times.

The paintings and bone fragments found at Bhimbetka record the variety of animals they saw and hunted—spotted deer, wild pig, tiger, leopard, elephant, birds, and fish. While the painted animal depictions are naturalistic, some are more imaginative, symbolic, and decorative. Though human beings are depicted in a stylized manner, the stick figures are animated and engaged in various activities—hunting, gathering honey, collecting fruit in baskets, and dancing. The hunting scenes show small groups of men while those of women depict them preparing food and collecting fruit, suggesting that a division of labour on the basis of gender had already taken place.

Painting of herds of animals, prehistoric period, Bhimbetka, Madhya Pradesh

In Bhimbetka, there are about 400 rock shelters with remains of prehistoric paintings and engravings. These paintings with dramatic scenes of wild animals, hunting and gathering expeditions, domestic life and rituals provide a fleeting glimpse of this prehistoric world and how the inhabitants saw and understood it. Archaeologists and specialists have studied the paintings and classified them into five distinct phases dating from the Upper Palaeolithic to the most prolific stage in the Mesolithic era, followed by those belonging to the early historic period, when horses and soldiers are depicted. The sorting into different eras was made according to the painting style, technique, and the colours used. In some places, paintings are superimposed over others, helping to determine which styles and pigments are older.

While the Palaeolithic and Mesolithic stages extended over a large span of time, the Neolithic period moved at a much faster pace. In India, Mesolithic sites begin to reveal many aspects of Neolithic culture such as the construction of semi-permanent settlements, a pastoral lifestyle with the domestication of animals like goats, sheep, and cattle, agriculture and food production, accompanied by a greater variety of well-crafted tools for farming, animal husbandry, and craft skills to service the new needs of the community. It must be stated that these phases and time periods are not watertight and there are many overlaps within the various stages. The duration and dates of these prehistoric time periods also differ from region to region.

The Neolithic period saw several dramatic changes. As the last Ice Age receded (it peaked about 21,000 years ago) and then began to retreat about 12,000 years ago, the climate became milder, warmer, and wetter. The monsoon rainfall probably doubled. Cereals like wild barley, millets, wheat, and, in some places, rice grew abundantly thus setting the conditions for a more settled way of life and the beginnings of agricultural practices. With the cultivation of crops came the development of new, more refined tools. The growing of crops and food production resulted in several major changes with the domestication of more plants, and changes in the lifestyle and food habits of human beings. Food production spurred innovations in methods of storing grain and cooking food. Farming required multiple skills and tools for growing plants, irrigation, collecting seeds, and also saving enough seeds to plant the next season's crop. The community's observation and knowledge of climate patterns, and preparation for the annual cycle of seasons was essential for its success.

The earliest evidence of the use of the wheel in India dates from c. 3,000–2,500 BCE. The invention of the wheel transformed life—it was used to make pottery, to develop transport, and later for the spinning of cloth. The ability to produce pots for storing grain and personal items, and to keep them safe from rodents and termites enabled the community to store surpluses between harvests and for seed stocks for the following season. Wheel technology and its continuous creative usage from this early period to the present have transformed cultures. As a symbol in India, the Wheel of Dharma and its position on the Indian flag are noteworthy.

Cultural adaptations to such changes led to the development of multiple human skills and saw a surge of inventions with the herding and domestication of animals with evidence from Madhya Pradesh and Rajasthan from c. 4500 BCE onwards. Initially goats and sheep were domesticated, and later cattle for milk and other

Prehistoric stone tools

Larger stone tools are associated with the Palaeolithic phase, while smaller geometrical flints are identified with Mesolithic times and are associated with activities of hunting and gathering. Microlithic tools with serrated edges of the Mesolithic era are usually small in size, often not more than 3 centimetres long, and many of them are carefully cut into geometric shapes. The long or oblong stone tools may have been used for scraping flesh off animal skin, or to cut fruits and plants. The triangular tool with serrated edges on two sides may have been attached to a wooden stick with resin and fibre to make a rudimentary arrow, or a point of a spear used for hunting. The microlithic tools disappeared gradually in the Neolithic period, when agriculture, ploughing, and harvesting required instruments shaped quite differently, such as the plough and sickle. Stone tools were then replaced by more durable materials—copper and iron—that are associated with the Chalcolithic and other historical periods that followed.

related products around 2500 BCE. At the same time temporary and permanent settlements were created, with skilled artisans making pottery and tools. Clay of various colours is found in different regions, and scholars use terminology such as grey ware, red ware, and black ware to distinguish the pottery of these early periods and the regions. Though they became settlers and farmers who tilled the land, these communities may have continued hunting, moving, and exploring for better prospects. The migration of humans continues to the present.

Mehrgarh, by the Bolan River in Baluchistan, was excavated in 1974 and provides some idea of the characteristic features of the Neolithic period over several phases, covering a span from c. 7000 BCE to c. 2200 BCE. There is evidence of early wheat cultivation and the domestication of cattle, sheep, and goats. The excavations also revealed remnants of houses made of handmade mud bricks, stores for grain, grinding stones and other implements like sickles and blades with wooden handles. The pottery was wheel-thrown (made using a potter's wheel) and of different shapes and sizes. The dead were buried in between houses and amidst the bones are found remains of stone and shell beads for necklaces.

Excavation at Burzahom, near the Jhelum River, a few miles from Srinagar, exposed dwellings that are termed 'subterranean pit dwellings'. Circular and oval pits were dug between 3 and 4 metres below ground level, using wooden poles to hold up the roofs. The 'burz' or branches of the birch tree were perhaps used for roofing material, giving the place its name. It is possible that this ingenious method of making pit dwellings was developed to protect inhabitants from wild animals and the harsh climatic conditions of this area—freezing winters with temperatures of -6 °C and warmer summers reaching 29 °C.

Interestingly, the next phase of human development referred to as the Chalcolithic phase saw the introduction of copper for the fashioning of tools. In some sites in Rajasthan, the Neolithic and Chalcolithic phases overlap. At the sites of Jodhpura and Ganeshwar, wheel-thrown and fired pottery was discovered along with tools made of stone, bone, and copper. The excavations reveal the nature of this transitory phase from handmade stone tools to acquiring the knowledge of mining, smelting, and making copper implements. In India, large copper deposits are found mainly in Rajasthan, Madhya Pradesh, and Bihar.

Burzahom site excavation, Kashmir, 1936

The site was first explored in 1936 by the Yale Cambridge Expedition and work continued under the Archaeological Survey of India in the 1960s and 1970s. Study and analysis of the material remains and tools suggest four main phases of habitation from 3000 BCE to 1000 BCE. Phases I–II represent the Neolithic, followed by the Megalithic and then the historical period, thus establishing the extent of early human habitation in this northern region of Kashmir.

Some of the Neolithic–Chalcolithic sites of this region may have evolved into centres of copper production that crafted and supplied copper instruments to rural farms. The use of efficient copper tools and skilled experience in farming gained over the centuries enabled these societies in the Neolithic and early Chalcolithic stages to create a surplus beyond the needs of their society, thus setting the stage for the transition from small rural settlements to larger towns and cities. These were the hub, not of agriculture, but of trade and commerce—introducing another turning point in the story of human development in India and, perhaps, linked to the rise of the Harappan urban culture.

Burzahom bone and stone tools

The Neolithic tools found at Burzahom were made of both stone and bone. Specialized tools were made for fishing and hunting—such as spearheads and arrowheads with finely worked microliths, scrapers for skinning animals, and heavier tools for pounding grain.

· CHAPTER 3 ·

HARAPPAN CULTURE

late 3000 BCE–c. 1750 BCE

In the early 1920s, the beginnings of Indian civilization and history were pushed back by almost 2,500 years due to a series of archaeological excavations in Punjab and Sind. What the archaeologists discovered were the remains of a highly developed urban culture that had existed around the same time as the civilizations of Egypt, China, and Mesopotamia. This urban culture had a network of large and small cities, with sophisticated town plans, markets, and houses that displayed a wide variety of highly developed skills and artefacts. What is noteworthy about this culture is that it was spread over a large area with more than 1,000 urban centres that evolved and endured for more than 1,000 years.

The first two sites to be excavated—Mohenjo-daro and Harappa (both now in Pakistan)—were situated near the Indus River. Archaeologists and historians called this civilization the Indus Valley Civilization. This label soon changed as more sites were discovered and, today, the term Harappan Culture is preferred, as Harappa was one of the earliest sites to be excavated. Harappa and Mohenjo-daro are important because of their size and features. Other large sites bearing features similar to Harappa and Mohenjo-daro have been discovered in Kalibangan in Rajasthan, Ropar in Haryana, Lothal and Dholavira in Gujarat, and Lurewala and Ganweriwala in Cholistan (on the dry bed of the river Ghaggar), to name a few. There are also a large number of smaller sites. On a rough count, there are 1,022 sites that can be identified as belonging to the Harappan Culture; of these 616 are in India of which only 97 have been excavated. The geographical expanse of this civilization was huge, covering between 680,000 and 800,000 square kilometres. The northernmost site lies in Manda in Jammu and Kashmir; the southernmost in Malvan in

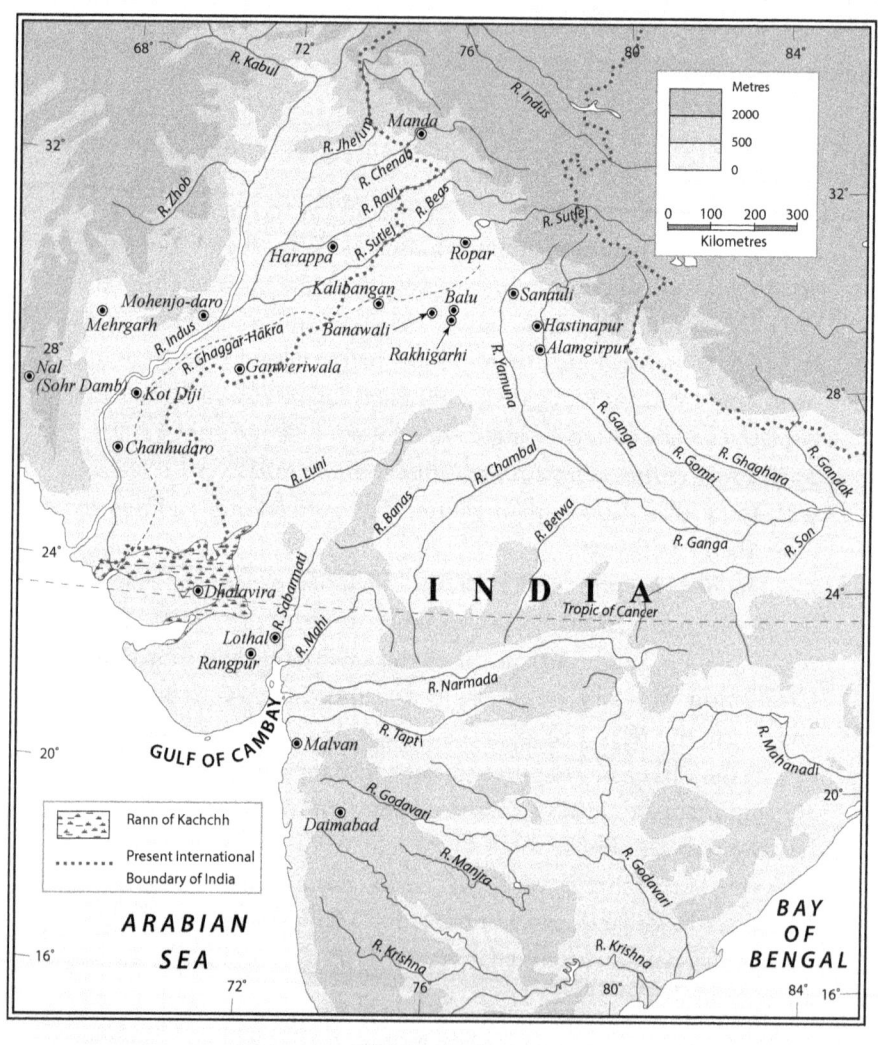

Harappan sites

Note: Not to scale. This map has been prepared in adherence to the 'Guidelines for acquiring and producing Geospatial Data and Geospatial Data Services including Maps' published vide DST F.No.SM/25/02/2020 (Part-I) dated 15th February, 2021.

Alamgirpur in the Saharanpur district of Uttar Pradesh; and the westernmost is Sutkagen Dor on the Makran coast of Pakistan. New sites continue to be discovered.

Since we began with the statement that the discoveries of Harappan Culture chronologically pushed back the beginnings of Indian history, it is important to have an idea of how old this culture was. According to archaeologists, this culture stretched from around

Excavation at Dholavira, 3000–1750 BCE, Kadir Island, Rann of Kutch, Gujarat

Unlike the structures at Harappa and Mohenjo-daro, the structures at Dholavira are often made of brick with sandstone outer facing. The city has a strong fortification wall with entrance gateways. An unusually large inscription with the Harappan script was found at the eastern entrance and it is believed to be either the name board of the city or the name of the ruler. Enclosed within these protective walls are distinctive parts of the city, the raised citadel area, the middle area with the workshops, and the lower town. Interestingly, excavations have revealed habitations outside the city walls, suggesting smaller suburban units along with a cemetery. The excavations at Dholavira, Lothal, and other Indian sites confirm that the Harappan Culture was dynamic—one that evolved to meet changing conditions and circumstances.

late 3000 BCE to about 1750 BCE. But this long stretch of about 1,300 years can be broken up into three phases: (*i*) the pre-Harappan from 3000 BCE to 2600 BCE, (*ii*) the mature Harappan from 2600 BCE to 1900 BCE, and finally (*iii*) the late Harappan from 1900 BCE to 1750 BCE. Specialists have arrived at these dates by collating radiocarbon data. But it should be remembered that these dates are approximate. The Harappan Culture was a long cultural process. The mature Harappan refers to the fully developed urban phase, which lasted for nearly 800 years. The existence of large urban complexes would logically suggest a surrounding economic environment in which agriculture and forms of exchange thrived. Such activities would make it possible for an urban population to be fed and to function. Food grain remains suggest that wheat, rice, and millet were the staples consumed along with vegetables and fruit.

Toy bullock cart, 3000–1750 BCE, Mohenjo-daro, Pakistan. National Museum, New Delhi.

Evidence from remains confirms that by c. 3000 BCE the wheel had been invented, animals had been domesticated and were used for agriculture and for the transportation of goods from villages to urban centres. Such carts may have also played a significant role during the construction of the city, transporting supplies of clay bricks, pipes for drainage, stone, and timber, much the way carts are used today.

Archaeological evidence collected from the pre-Harappan phase revealed that the inhabitants of these sites had a degree of expertise in stoneworking and metalwork, which they used to make a range of objects from agricultural implements to gold and silver jewellery to wheel-thrown pottery. The latter was used to make household necessities like cooking utensils and storage jars. Beads, bracelets, and necklaces were made from semi-precious stones. Cotton was grown and along with wool was used to make fabrics and clothes. They used wheeled transport and were familiar with trade and exchange. These features linked the pre-Harappan with the mature phase when the existence of large cities was evident.

Necklaces, 3000–1750 BCE. National Museum, New Delhi.

Limited supply of stone in the Harappan region meant that stone was rarely used in construction and to make household objects, while semi-precious stones—agate, carnelian, amazonite—were used to make jewellery (lapis lazuli was a luxury item, perhaps imported). The semi-precious stones were mined and transported to city workshops where they were cut and polished to create colourful necklaces and bracelets. Shells and bone were also carved and assembled to make of a variety of jewellery. Clay and metal figurative sculptures of this period are adorned with bangles, necklaces, and belts, suggesting that jewellery was popular 5,000 years ago, as it continues to be today in India.

Large urban complexes that lived off the agricultural surplus produced in the countryside would imply that there must have existed a mechanism of and institutions for the coordinated collection of raw materials. Archaeological finds show evidence of mining—copper in Rajasthan and Baluchistan; semi-precious stones from western India were widely available; lapis lazuli came from the Chagai Hills or the Pamirs; and these were crafted into beads or even exchanged as raw materials. Teak was available in Gujarat and ornaments were made from shell and stone and clay beads that came from the coast. All these provide evidence of trading networks and communication. The most distinctive feature of this culture is its pottery with designs in black, of plants, birds, and even of abstract forms; Harappan pottery was usually painted on a red surface. The crafted items were made by skilled and specialized artisans whose products were traded overland and overseas. Bead-making was very common and bead-makers frequently used gold, copper, ivory, and semi-precious stones.

Bronze and stone tools were common and were also used as items of exchange. The level of exchange is suggested by the presence of fixed weights and rods for measurement. Lothal has the remains of a structure that many scholars think was originally a dockyard but this is not an issue on which there is a consensus. But near this structure there was a warehouse and this leads to the conclusion that Lothal was a hub of exchange with facilities for storage and from which products could be transported. Evidence suggests that sea and land trade networks extended to the Persian Gulf and Mesopotamia. Earnings and profits from this trade contributed to the economic advantage of the urban complexes whose proximity to rivers facilitated the transportation of goods.

Dockyard of the port area of Lothal, 3000–1750 BCE, Saurashtra, Gujarat

Today, Lothal is situated more than 15–20 kilometres away from the sea, on the Gulf of Khambhat (historically known as the Gulf of Cambay). Five thousand years ago, the city may have been built as a port for sea trade. The dockyard appears to have been cleverly designed to maintain the right level of seawater for the easy access of boats to the wharf and the docking area. Remains of seal impressions found here further confirm trade activity. Workshop areas were built nearby to manufacture and package high-value goods, such as beads and gems for long-distance trade.

The remains of the cities display sophisticated levels of civic planning and organization. The urban settlements were clearly demarcated into what archaeologists have designated as a 'citadel area', which was to the west of the settlements, and a residential area to the east. The distinguishing features of the citadel area were buildings that probably housed institutions of civic life and for public rituals. The layout of the Harappan cities displays a concern for maintaining an ordered urban life and an efficiently run economic system, especially the management of land, labour, and water. The buildings in the citadel area were erected on brick platforms to protect them from floods since many of the cities were close to riverbanks. Streets were laid out in a planned way often following a grid pattern. The cities had an elaborate drainage system; drains in houses were linked to the drainage in the streets.

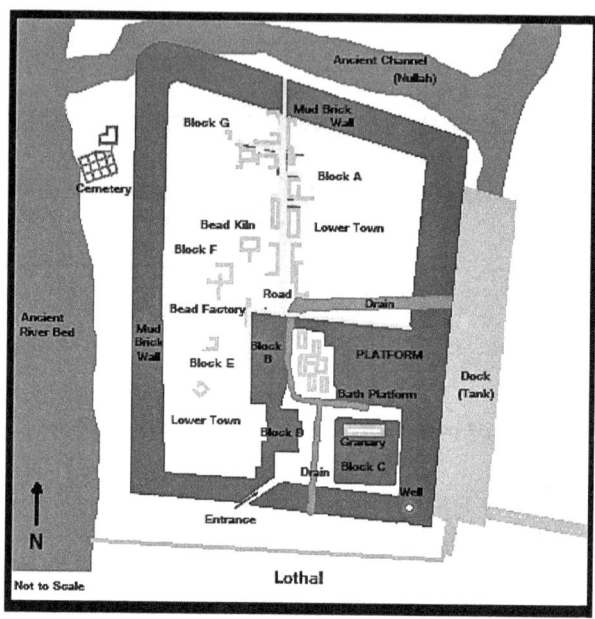

Plan of the city of Lothal, Gujarat

Lothal was discovered and excavated in the 1950s by the Archaeological Survey of India. The remains suggest it was a small port town with a dockyard, workshops, warehouses to store items of trade, and a planned residential area for the inhabitants. Some large houses were found here with several rooms and courtyards. The town had streets and side lanes, pavements, and a complex drainage system similar to the cities of Harappa and Mohenjo-daro.

The houses were built according to a given design: all of them had courtyards with rooms opening onto it; they had wells and designated bathing areas and, of course, drains. The drains were made with kiln-burnt bricks but the houses were made of mud bricks. Interestingly, the bricks were made to a standard size in most of the large urban centres. All these features suggest a high level of skill and expertise, a deep understanding of the environmental conditions, and how to adapt to them. The citadel area was protected by walls and bastions with entrances. This suggests that the area was guarded. In some cases the city was also fortified. Why this need for protection and demarcation from the surrounding countryside? The city, in socio-economic terms, was a new phenomenon in comparison to the rural world: its wealth was different as was its management. The city, thus, represented a new way of life. But it is worth highlighting the fact that the Harappan cities do not exhibit any signs of ostentatious display of wealth in the houses or in the graves. There are no definite answers, based on firm evidence, on why the demarcation and protection were needed. The cities lived off the surplus produced by the nearby villages.

Clay pot used in the drainage system, 3000–1750 BCE, Lothal, Gujarat

In the Harappan Culture the wheel was used to create fine glazed and painted pottery. Wheel-thrown pots of different sizes and shapes were designed to serve a variety of functions such as storage jars for perfume and oil, water and grain, and for the burial of bones. Clay was also used to make pipes for the elaborate drainage system beneath the city roads that transported waste water for disposal into the river.

The most puzzling remains of the Harappan Culture are the seals. They were most often made of steatite and were small and flat; in shape they were square or rectangular. The steatite was cut, carved with intaglio images (carved in reverse) so that when it was used as a seal, an inverted impression appeared as a relief on the soft clay on which it was stamped. On one side of the seals are carved pictorial motifs that depict humans and animals. They have inscriptions on them but they have still not been deciphered. The inscriptions contain over 400 different symbols and it is still unclear whether each symbol represents a word or a name or a sound like modern alphabets. Moreover, we will never know what this language sounded like and if it had any similarities with any of the known languages. While research continues to attempt to decipher the script, the only point of certainty is that the script or the signs should be read from right to left. What purpose did these seals serve? Every seal had a perforated boss at the back to facilitate handling. Were they used to stamp packages? If they were, then they were identifying marks for civic authorities, for merchants, and for those regulating trade, and could even have indicated family/clan affiliations. If they were indeed signs of identification, the seals could have related to professions and religious and social groups. The undeciphered script has also been noted on pots and items of jewellery like amulets and bangles. In Dholavira, archaeologists discovered what they think is a sign because it is a short inscription in large letters. If the script is a puzzle, so are the animals depicted on the seals. The most common animal looks like a rhinoceros but some scholars see it as a mythical unicorn. This animal is very often shown with what seems like an altar. Elephants and bulls are common on the seals; tigers make rare appearances and almost always as part of a scene. The horse is conspicuous by its absence on the seals. Some bones, said to be that of the horse, and small terracotta forms have been discovered in levels of later periods in Pirak in Baluchistan and these have been dated to the second millennium BCE. The horse was probably unimportant, functionally and ritually, in Harappan Culture. This suggests that the horse was a late arrival in India and it was not an indigenous animal. Even in West Asia its presence is recorded only in the second millennium BCE.

Unicorn Seal, 3000–1750 BCE. National Museum, New Delhi.

The most abundant object found in the cities were seals. The main trade routes established at this time were to the west of India—through Afghanistan, northern Iran, Turkmenistan to the distant lands of ancient Mesopotamia where Harappan seals were also found. When the Harappan script is deciphered, it may open a window to the Harappan Culture—their language, culture, beliefs, and provide answers to many tantalizing questions such as the meaning of this seal and its depiction of the one-horned animal.

Two other significant absences in the Harappan cities are buildings that can be identified as temples or places of worship, and elaborate burials. In the absence of identifiable temples, it is clear that temples did not serve as sites for social bonding and prayer. What and how the people of these cities worshipped remains a mystery. From some of the western sites have come female figurines and these have been interpreted as representations of goddesses that were worshipped. There is some evidence for the prevalence of fertility cults but how elaborate and popular they were is not known. It is difficult to conceive of an ancient culture that did not have a significant religious dimension. But for Harappan Culture what this dimension was—or what these dimensions were—remains shrouded in obscurity.

Harappan pottery, Nal, Pakistan. National Museum, New Delhi.

The gradual waning of this extraordinary culture is also a mystery. The decline of the cities was at one time related to an assumed Aryan invasion. But there is very little archaeological evidence of an invasion that caused the defeat and decline of a well-established social, economic, and political order, and the complete disappearance of a culture. The theory or the idea of an Aryan invasion no longer carries any credibility. One kind of evidence that bolstered the invasion theory was the discovery of skeletons in the residential parts of Mohenjo-daro. But once the skeletons were analysed, it was discovered that these were the remains of persons whose death had been caused by diseases like anaemia. But it needs to be underlined that the role of diseases in the decline of the Harappan cities has not received adequate scientific and forensic attention. It also needs to be emphasized that evidence of deaths caused by violence does not necessarily imply invasion or conquest. Such deaths could have been caused by local disturbances such as epidemics. Changes in the environment, especially recurrent flooding of the area around Mohenjo-daro, have also been put forward as a major factor in the decline. The striations found in the top soil suggest fire and floods destroyed the cities time and again, and each time the cities were rebuilt. In the formative and mature phase there were improvements on the previous phase and then in the Late Phase gradually the reconstruction shows signs of haste and clumsiness; some cities were even abandoned. But the impact of such changes is not too clear. It is reasonable to suggest that a whole range of factors determined the decline of Harappan cities and culture. Since this civilization was spread over a large geographical area, there may not have been a uniform cause and the weightage of factors could have varied over regions and terrain. Also, this was not a culture that came to a sudden and abrupt end. The decline was spread over a chronological period which scholars call the late Harappan phase.

The Harappan civilization was the earliest urban culture in South Asia. The discovery of this culture is still a work in progress. More archaeological evidence and the decipherment of the script will add to our knowledge of this civilization and will provide answers (hopefully) to the many unanswered questions. It may also help in the understanding of how this culture influenced later ones that developed in the subcontinent. What is remarkable is that the next phase of Indian history was for the most part rural in contrast to the urban world of Harappan civilization and our knowledge of the next phase is largely text based and not archaeological, as we shall see in Chapter 4.

'Mother Goddess', 3000–1750 BCE, Mohenjo-daro, Pakistan. National Museum, New Delhi.

Such figurines (found in excavations at Mohenjo-daro, Harappa, and Banawali) are of women wearing a wide heavy belt to hold up their lower garment, rows of necklaces (perhaps of silver, gold, and semi-precious stones, and coloured clay beads similar to those discovered at these sites) and a tall, high, fan-shaped headdress or hairstyle. These female clay figurines were made using simple clay modelling techniques that involved patting and pinching the clay to form the face, nose, and figure; while rolled, thin strands of clay were used to create necklaces and earrings. Their extraordinary ornamentation and headgear have earned them the title of 'Mother Goddess'. Several such figurines were found broken, suggesting their temporary significance as ritual objects.

Dancing Girl, 3000–1750 BCE, Mohenjo-daro, Pakistan. National Museum, New Delhi.

The Harappan Culture also ushered in the Chalcolithic or Bronze Age. Bronze objects found in these urban centres exhibit a profound knowledge of mining metals (like copper), and mastery over techniques to mix alloys of metals. The lost wax process was used to create metal sculptures. The image was first made in wax with exact proportions and details of hair and jewellery as desired in the finished product. The wax figure was coated with mud to make a mould that was dried and then heated. As the wax melted, it was let out through an opening at the base. In its place molten metal was poured into the mould, to replace the wax. The mould was cooled, and then broken. The metal (brass, silver, or gold) image emerged as the exact replica of the original wax figure, and still retained the fluid and soft textures of wax.

The so-called 'Dancing Girl' is a youthful figurine (10.5 centimetres high), with half-closed, contemplative eyes. She wears bangles covering one arm and a necklace. Her head is held high, and her long hair is swept into a long roll that hangs to the side of her neck. The statue has been called the 'Dancing Girl' perhaps because of the way the girl stands—with one arm on her hip and her leg bent. Yet her true identity continues to remain a mystery.

EXPLORATIONS OF RAKHIGARHI

Rakhigarhi is a small village in the Hisar district of Haryana, 150 kilometres from Delhi. It is considered one of the largest Harappan settlements to be found in India. The site was excavated by the ASI and Professor Vasant Shinde, former vice chancellor of Deccan College, Pune, over several seasons from 1997 to the present. Only a small part of the site has been revealed so far, as it is greatly constrained by the villages built over it, making access to the ruins below extremely difficult.

This settlement, like many other Harappan sites, was built near the floodplain of a river, in this case the Ghaggar that must have supplied water for irrigation for agriculture, and to the neighbouring villages and the city. Finds have revealed pre- and mature phases of development of this Harappan city, making it one of the most ancient sites to be excavated in India. Similar to other Harappan cities there is evidence of paved roads, a drainage system, houses made of baked bricks, remains of metal products, and stone items like grinding stones. The remains of a large brick structure suggest it may have been used as a granary.

Jewellery, made of terracotta, conch shell, silver, gold, and semi-precious stones was found here. Also common to other Harappan sites was the use of agate and carnelian to make beads. Some were found in Rakhigarhi, suggesting trade, commerce, and the movement of semi-precious stones from distant cities and regions for manufacture and trade.

As in other Harappan sites, pottery, steatite beads, and seals were unearthed. Especially interesting is the seal with a depiction of the one-horned rhinoceros. This animal is no longer found in this region of India, as the remaining rhinoceros population is found thousands of kilometres away in Assam. There are many possible reasons for this. The rhinoceros and other water-loving creatures like elephants and water buffaloes that are represented on seals of the Harappan period once lived in this region at a time when it was covered with grasslands and well-watered moist forests. When the climate and environment changed, the loss of habitat forced these animals to migrate to more suitable habitations. On the other hand, travellers of this culture may have encountered such water-loving animals when they explored lands beyond their cities.

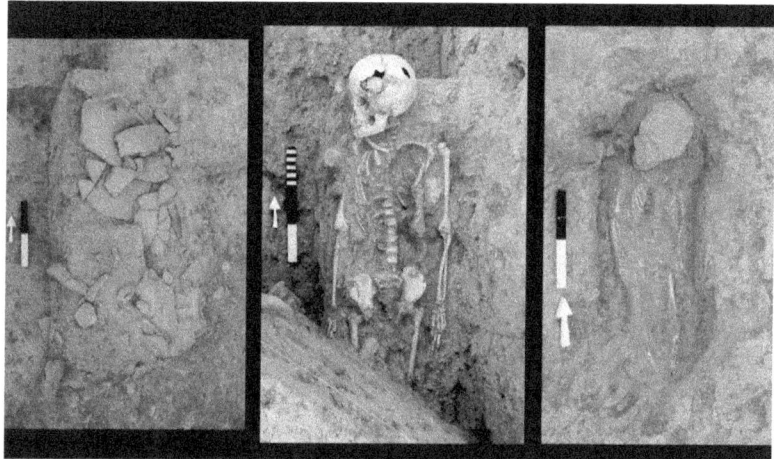

Burial excavations at Rakhigarhi, Haryana

One of the most significant findings at Rakhigarhi are several burial sites with human skeletons, often buried with everyday utensils, bangles made of shell, and the remains of necklaces. The use of the latest twenty-first century scientific techniques, research, and analysis of recent findings may provide answers to some of the many mysteries and unanswered questions about the origin and the people of the Harappan Culture.

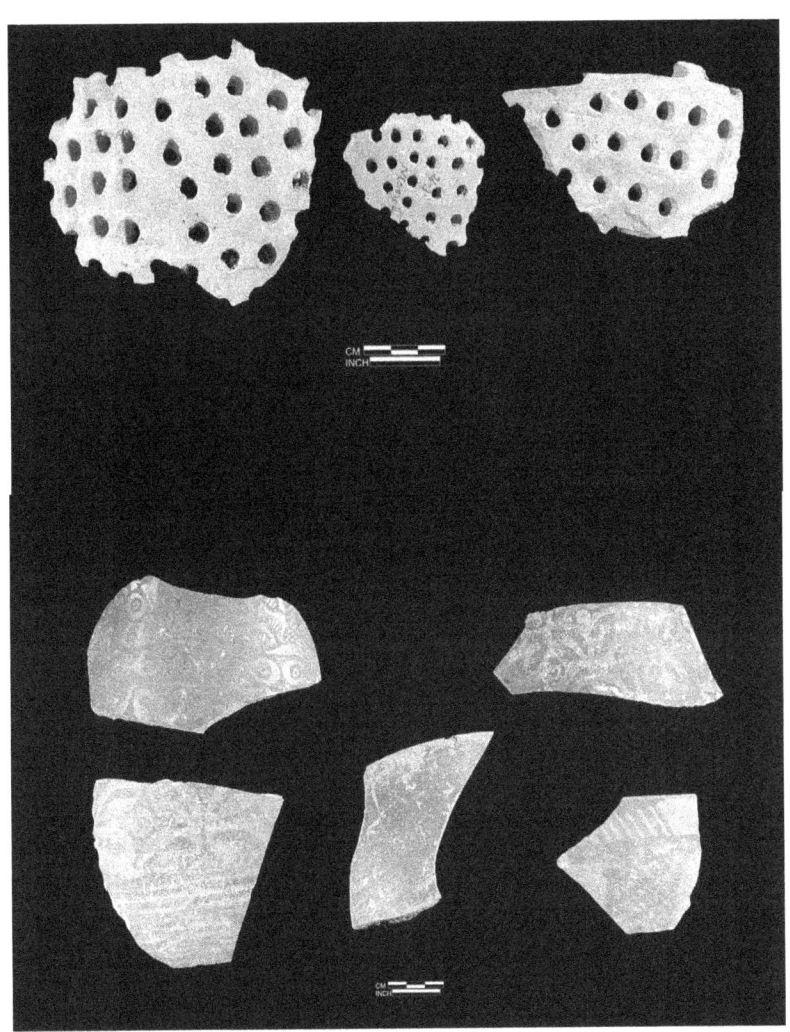

Pot shards, Rakhigarhi, Haryana

City street, excavations at Kalibangan, Rajasthan

From the excavated remains at Kalibangan, archaeologists were able to reconstruct the grid pattern of the city streets, the plan of the individual houses, the position of wells, and the network of drains in this city. The excavations also gave them an idea of the scale of the city and the different sections within it—the residential and workshop areas. The excavated remains of Kalibangan have since been covered over with earth, and cordoned off to preserve them for posterity.

· CHAPTER 4 ·

SOCIETY AND IDEAS IN THE AGE OF THE VEDAS

c. 1200 BCE–c. 600 BCE

The Vedas refer to a body of literature that was composed between c. 1200 BCE and c. 600 BCE. They serve as sources to reconstruct the culture and civilization that prevailed in large parts of North India during this period; the Vedas are also a source of philosophical and spiritual ideas that describe rituals and reflect upon abstract philosophical concepts that continued to evolve through the subsequent centuries.

The Vedas were composed by a group of people described as the Aryans. There is a widely held belief that the Aryans constituted a race. This is erroneous. The term Aryans refers to a group of people who originated from Central Asia and spoke versions of the Indo-European group of languages. Aryan is thus a linguistic term and not a racial category. Aryans should be correctly referred to as Indo-European-speaking people. In the earliest texts they composed—the Avesta in present-day Iran and the Ṛig Veda in India—they refer to themselves as ariia and arya. It is possible that these terms were etymologically derived from ar (to cultivate). The second misconception is the belief that the Aryans came to India as invaders. There was no Aryan invasion of India. The Aryans (Indo-European-speaking people) migrated in small groups—settling first in the north-west of India and then gradually moving eastward into Punjab and on to the Gangetic plain.

Migration, by definition, indicates movement; so the culture that the Vedas describe was not a static one. It evolved over a very long period of time and was also spread over a large geographical area. There is also a noticeable shift from cattle-rearing to settled agriculture. The bulk of the evidence of this culture, in contrast to the Harappan, does not come from archaeological remains but from textual evidence.

A body of literature collectively referred to as the Vedas make up this textual evidence. Veda means to know and the Vedas consist of four kinds of compositions—the Samhitas (collection of verses), the Brahmanas (explanation of the rituals), the Aranyakas (forest treatises), and the Upanishads (largely philosophical discourses)—which were in prose and in verse. The most important point here is that originally these compositions were heard, remembered, and orally transmitted—a fusion of sruti (hearing) and smriti (memory or remembering). The Vedas have no known or identifiable author and are thought to have been revealed and, therefore, considered sacred or holy. The Vedas are best seen as part of an oral tradition, as they were written down much later. The fascinating aspect of the oral tradition, chanting of the Vedas, is the way that they were composed for recitation, using different techniques to facilitate memorization.

The Samhitas consist of four collections—Rig Veda, Sama Veda, Yajur Veda, and Atharva Veda. The Rig Veda is the earliest; the Sama Veda has little independent value, except for seventy-five stanzas, since it repeats verses from the Rig Veda though the arrangement varies with reference to a particular ritual of sacrifice. The Yajur Veda also contains verses from the Rig Veda but it adds prose formulae to them as instructions to be followed in rituals and sacrifices. There are also sacrificial prayers in the Yajur Veda. The Atharva Veda is much later than the Rig Veda and consists largely of spells for the demon world.

The Brahmanas, set in prose, highlight the significance of the different rituals and the importance of sacrifice. They describe the different kinds of priests to carry out the functions involved in a ritual. This suggests the emerging complexities of an evolving society. There is a movement in these compositions from the simple to the complex over time.

The Aranyakas refer to life and thought related to those, possibly the elderly, who retired to the forest. Here the rituals are simplified, and in this sense they pave the way for the Upanishads, often considered the fountainhead of Indian philosophy, to which we will turn later on in this chapter.

Meditating in the forest

There are several sculptures and textural references to the notion that when a man reaches old age, he should disengage from his family, social and economic aspects of life, and retreat to the forest for meditation and philosophical reflection.

The people who composed these texts inhabited a large geographical area which is suggested by the reference to rivers. These areas stretched from eastern Afghanistan, the Swat valley, to Punjab, and the Gangetic plain. There are references to Sapta Sindhu. The sapta or seven rivers of northwestern India are identified as the Indus, Chenab, Ravi, Beas, Sutlej, Jhelum, and Saraswati. Some of the rivers are also paired—the Yamuna with the Ganga, the Beas with the Sutlej. These people were cattle rearers who gradually shifted to agriculture. For both the activities land had to be cleared, which required the use of metals. The people knew the use of copper and bronze and, a little later, of iron as well. Archaeological evidence in this area shows habitations, metal tools used for agriculture and clearing of forests, and also the use of pottery for cooking and storage. Cattle were the initial source of wealth before the emergence of settled agriculture. It is believed that the Aryans migrated to the Gangetic plain to find rich pastures for their herds of cattle. Later, some groups settled in permanent habitations and developed skills in agriculture and cattle rearing. It is also important to highlight the fact that the Aryans did not come into empty and uninhabited spaces. In the process of migration, they encountered and confronted the original occupants of these areas who are referred to as panis and dasas. The latter was used as a derogatory term to denote cattle lifters. The dasas were both feared and treated with contempt. There are mentions of dasa chiefs but the term came to mean subordinates and slaves. This would suggest that over time the dasas were subjugated.

Migration was obviously an ongoing process occurring over a large span of time. It is evident that agriculture and cattle rearing were the principal occupations. There is evidence of the plough being driven by oxen and hence the latter became an icon of strength and fertility. In terms of agricultural activity and production, as the migrants moved eastward down the Gangetic plain, there was a shift from wheat to rice cultivation. Wet rice cultivation produced a dramatic increase in yield and thus led to surplus. This was reflected in the texts through elaborate rituals which involved dana and dakshina, the giving of gifts of land, produce, and other valuable items. Land was cultivated in common, but this period saw the emergence of the rights of usage, demarcation of cultivated areas, and of family holdings. The development of other non-agricultural occupations—carpenters, metalsmiths, potters, tanners, weavers, and so on—is noticeable. Simple forms of division of labour and specialization were emerging. Surplus and specialization preceded urbanization and encouraged exchange through barter. Exchange was, of course, facilitated by the use of rivers as a means of transportation. The Vedas offer some insight into the society and occupations of this period, and also details of family life and rituals.

At the centre of social life was the family—the kula, a term that denoted family, rituals, and customs specific to a kinship group. Sociologists have struggled to classify Indian society, and have found that more than religion, caste, and region, it is the extended family that determines customs and rituals, food, and other norms. Patriarchy was the norm and groups of families living in the same area formed a grama or village. Marriage was customary with monogamy (having one married partner only) as the predominant practice but men belonging to the ruling class practised polygamy (having more than one married partner). Polyandry (a woman having more than one husband) was not entirely unknown. The position of women varied from relative freedom to restrictions, a position that continues to exist today in varying degrees in different communities. Clans based on kinship ties emerged and the head of a clan was referred to as raja. This was the beginning of kingship, a form of rule that dominated later periods of Indian history for centuries.

As mentioned earlier, the Vedas not only serve as a source of information for the society in which they were composed, they also reveal ideas and reflections on a large variety of themes and aspects of reality. One prominent theme was of nature's power over human life, the convergence of natural phenomenon with divinity. Indra, one of the more important divine figures in the Vedas, is described as the god of rain and thunder. Ushas (dawn) was deified as was Vak (speech); the concepts of time and measurement, seasons and language evolved in association with the growing awareness of the agricultural cycle. Most of the hymns are about gods. Abstract ideas like space and time are also present.

At the heart of the Vedic compositions was sacrifice and the principal ritual associated with it was the yagna, accompanied by elaborate chanting of prescribed verses (mantras). The yagna involved offerings to Agni, the god of fire. At one level, the offerings, consisting of what was valuable to the person performing the ritual, were meant to appease the gods. At another, second level, it was indicative of obedience and allegiance. At yet another, third level, it was a sign of renunciation. Over time, there may have been a shift from the first level to the third. What is important is that these rituals were all performed by priests with specified functions. Priestcraft was clearly a specialized occupation.

The Vedas mention many gods and goddesses, but a strand emphasizing only one god is also noticeable. At the centre of this strand is the figure of Prajapati about whom the Rig Veda says, 'He is one, though the wise men call Him by many names.'

It is difficult to put a definite date to the Vedic compositions: they were composed over a very long period of time beginning with the Rig Veda c. 1200 BCE. The collection of texts was certainly known from around 800 BCE to 600 BCE. The reason for saying this is that Gautama Buddha, who was born in or around 560 BCE, knew of the ideas of the Vedas and was almost certainly influenced by the teachings of the Upanishads.

The Upanishads are often referred to as Vedanta—the last portion or the end of the Vedas as indicated by the word anta, meaning end.

Guru training shishyas in a Vedic school, Kerala

Veda Pathshalas – schools that specialize in teaching the Vedas-are still found in Kashmir, Kerala, Maharashtra, Karnataka, and Odisha. Years of daily training and practice are required to master the recitation of the Vedas, while it takes decades of dedicated study of the Upanishads to understand, debate, and interpret their philosophic content.

· CHAPTER 5 ·

BEFORE EMPIRES AND THE AGE OF MAHAVIRA AND THE BUDDHA

c. 600 BCE–c. 300 BCE

Around the sixth century BCE, certain new social, political, and economic features were noticeable in the Gangetic plain that were building blocks for the future. These were the development of urban centres and trade, both inland over rivers and along land routes and overseas; certain ways of organizing society and different forms of political power were established. Groups of kinsmen were beginning to wield power locally; this was referred to as gana sangha. Power was diffused rather than centralized. In many localities such power structures persisted till the first century CE. There are references also to mahajanapadas (large human settlements); sixteen of these mahajanapadas are clearly identified and these were spread across the whole of North India from Taxila (in present-day Rawalpindi) in the north-west to present-day Bihar in the east. The most important of these were Anga and Magadha in the middle Gangetic valley; Kashi and Kosala a bit further west; Avanti and Chedi in western and central India; Gandhara in the north-west and Assaka in the Deccan. In most of these, power was wielded by ruling clans which tended to evolve into ruling lineages and then in certain cases became full-blown monarchies as, most prominently, in the case of Magadha.

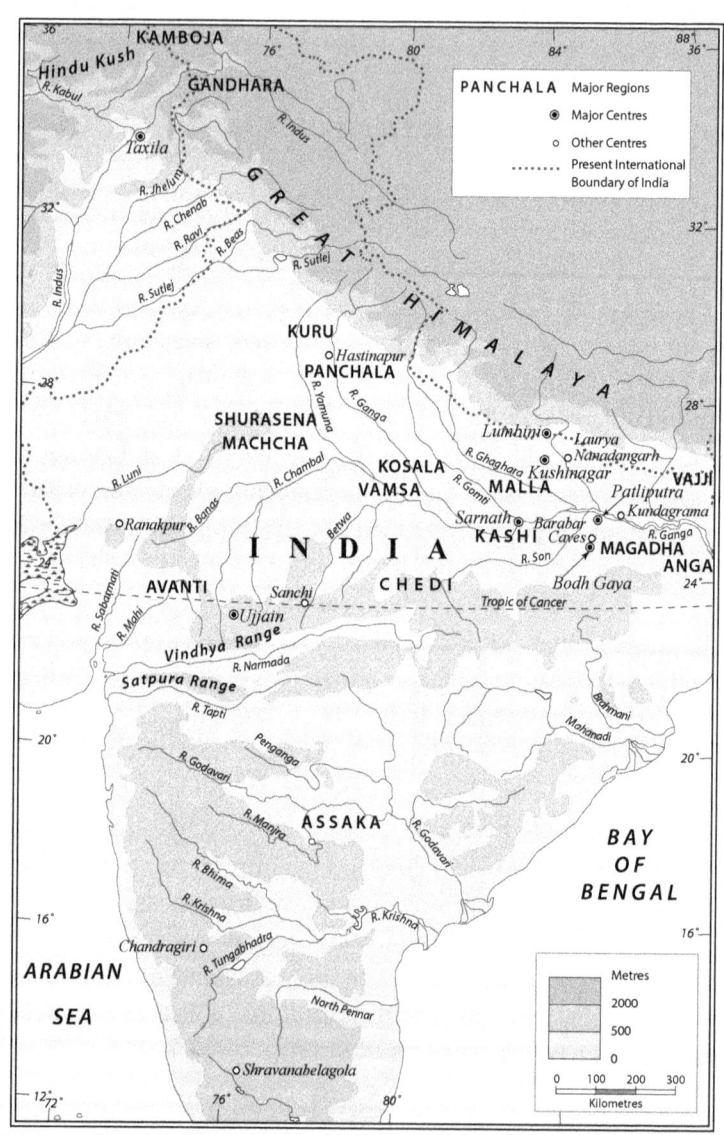

The sixteen mahajanapadas

Not to scale. This map has been prepared in adherence to the 'Guidelines for acquiring and producing Geospatial Data and Geospatial Data Services including Maps' published vide DST F.No.SM/25/02/2020 (Part-I) dated 15th February, 2021.

This gradual development of state formation was often associated with processes of urbanization. The origins and evolution of cities varied. Some, like Hastinapur, developed as administrative centres; others, like Magadha, evolved as a capital of an empire; some others originated as a market or a centre of exchange—the history of Ujjain illustrates this; towns also developed around sacred places where people gathered to worship or for pilgrimage. The cities of the Gangetic plain display certain common features: they all had either moats or ramparts and there was a shift from mud to brick buildings. They had drains, wells, and soakage pits. Houses had rooms around a courtyard. The rooms that faced the streets were shops. The streets were levelled to facilitate wheeled traffic. These urban settlements reveal the use of iron tools—hoes, sickles, knives, hooks, and so on. Trade was quite extensive in items like textiles, beads, pottery, ivory objects, glassware, horses from the Northwest and also blankets and woollen goods.

The production and exchange of these items suggest that division of labour was prevalent. Society was also becoming more structured and organized and this was giving rise to hierarchies and inequalities both in terms of status and wealth. One form of structuring society emerged from the Brahmanical tradition—the four-fold varna system. In its idealized version the four varnas were arranged in order of importance and members of each varna followed vocations prescribed to them. At the top of the hierarchy were the Brahmins who studied and interpreted the Vedas and performed various ritual functions. Immediately below them were the Kshatriyas who studied, bestowed gifts to the Brahmins, and protected the people. The Vaishyas followed agricultural and trading occupations. The Shudras, at the very bottom of the hierarchy, were supposed to earn their living by serving the other three varnas. The varnas were considered to be self-contained units: they were endogamous, in other words, marriages took place within the group. But certain inter-varna marriages were accepted. For example, anuloma marriages—a man of a higher varna marrying a woman of a lower varna. But the converse, a man of a lower varna marrying a woman of a higher varna (pratiloma marriage) was not recognized or accepted. But the very fact that within Brahmanical discourse such marriages were discussed suggests that such marriages did take place and that the varnas were not strictly endogamous.

Another social institution that emerged with varna, often competing with it and sometimes complementing it, was jati (caste). The Brahmanical texts conveniently explain and justify jatis as products of various kinds of inter-varna marriages. The emergence and existence of jati can be traced to the sixth century BCE but what is uncertain is whether endogamy, prohibitions on inter-dining, accepting water and food from others that became markers of the caste system were already prevalent in their rigid form in the sixth century BCE. There is no doubt that there was a connection between varna and jati and often in ancient texts the two terms were used interchangeably. It might be worthwhile to note some of the similarities and differences between the varna system and the jati system. The varnas numbered four while jatis are innumerable. Both varna and jati are ordered by importance and status but in the former, the ranking is fixed; in the latter there is or was fluidity, and castes could move up the ladder (this process is referred to by scholars as Sanskritization). Rules governing the varna system disapproved of social interaction and acceptance of food from Shudras but in the caste (jati) system, disapproval became prohibition based on ideas of purity and pollution. Over time and with practice, the distinction between the varna and the jati system became blurred. This blurring served to place the jati system within the Brahmanical tradition and thus give it legitimacy.

The varna and the jati systems—the term caste system is a convenient shorthand for both forms of discrimination and prejudice—are enduring and ugly features of contemporary Indian society. But it would be incorrect to assume that these forms of organizing and perceiving society passed without protest and dissent in the sixth century BCE and the centuries following it. New social groups, new occupations, new forms of wealth came together to start a churn in the world of ideas that had an impact on religious beliefs and practices. The spread of diverse ideas created a space for public debate and discussion; urban life also encouraged the presence of multiple and competing ideas and views of the world. Many of the urban settlements had halls for public discussion. These were called kutuhala shalas—literally a space for nurturing curiosity. Such discussions also took place in parks and groves on the fringes of towns. These features suggest that intellectual discussion was becoming public, open, and inclusive. This was a radical shift from the world of Vedic learning where intellectual quest was exclusive—a private disputation between a guru and his students. There was a parallel shift taking place in the realm of language. Brahmanical learning and rituals were all carried out in Sanskrit while common people in towns and villages spoke Prakrit, which was a term that included many local variants and dialects. Prakrit was derivative of Indo-Aryan; the western variety of it was called Shauraseni and the eastern variety was called Magadhi. In subsequent years, Pali, a Prakrit language, would become very important.

Out of this social and intellectual context, Jainism and Buddhism were two major and enduring movements that talked about organizing society and piety in ways that were very different from those that the Brahmanical tradition attempted to impose on people. The Jaina traditions predate the Buddhist doctrines, but it is difficult to be precise about the dating. The Buddha and Mahavira taught around the same time and there are some similarities in their ideas. These two traditions cannot really be described as religions, in the way Christianity and Islam are defined, but rather a code of conduct held together by an understanding of piety and the world. Both reject the authority of the Vedas, emphasize renunciation and human action in the attainment of salvation, and the establishment of a monastic order for men and women. The word Jaina denotes a follower of a Jina—a victor, an individual who has acquired infinite knowledge and teaches others how to attain liberation from the cycle of rebirth—moksha. A synonym for Jina is Tirthankara—a ford builder, someone who builds bridges to help people cross the ocean of suffering.

According to the Jaina tradition, there were many Tirthankaras—Mahavira was the twenty-fourth Tirthankara. Around 300 CE, there was a split among the Jainas: one sect came to be called the Digambara and the other Shvetambara, and both produced their own stories of Mahavira. According to these accounts, Mahavira was born c. 599 BCE at Kundagrama near Vaishali, the capital of Videha. His lineage was Kshatriya and aristocratic. The Shvetambara version says that Mahavira began his life as a householder and then became a wandering ascetic. Both versions agree that this wandering phase of Mahavira's life lasted for twelve years and during this time he underwent severe austerities like fasting and meditation. He is supposed to have attained kevalajnana (infinite knowledge) on the outskirts of the town of Jrimbhikagrama, on the banks of the Rijupalika River, on the field of a householder named Samaga.

The responsibility of spreading the teachings of Mahavira fell on his chief disciples who were known as ganadharas. The first to become chief disciples were the Brahmin Indrabhuti Gautama and his two brothers who also became the first members of the Jaina sangha (monastic order). The number of ganadharas increased to eleven; they were all Brahmins. Thus a monastic order was established. Mahavira died at the age of seventy-two near Patna.

The teachings of Gautama Buddha—or what has come to be known as Buddhism—also presented a formidable critique of and challenge to Brahmanical orthodoxy. Gautama Buddha was born Siddhartha, the son of the chief of the Sakya clan, Suddhodana. He was born around 560 BCE in Lumbini, Nepal. He lived the sheltered life of a royal prince, married a young woman named Yashodhara, and had a son named Rahula. It is said that when Siddhartha was twenty-nine years old, he ventured out of the palace, and saw an old man, a sick man, a corpse, and a monk. These encounters made him question his own life and brought him face to face with facets of reality which were inevitable. He renounced his royal life and adopted the life of a wandering ascetic in a quest for truth. He sought out teachers, learnt from them but was not entirely satisfied with what he had been taught. He practised severe austerities, which emaciated his body, but he came around to believing that without nourishing his body he could never achieve calmness of mind. Legend has it that a young woman, Sujata, offered him a bowl of milk-rice. Thus nourished, he sat under a peepul tree to meditate and attain enlightenment which he did attain on the forty-ninth day and came to be known as the Buddha—the Enlightened One.

Mahavira in meditation, relief carving, Gwalior Fort, Madhya Pradesh

Though damaged, this image is no less powerful, showing Mahavira sitting cross-legged and deep in meditation, surrounded by an aura of calm. There are many similarities in early Buddhist and Jain art, but as the faiths spread, each of them developed their own distinct regional styles. Local artisans in different parts of India gave expression to philosophical ideas in materials available to them, thus creating a plethora of styles, with their own vocabulary of motifs and symbols.

Parshvanatha, bronze sculpture, ninth century, Maitraka, Gujarat. National Museum, New Delhi.

Parshvanatha was the twenty-third of the twenty-four Jain Tirthankaras. In this sculpture, he is seated under the protection of a gigantic serpent's hood and is surrounded by his faithful students.

The Bodhi Tree, Bodh Gaya, Bihar

This famous Buddhist pilgrimage site is associated with the sacred Bodhi Tree under which the Buddha meditated for forty-nine days to attain enlightenment. An old peepul tree (*Ficus religiosa*) stands to the west of the Mahabodhi Temple, and is believed to be a direct descendant of the original tree. Emperor Ashoka visited Bodh Gaya and constructed a small temple near the tree. The Chinese Buddhist monk and translator Faxian first makes reference to the main temple and the Bodhi Tree in 404–405 CE. Xuanzang, the Chinese Buddhist monk, visited the site later around 637 CE and mentions the presence of railings around the Bodhi Tree.

The Mahabodhi Temple, Bodh Gaya, Bihar

The word Bodh/Budh means 'wisdom' and is the root of the name given to the Buddha, the Enlightened One, the Bodhi Tree and the site, Bodh Gaya, where he attained enlightenment. The Mahabodhi Temple (Temple of Great Wisdom), is over 55 metres high and has seen many additions and alterations. During the nineteenth century, Burmese kings made certain repairs; this continued during the British era. This complex was declared a World Heritage Site along with Sarnath in India and Lumbini in Nepal.

Dhamek Stupa, Sarnath, Uttar Pradesh

After attaining enlightenment in Bodh Gaya, the Buddha went to Sarnath, where he was persuaded by his disciples to share his wisdom. The Dhamek Stupa marks the site of the Buddha's first sermon. The remains of the Lion Capital now kept in the Archaeological Site Museum were found when several stupas and burial mounds were excavated here. Sarnath is also associated with the foundation of the order of monks (sangha) by the Buddha. It was a flourishing pilgrimage centre for over 2,000 years, visited by kings and pilgrims like Xuanzang who left records of his visit to this revered site.

On the basis of this enlightenment, the Buddha gave his first sermon or discourse to five disciples in a deer park at Sarnath near Banaras, present-day Varanasi. This sermon came to be known as the 'Discourse on Turning the Wheel of Dhamma'. Beginning with the first sermon, the Buddha's teachings consistently emphasized the Four Noble Truths: the world is full of suffering; this suffering is caused by human desires; the renunciation of desires is the path to nirvana or liberation from the cycle of rebirth; and the attainment of nirvana was possible by following the Eightfold Path. The latter, according to the Buddha, consisted of right views, intention, speech, action, livelihood, effort, mindfulness, and meditation. This path is also referred to as the Middle Way—avoiding the two extremes of indulgence and asceticism. What is important here is that following the Middle Way or the Eightfold Path did not require the help of priests and rituals. The Buddha emphasized ethical behaviour and this behaviour was not confined to any one varna; any individual could follow the Middle Way.

The Buddha did not directly attack the varna system but opened up the possibilities for an individual to enhance his/her status without the dependence on priests.

At the very core of the Buddha's teaching was the idea of dukkha (suffering) and its removal. He taught that dukkha was all-encompassing and was related to certain ingrained human tendencies like desire, attachment, greed, vanity, ignorance, and so on. If by following an ethical life—the Eightfold Path—human beings eliminated these tendencies, suffering could be eliminated. The Buddha taught that nothing was permanent except change. This led to the rejection of any doctrine or practice that was rigid and inflexible. The ultimate goal of human life, according to the Buddha, was the attainment or the experience of nirvana which was possible in this life

The Buddha lived until the age of eighty and he wandered around spreading his teachings. He established an order of monks and later of nuns. This came to be known as the sangha and was a key instrument in the spread of the Buddha's message during his lifetime but more significantly after his death. The establishment of an order of monks resulted in the creation of monasteries, which emerged as centres of learning. It should be noted that by allowing women to join the sangha as nuns, the Buddha was providing women the freedom to make a life outside the institution of marriage. The Buddha did not treat courtesans with contempt and allowed them to make presents or gifts to the sangha. He made it clear that women could also attain nirvana.

Worship of the Bodhi Tree, relief panel, second BCE–fifth century CE, Sanchi Stupa No. 1, Madhya Pradesh

This sculptured scene depicts several men worshipping the Bodhi Tree, under which the Buddha attained his enlightenment. Tree worship is both an ancient and a contemporary practice in India—offerings of water and flowers to trees in villages and on city roadsides is a common sight. The tree symbolizes growth and generous fertility as it gives sustenance to birds and small creatures; provides shade and clean air; fruit and nuts; and wood for construction and fodder for cattle. It is interesting to note that rituals that honour trees feature in several cultures around the world.

Over the centuries, the Buddha's teaching travelled along sea trade routes to Sri Lanka, Myanmar, Indonesia, Thailand, Cambodia, China, and finally to Japan, and through land routes and the silk trade routes from India to Pakistan, Afghanistan, Central Asia, and China.

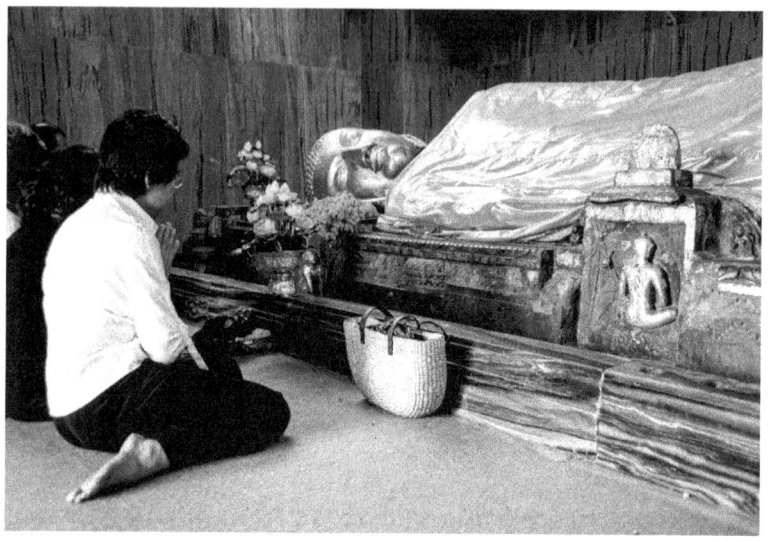

Pilgrims worshipping the Buddha image at Kushinagar, Uttar Pradesh

The site at Kushinagar is associated with the final parinirvana, the death of the Buddha. It is believed he made his last journey here at the venerable age of eighty and spent time walking through the sal forests before he laid himself to rest. After his death and cremation, his remains were distributed to different locations and were enshrined in stupas.

The period c. 600 BCE to c. 300 BCE was thus a period of transition in North India. Life was becoming more complex than it was in the lifestyle described in the Vedic texts. These complexities were reflected in the emergence of new occupations, the growth of trade and exchange, and new ways of organizing society and structures of authority. Prevailing ideas were being challenged and the two most important articulations of these challenges were Jainism and Buddhism. At the political level, there was the drive to build a more centralized power centre of which the Magadhan empire was the first important expression.

**Buddhist monks and pilgrims at Kushinagar,
Uttar Pradesh**

Pilgrimage sites like Lumbini, Sarnath, Bodh Gaya, and Kushinagar attract pilgrims and visitors from around the world, particularly from other Buddhist nations in Asia. The sanctity of this site carries special meaning as this is where the Buddha's body was said to have been cremated. Out of respect, the pilgrims walk in procession, keeping their right shoulder aligned and parallel to the sacred stupa and perform a pradakshina or procession circling around the stupa, either once, thrice, seven times, or as their custom demands.

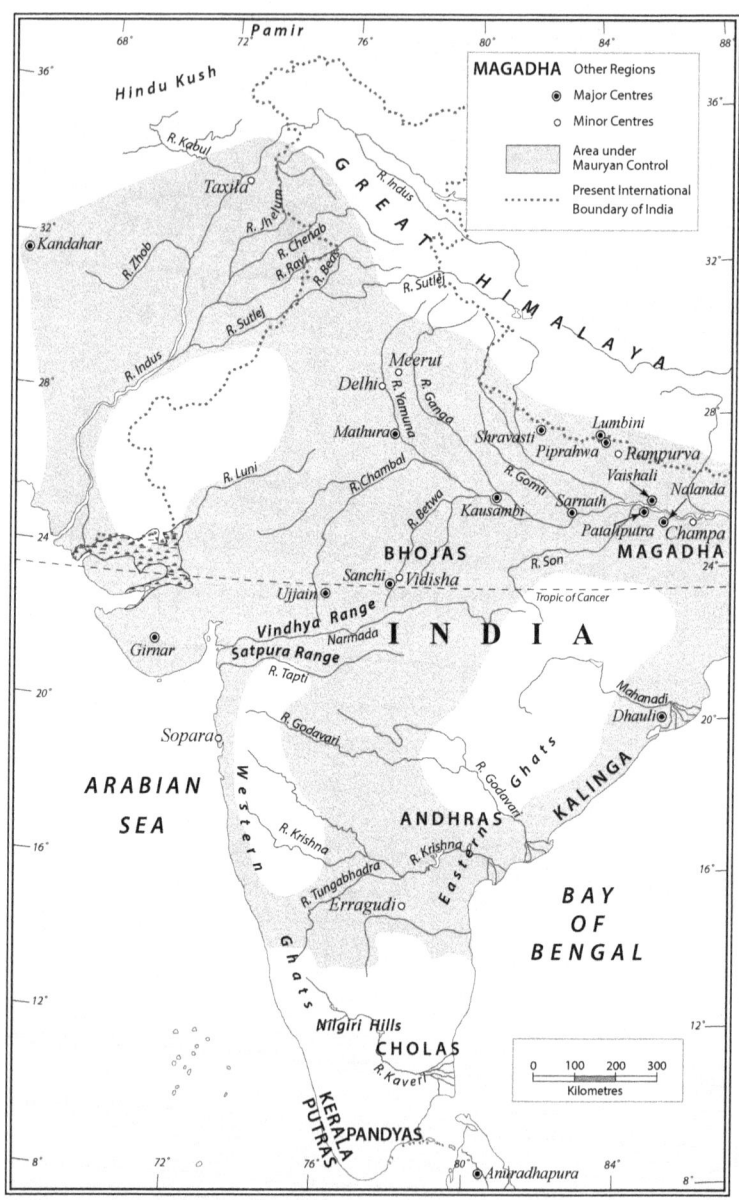

Ashoka's empire

Note: Not to scale. This map has been prepared in adherence to the 'Guidelines for acquiring and producing Geospatial Data and Geospatial Data Services including Maps' published vide DST F.No.SM/25/02/2020 (Part-I) dated 15th February, 2021.

· CHAPTER 6 ·

THE FIRST EMPIRE AND ASHOKA

c. 324 BCE–c. 187 BCE

The Mauryas ruled over large parts of India between c. 324 BCE and c. 187 BCE. Their rule extended practically over the entire subcontinent and extended beyond into the north-west, present-day Afghanistan. The geographical spread of their control and influence merits the term 'empire', the first in the history of India. The empire lasted for more than 130 years and was based on the dynastic principle (rule by members of the same family). Chandragupta Maurya (c. 324–297 BCE) established the Maurya dynasty and the empire; he was followed by Bindusara (c. 297–273 BCE) and then Ashoka (c. 273–232 BCE). The later Mauryas, not as important as the first three emperors, continued to rule until 187 BCE.

Chandragupta probably first established himself in Punjab and then moved eastward until he came to control the area around Magadha. According to one tradition, Chandragupta overthrew the Nandas and in this he was aided by a Brahmin from Taxila named Chanakya/Kautilya/Vishnugupta. The Punjab period of Chandragupta's career is based on Greek sources which mention that when Alexander of Macedon (356–23 BCE) invaded the Northwest, he encountered Chandragupta. The same sources also refer to a hostile encounter between Chandragupta and Seleucus Nikator who had inherited the eastern provinces of Alexander's empire. This conflict probably took place around 301 BCE and was settled by negotiations through which Chandragupta gained the territories corresponding to present-day Kandahar, South Baluchistan, and the area between Afghanistan and the Indian subcontinent. In return, Chandragupta gave Seleucus Nikator 500 elephants. Graeco-Roman sources also speak of Chandragupta's trans-Vindhyan conquests.

Dharmarajika Stupa at Taxila, Pakistan

Excavations in Taxila and other sites in Pakistan and Afghanistan were undertaken by Alexander Cunningham (who went on to found the Archaeological Survey of India) in 1863–64 and later under John Marshall. Taxila was one of the most important archaeological sites in the Indian subcontinent with the remains of three cities, a university complex, Buddhist monasteries, and stupas. The university grew over centuries from the sixth century BCE to the eleventh century CE drawing students of mathematics, astronomy, law, sciences, and the arts from near and far. The stone and stucco sculptures of this region exhibit a strong synthesis of Graeco–Roman influences.

To understand the political and economic structure of the empire of the Mauryas, the major source is the *Arthashastra,* which discusses how a kingdom should be governed. The dating of this Sanskrit text that first surfaced in 1905 is uncertain, as is its authorship. It is assumed to have been written by Kautilya/Chanakya/Vishnugupta who was supposed to have been the chief minister of Chandragupta. The text as it exists today is the work of Vishnugupta, who lived in the third century CE. So, which parts of the text, if any, can be dated back to the Mauryan period is a matter of debate.

Some features of the political economy of the Mauryan empire are clear. It was a monarchy under powerful monarchs (at least for its first ninety years) and it was an empire based on a predominantly agrarian economy. Large parts of the empire were under cultivation and land revenue was the principal source of the government's income. There appear to have been regular assessments of the area of land cultivated and of what and how much the land produced. These assessments made for a degree of predictability and created a sense of revenue security. It follows therefore that the administrative system was geared to the collection of land revenue. But the land tax was not the sole source of income because non-agrarian activities were known. For example, villages had herds of cattle which were listed and taxed; goods in transit were also taxed through tolls and customs duties.

Land was cultivated by individuals—either by landowners or by farmers who worked for the landowners. The landowners earned rent from the tenants. From this, it would appear that private property ownership in land was coming to be recognized. This is also suggested by the fact that when landed property was sold, the proceeds of the sale would first go to the kinsmen and creditors before others. The state also owned extensive tracts of cultivated land and wasteland—this crown land could be directly cultivated by appointed persons or by sharecroppers or tenant farmers who paid the state a tax; wage labourers directly employed by the state could also cultivate the crown lands.

The administrative unification and political stability that the Mauryan empire established facilitated trade which, in turn, encouraged artisans and craftsmen to form associations known as shreni. Artisans, except those who were employed by the state to make weapons, or those who worked in state workshops and state mines, had to pay taxes. Artisans joined the associations since the latter were more convenient than working alone. Over time these associations acquired complex structures. From the state's point of view, the presence of these associations made the collection of taxes easier. The sale of goods was strictly supervised; goods had to be stamped so that the old could be distinguished from the new. There was a superintendent of commerce who assessed the goods on current price, demand and supply, and cost of production. Tolls were fixed at one-fifth of the value and evasion of taxes and tolls was severely punished. Profiteering was discouraged and to this end prices were controlled. Taxes were used to build highways for trade, maintain an army, and a large bureaucracy to maintain law and order, collect taxes, develop irrigation, and so on. There was no banking system but moneylending was prevalent and the rate of interest on money borrowed was 15 per cent per annum. Silver and copper coins bearing symbols have been found but the meanings of these symbols have not yet been deciphered.

Forest dwellers, relief panel, second century BCE– fifth century CE, Sanchi Stupa No. 1, Madhya Pradesh

This relief from the toran (ornamental gateway) provides a vivid picture of forest dwellers, their huts, and activities. The forest is depicted with wild animals; elephants and lions. The panel suggests that in this period there were communities whose livelihood depended on forest produce and hunting. Other relief panels show land being tilled by farmers using bullock carts and scenes from city life.

The excavation of the urban centres of the Mauryan empire—the most important one being Pataliputra (present-day Patna)—show signs of improvement in the standards of living. The houses were made of bricks and the palaces were of wood and stone. Greek historian Megasthenes wrote that Pataliputra was surrounded by towers and gateways made of wood. These observations have been corroborated by archaeological excavations. Since many of the buildings of Pataliputra were made of wood, fire was a major hazard. The remnants of the architecture of Pataliputra suggest the grandeur associated with an imperial city.

Megasthenes, who served as the ambassador of the Greek general Seleucus to the court of Chandragupta, spoke of Mauryan society being divided into seven sections—philosophers, farmers, soldiers, herdsmen, artisans, magistrates, and councillors. These divisions have been taken to indicate castes since intermarriage between the sections was not allowed, neither was the change of occupations. He made no mention of untouchability. He was probably referring to occupations and not to varnas, of which there were only four. Farmers who cultivated the land were the largest category. The mention of soldiers is indicative of the importance of the army. The Mauryas probably had a standing army. The mention of herdsmen suggests that cattle rearers still existed.

The son of Bindusara and the grandson of Chandragupta, Ashoka came to the throne around 272/3 BCE. As a young prince, Ashoka had won his spurs as the governor of Taxila where he had been sent by his father to suppress a rebellion, which he did successfully. Taxila was strategically located, controlling the northwestern trade routes; it was the meeting place of people and cultures and hence had a cosmopolitan character. It was also a major centre of learning. The exposure Ashoka had in Taxila possibly had a formative influence on his outlook and tastes. From Taxila he moved to Ujjain. His accession to the throne was not smooth; it was, in fact, paved with blood. He was not the crown prince and so he was involved in a succession struggle against his brothers. Ashoka had his brothers killed—as many as ninety-seven of them, the sons of the various wives of Bindusara. Ashoka's path to the throne thus bore some of the usual features of the road to kingship in ancient and medieval times.

His career as a king, however, was remarkable. The first remarkable feature was that he spoke directly to his subjects about himself and his policies. He did this through edicts that were inscribed on rocks and pillars. Historians have divided these edicts into three categories—Minor Rock Edicts (the earliest), Major Rock Edicts (later), and the Pillar Edicts (the last ones to be erected). The Major Rock Edicts number sixteen and there are six or seven Pillar Edicts. It is entirely possible that all of Ashoka's inscriptions and edicts have still not been discovered. Most of the inscriptions that have been found are in the Prakrit language and in the Brahmi script. There are some inscriptions in the Kharoshthi script and some others in Greek and Aramaic. The most important theme in most of these edicts of Ashoka is his understanding of dhamma. These edicts were located in various parts of India and beyond—Karnataka, Gujarat, Odisha, the Gangetic plain, Punjab, and near Taxila. The geographical spread of the edicts is suggestive of the extent of Ashoka's empire and the spheres of his influence. Many of his edicts begin with the declaration 'Devanampiya piyadasi evam aho' (Piyadasi, the favourite of the gods, says thus); thus making the authorship of the edicts beyond doubt.

The other noteworthy feature of Ashoka's reign was the conquest of Kalinga in c. 262/3 BCE. This was a bloody campaign: the bloodshed and the loss of lives filled Ashoka with horror. He went into a period of deep introspection for over two years. He emerged from this phase and converted to Buddhism c. 260 BCE. He articulated his introspection in Major Rock Edict XIII in which he announced that he was abandoning military conquest.

Detail of the 13th Major Rock Edict, Dhauli, Odisha

This stone edict marks the site of the Battle of Kalinga. An extract from this edict reads: 'When he had been consecrated eight years the Beloved of the Gods, "Devanampiya Piyadasi", conquered Kalinga. One hundred and fifty thousand were deported, one hundred thousand were killed and many times that number perished. After Kalinga was annexed, Devanampiya very earnestly practised Dhamma, desired Dhamma and taught Dhamma. On conquering Kalinga, the Beloved of the Gods felt remorse....'

Ashoka's conversion to Buddhism was a profoundly personal thing. He never made Buddhism the religion of the empire and of the people who lived in his empire. But he did use what he called his dhamma as an instrument of statecraft. It is entirely possible that during the long period of introspection the question of how to rule a diverse and vast empire without recourse to force occurred to Ashoka. He was looking for a bond that would hold his empire together. Ashoka formulated in his edicts and inscriptions a new social ethic that addressed the question of how an individual should live his or her own life: this has come to be known as Ashoka's dhamma. At the heart of this dhamma were the principles of ahimsa and tolerance. Lives governed by this ethical code needed no divine inspiration or dependence. Moreover, its appeal was universal. Even where Ashoka did not clearly mention Buddhism, the latter's influence was apparent. He drew on the teachings of the Buddha and gave them a wider meaning in a social and religious order where Brahmanism was the norm. Ashoka located himself as a king within the social and intellectual movement that Buddhism represented. He also wanted to ensure that his dhamma should have an impact on society and on the people who lived in the vast empire over which he ruled. His edicts are obvious examples of how seriously he took this matter.

Unfinished carving of elephant, Dhauli, Odisha

The half-cut elephant, emerging out of the rock, gives a vivid picture of how such sculptures were carved in situ. This image is unlike the Ashokan Pillars where the stone was transported great distances from Chunar in Uttar Pradesh to mark religious sites along well-known trade routes across the Ashokan empire. The purpose of this elephant is unknown and it was probably carved by local craftsmen. It is unlike the Ashokan Pillar edicts, both in scale and detail, and does not have the polished surface of their finely carved capitals.

11th Major Rock Edict, Girnar, Junagarh, Gujarat

This picture shows the nineteenth-century structure built by the Archaeological Survey of India to protect the natural rock on which the edict of Girnar was carved.

At a time when the ideas of Jainism, Buddhism, Ajivikas, and other sects were challenging Brahmanical orthodoxy, and were suggesting ways of living that were contrary to Brahmanical doctrines, there was a competition of ideas. This competition inevitably created tension. How to rule while preserving this plurality of ideas? One way was through coercion; Ashoka moved away from this and preferred to rule his vast empire through persuading his subjects to live by recognizing each other's dignity and by tolerating each other's beliefs. His dhamma was not necessarily religious; it could be followed by anybody and everybody, irrespective of their religious beliefs. It was a remarkable experiment in which social ethics became an integral part of statecraft.

Ashoka thus emphasized tolerance and the accommodation of difference—harmony was preferable to its opposite. There were occasions that had the potential of breaking the spirit of harmony—assemblies, for example—and these were discouraged. The principle of non-violence was also not treated as an absolute; sometimes violence became unavoidable, for example, when forest dwellers became troublesome. Ashoka did not restrict ahimsa to only war and conquest, he extended it to the killing of animals. However, the royal kitchen prepared meals of venison and peacock. His injunction to his descendants was that they should try and avoid conquest by force but if violent conquests became necessary, they should temper that violence through gestures of mercy and clemency.

Detail of 11th Major Rock Edict, Girnar, Junagarh, Gujarat

Several major edicts, such as this one, were copied many times and situated across the Ashokan empire. An extract from this edict reads: 'Thus speaks the Beloved of the Gods, Devanampiya Piyadasi—there is no gift comparable to Dhamma…and this is—good behaviour towards slaves and servants, obedience to mother and father, generosity towards friends, acquaintances, relatives …and abstention from killing living beings….'

As a king, Ashoka was concerned with the welfare of his subjects. He planted trees alongside roads and dug wells to provide travellers with shade and water. He criticized 'useless ceremonies and sacrifices' and superstitions relating to journeys as the stock-in-trade of low-level priests. He was, however, not averse to the use of spectacle to attract audiences to listen to his doctrine of dhamma. He did not attempt to validate his own imperial rule by way of appealing to a deity or to gods.

Ashoka died around 232 BCE. After his death, a process of political decline set in, and the empire began to disintegrate. While the core of the empire, the Gangetic plain, remained under the Mauryas, the far flung parts came under the control of regional powers. Historians believe that this decline was probably caused by financial pressure that the Maurya economy was unable to bear. Costs of maintaining an army, paying the salaries of an expanding bureaucracy, and the expenses involved in clearing land for cultivation, which would lead to increase in revenue—all these were sources of pressure. One sign of this strain was the reduction in value of silver coins in the later Mauryan period.

It is important to note that several symbols of Ashoka's reign were adopted in independent India—the Ashokan Lion Capital was chosen as the symbol of the Indian republic and is found on all Indian currency, government stationery, and property; the Buddhist symbol of the wheel found on the Lion Capital and other sculptures was selected as the central emblem of the national flag of India. Most importantly, Ashoka's message of peace, harmony, and tolerance of dissent continues to have relevance in the lives of Indians.

Sri Maha Bodhi Tree, Anuradhapura, Sri Lanka

It is believed that Sanghamitra, Ashoka's daughter, brought a sapling of the original Bodhi Tree under which the Buddha attained his enlightenment in Bodh Gaya to Sri Lanka. She came with a retinue of monks and scholars who carried the message of the Buddha to the people of Sri Lanka, where it continues to be the dominant religion.

Lion Capital, Sarnath, Uttar Pradesh

The Lion Capital (2.31 metres high) was unearthed during excavations at Sarnath in 1904. This site commemorates the place where the Buddha gave his first sermon. The finely polished capital, belonging to the reign of Ashoka, was adopted as the emblem of the republic of India in 1948. The capital comprises four lions seated back to back, guarding the four cardinal directions. They carry on their backs the Dharmachakra or the Wheel of Dharma, that was unfortunately damaged. Below the lions is a band with four evenly spaced smaller wheels or chakras with twenty-four spokes, to represent the turning wheel—and the aspiration for constant movement towards spiritual progress. Between the smaller wheels are the figures of an elephant, bull, lion, and horse that are symbols of strength, devotion, power, and speed respectively.

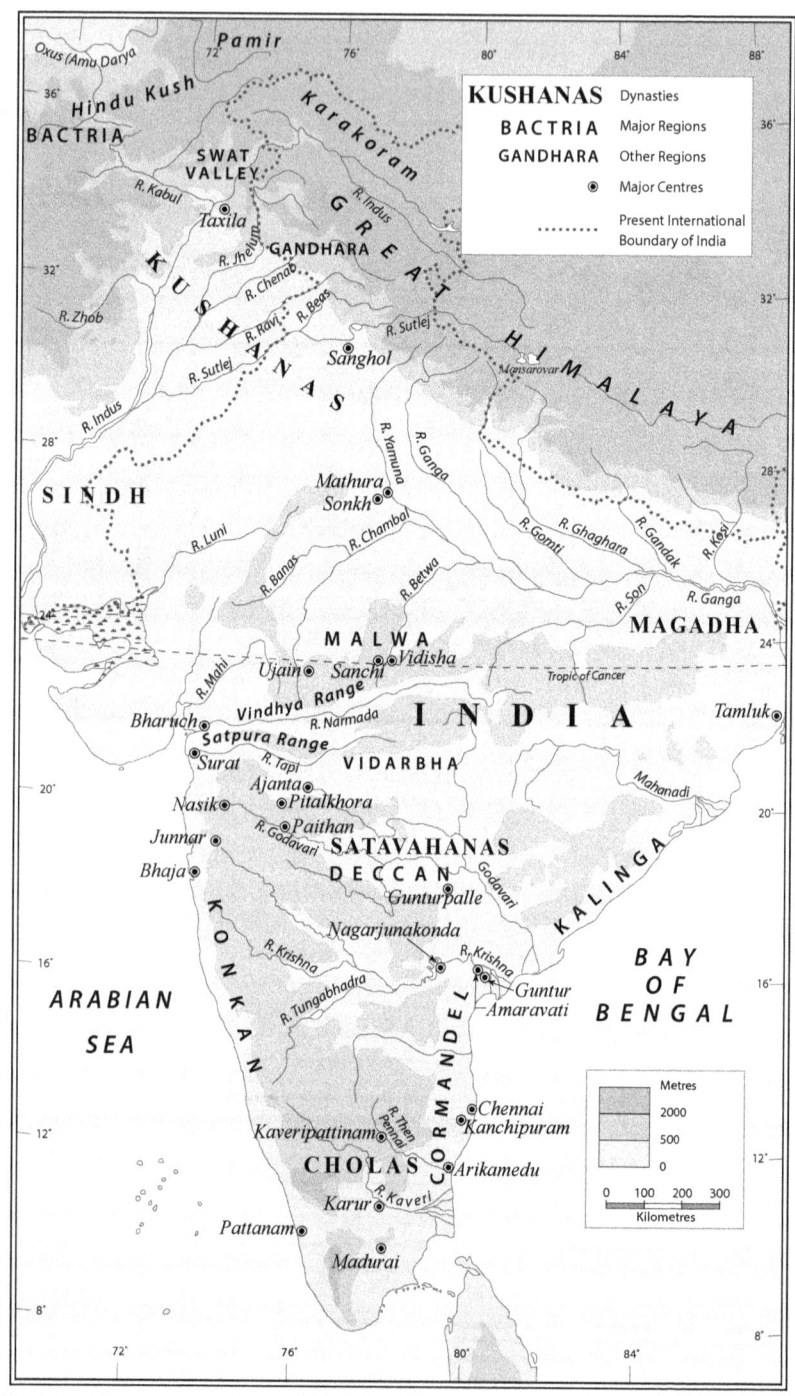

The Satavahana empire

Note: Not to scale. This map has been prepared in adherence to the 'Guidelines for acquiring and producing Geospatial Data and Geospatial Data Services including Maps' published vide DST F.No.SM/25/02/2020 (Part-I) dated 15th February, 2021

· CHAPTER 7 ·

BETWEEN EMPIRES

c. 200 BCE–c. 300 CE

The decline and the eventual collapse of the Mauryan empire left the structure of political authority diffused. Different types of political formations emerged in different parts of India from the second century BCE to the third century CE. In North India, the immediate successors of the Mauryas were the Shungas, a Brahmin family that had served the Mauryas. The founder of the Shunga dynasty, Pushyamitra, usurped the throne after killing the last of the Mauryas.

Other monarchies had emerged in Kalinga and the Deccan and there were threatening inroads of the Greeks in the Northwest. This involved the Shungas in wars in which they were not always victorious. Within a hundred years of their rise, the rule of the Shungas had shrunk to the area around Magadha. But here too their control was at best tenuous, and they were soon overthrown by another Brahmin dynasty, the Kanvas, who ruled the area around Magadha rather uneventfully, until the late first century BCE. It is possible that the rich iron mines of this region of Bihar may have given Magadha its significance. Iron gained supremacy over brass and copper as it was best suited to produce farm tools and implements to construct cities, roadways, and weapons of war.

Beyond the political phenomenon of monarchies, this period saw the resurfacing of clan-based polities (societies as political units) in Punjab, Haryana, and Rajasthan. Their existence is corroborated by their coins. Many of these clans migrated even as far as the northern Deccan. These clans claimed Kshatriya status, drawing their lineage and legitimacy from the heroes of epics and legends. Though some of their leaders took titles that suggested kingship, their coins were minted in the name of the gana or janapada, harking back to the gana sangha. There are repeated references in the sources to these leaders attacking Kshatriyas—this is suggestive of a persistent challenge to monarchy from other forms of political authority.

There were significant political and economic developments in the Deccan in the post-Mauryan era. The Deccan came to be ruled by the Satavahanas for nearly 450 years from c. 250 BCE. At its peak, the Satavahana empire extended beyond the Deccan into North India, as far as Magadha. Historians identify the dynasty of the Satavahanas with the Andhras in the Puranic lists of kings. The Satavahanas rose to power in the western Deccan, possibly in the region around Paithan (present-day Pratishthana) and then extended their rule in all directions. The first areas that they conquered were north and south Maharashtra and then eastern and western Malwa in present-day Madhya Pradesh. It is difficult to pinpoint when the rule of the Satavahanas started but 230 BCE seems to be the accepted date for the beginning of the rule of the first king, Simuka. Coins and inscriptions bear witness to the spread of Satavahana power first from Pratishthana to Ujjain and then to Vidisha. Satakarni II, who came to the throne c. 166 CE, was the sixth king and he ruled for fifty-six years—the longest reign by any Satavahana king. He annexed Malwa from the Shungas.

The four kings who succeeded Hala, the seventeenth Satavahana king (c. 20-24 CE), ruled for very short periods—twelve years between the four of them. This would suggest that these were years of turbulence for the Satavahanas. It is around this time that the Sakas, the 'western satrap' of the Satavahanas, came into prominence: first under Bhumaka and more powerfully under Nahapana who was a great conqueror. Between 40 and 80 CE, Nahapana extended his rule over Gujarat, Kathiawar, northern Maharashtra, Konkan, and even parts of southern Maharashtra for a few years. Satavahana power revived under Gautamiputra Satakarni (c. 80–104 CE) who defeated the Sakas, Pahlavas, and Yavanas. He overthrew Nahapana and from the Sakas recovered northern Maharashtra, the Konkan, Narmada valley, Saurashtra, Malwa, and western Rajasthan. His empire was vast, extending to Vidarbha (present-day Berar) in the south. He may not have ruled over Andhra but coins indicate that his rule and influence and that of his son, Pulumayi II, went as far as the Godavari and the Guntur districts and to the south on the Coromandel coast. The best known Satavahana ruler is Yajna Satakarni (c.170–99 CE). He retained control over both the eastern and western provinces in spite of opposition from the Sakas in the western parts. The Satavahana empire began to dwindle under his successors.

Trade flourished under the Satavahanas. The western and the eastern coasts had many active ports. In the western Deccan, Barygaza (present-day Bharuch) was the northernmost port and the largest was Kalyan. There were many market towns in the interiors, away from the ports. Traders were organized into guilds. Luxuries like wine and fine cloth were imported; common cotton cloth was the staple export. Roads were absent and this hindered trade but by the end of the first century CE, currency was plentiful and this facilitated trade. Around the first century CE, the eastern Deccan emerged as a hub of industrial and commercial activity, and this peaked at the end of the second century. Even though the Satavahana rulers were devoted to Brahmanism, Buddhism flourished throughout their rule. In fact, the first two centuries of the Common Era were the most glorious epochs for Buddhism in the Deccan. In society, women had a place of importance and they were even allowed to own property in their own right. Foreigners—people from outside the Satavahana realm like the Sakas—were assimilated into society but as Buddhists or as degraded Kshatriyas.

Around the time the Satavahanas were attaining prominence in South India, certain developments were taking place far away in Central Asia which would affect the history of India. In the third century BCE, the Chinese emperor Qin Shi Huang consolidated his position and this led to the movements of certain people. The Sakas of Scythia who had lived on the plains of the Syr Darya in Central Asia were displaced by the Great Yueh Chi tribe in the second century BCE. They moved southward into Afghanistan and then into

Northwest India. There was another group, known as the Parthians or the Pahlavas who came from the area called Parthia, south-east of the Caspian Sea. The people who came from Parthia into Northwest India in the first century BCE were referred to as the Saka–Pahlava or Scytho-Parthian. The rule of these people is known from their inscriptions. The Sakas ruled through governors known as kshatrapas. Some of these kshatrapas ruled in western India and were a thorn in the side of the Satavahanas. The Pahlavas came to rule over Southeast Deccan and made Kanchipuram their capital.

The movement of the Great Yueh Chi tribe and the consolidation of their power led to five Great Yueh principalities (political units ruled by a prince), of which one was the Kushanas. In the first century CE, the Kushanas merged these principalities and laid the foundations of the Kushana empire. The Kushana movement into India began around this time. The Kushana empire reached its peak under Kanishka who came to the throne in 78 CE. Kanishka extended his empire into the Gangetic plain and into Malwa. His power was also felt in other parts of central India and western India as the Saka kshatrapas of these areas acknowledged his right to rule. Economic motives—the trade potential of the lower Indus area and the diamond mines in Malwa—were probable factors behind this expansion. Kanishka's empire was vast. Apart from the areas in India just described, it included Afghanistan, eastern parts of Xinjiang in China, and Central Asia, north of the Oxus. The political unification of these areas facilitated trade. Kanishka was a patron of Buddhism; he patronized monasteries and Buddhist scholars like Ashvaghosha and Vasumitra. His coins, however, carry the motifs of various gods—the Buddha, Shiva, Greek, and Persian gods. This suggests that Kanishka tolerated all religions and through his coins recognized the religious and cultural diversity of his empire. The Bactrian language was used on Kanishka's coins, indicating the importance of Bactria in his empire. The Kushana kings were referred to as devaputra (sons of god).

Gold coin of Kanishka I, first century CE. National Museum, New Delhi.
This gold coin offers a striking image of Kanishka, the Kushana statesman and king. His broad shoulders are draped in a stiff, heavy coat and a cloak, presumably to protect the king against the bitter cold of the northern mountainous regions of Pakistan and Afghanistan over which he ruled. Grasped in one hand is a curved bow and arrow and in the other is perhaps a lantern. He sports a beard and a tall cap, and his boots point dramatically outwards, to present an image of authority, stability, and power.

The years between 200 BCE and 300 CE were marked by urban prosperity all over India. This is clear from archaeological remains and though this evidence is limited, it is spread over a large geographical area—from the Northwest to the Gangetic valley to eastern India to central and western India to the Deccan and the far south. The urbanization and prosperity were nurtured by artisanal production and trade. Artisanal production not only thrived but was also highly specialized. This is borne out by both archaeological and literary evidence. There is reference to as many as sixty types of crafts; crafts tended to be localized as is suggested by villages named after the main profession of the inhabitants. In the towns, people pursuing the same crafts tended to live in the same localities. There is the mention of potters, carpenters, metalsmiths, foresters, hunters, fishermen, and salt-makers. Crafts were hereditary with the sons following the fathers' occupation. This period also saw a notable increase in the number of guilds and in the scale of their operations. Guilds probably had a close relationship with kings and were often part of the royal entourage. The importance of guilds is evident from coins and seals that they issued. The specialization, scale, and organization of artisanal production suggest an obvious link with the expansion of trade that occurred between 200 BCE and 300 CE. This expansion was not just within the subcontinent but also with other lands.

The growth of the money economy is indicated by the availability of coins, which facilitated inland trade. There exist accounts of caravan journeys of people travelling by bullock carts and on foot; the rich travelled by chariots or palanquins. Ports were connected to the manufacturing centres in the countryside. There are descriptions of markets selling a large variety of commodities. There appear to have been some major trade arteries. One of them—the Uttarapath—linked Taxila in the north-west to Tamralipti in the Gangetic delta. Another route was the sea route connecting Sindh and Gujarat. Another began from Mathura and via the Chambal valley travelled to Ujjain and moved from there into the Narmada valley. This same route after crossing the Satpura Hills and the Tapti River split into two—one crossed the Western Ghats to Surat and another went on to the Deccan. In South India, trade routes followed the rivers. There is a great deal of evidence regarding the growth of trade beyond the subcontinent in this period. One area with which trade flourished was the East and Southeast Asia. The areas around the Pamirs and Gandhara served as hubs for trade with China that was principally dominated by silk.

In the first century CE, overseas trade with Southeast Asia increased and a variety of goods were exported from India to that region. The principal items of trade were gold, spices, cotton cloth, sugar, beads, pottery, aromatics, sandalwood, and camphor. These commodities were also valued in the Mediterranean region. Sources for this period mention the term yavana—a term initially used for Greeks but later included anyone who came from the west of the subcontinent. The period under discussion witnessed a flourishing trade between India

Standing Buddha, second–third century CE, Kushana period, Gandhara region. National Museum, New Delhi.

The distinctive elements of the images of the Buddha and attendant figures of the Gandhara region are seen in the natural treatment of the body and clothing; wavy hair, strong features—sharp nose, arched eyebrows, and elongated earlobes. This sculpture of the Buddha conveys a sense of calm repose and the thick folds of the clothing provide a flowing outline to the figure.

and the Roman empire. The latter had an interest in the Chinese silk trade but when between 27 BCE and 14 CE there was turbulence in Parthia, traders avoided the Central Asian route and travelled through India. Goods came overland to India and from there reached the shores of the Roman empire by sea. It is worth noting that a large number of Roman coins have been discovered in India. One immediate consequence of trade was the prominence of merchants in society. This is borne out by inscriptions from various regions in which merchants are identified as donors. Merchants began to patronize religious institutions with financial support. This was in one obvious way an expression of their piety but it was also a sign of their importance in society. Even Buddhist monasteries were not left unaffected by this expansion of mercantile and financial activities.

Trade with Europe via the Middle East brought Jews and Christians to India's shores. These small trading groups settled in Kerala and Tamil Nadu around the first century CE and their descendant communities continue to live here. They brought with them their faith and culture, but assimilated with local people and adopted their language and ways of life.

St. Thomas Cathedral, Chennai, Tamil Nadu

Over the trade routes established from the Mediterranean region to India came people and ideas. Saint Thomas, one of the twelve apostles of Jesus Christ, is said to have come to India in 52 CE to spread the Christian faith. He was martyred in 72 CE and buried in Chennai. The original modest shrine over his grave was redeveloped when Portuguese explorers built the large San Thome Church in the 1500s. In 1893, the British rebuilt it to the proportions of a Catholic cathedral, and it soon became the famous pilgrimage centre that it is today.

As suggested by the discussion above, this period was one of social churn as well. Merchants were not just carriers of goods, they were also carriers of ideas and different practices. Trade was often the driver of social and cultural change. While the four varnas remained fundamental to Brahmanical orthodoxy, some changes are noticeable. Outsiders, such as the yavanas, were being absorbed into the varna system and this was justified by the theory of mixture of varnas (varna–samkara). Offspring of unequal marriages were being recognized thus showing that caste distinctions were losing some of their rigidities. Women were generally seen as inferior and subordinate but from the second century BCE women's right to inheritance was being sanctioned. Women, as inscriptions from the era of the Satavahanas show, began to take the initiative in making donations. The use of matronyms (the mother's surname) was not uncommon. This period also saw greater interaction between the predominantly Sanskritic culture of the north with the Tamil cultures of the south. And in the south, this period saw the emergence of Sangam literature with its celebration of war and love.

This was also a period of experimentation as wooden architecture was replaced with more permanent stone structures. Temples were built in stone, often mimicking the wooden prototype to enshrine the images, and markets and settlements developed around them.

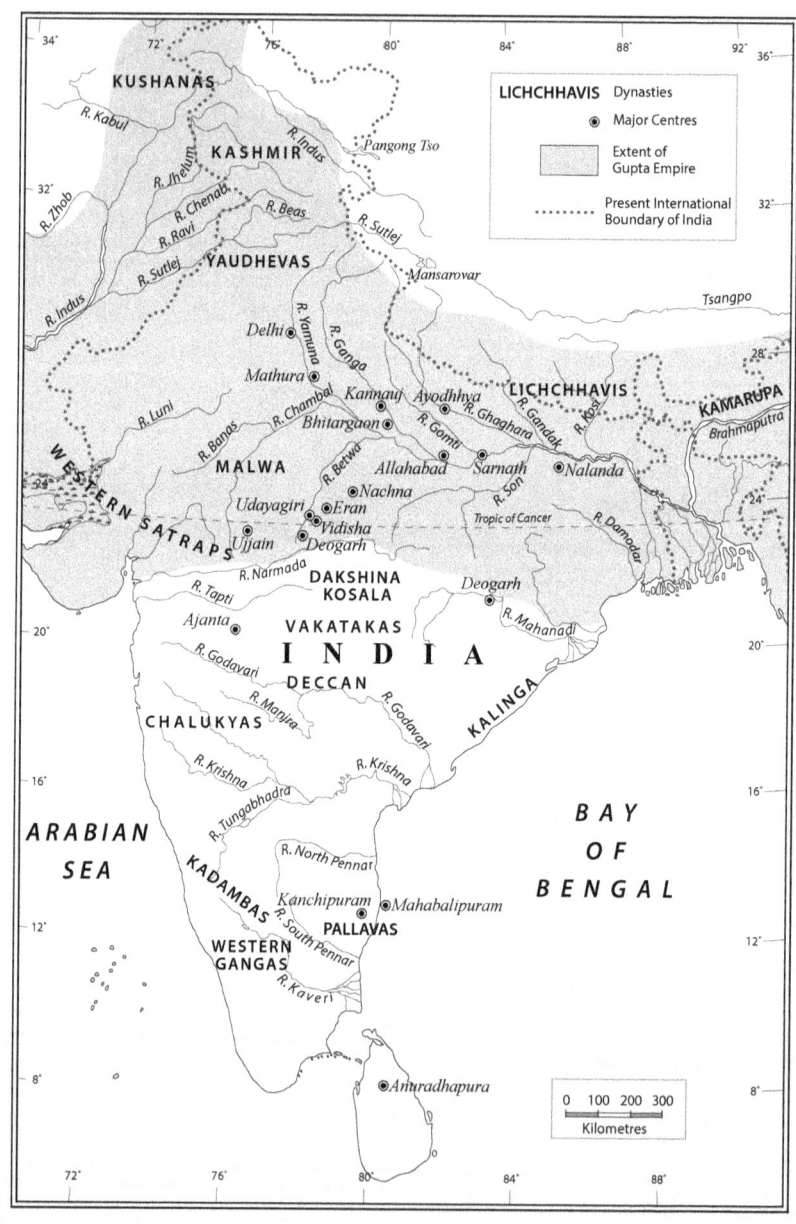

The Gupta empire

Not to scale. This map has been prepared in adherence to the 'Guidelines for acquiring and producing Geospatial Data and Geospatial Data Services including Maps' published vide DST F.No.SM/25/02/2020 (Part-I) dated 15th February, 2021

· CHAPTER 8 ·

THE GUPTA AGE AND BEYOND

c. 320 CE–c. 900 CE

Many of the changes noted in the previous chapter continued and matured over the next three centuries but the political configuration underwent a dramatic transformation. From around 320 CE, a new centralizing political power began to emerge. This was the beginning of the Gupta empire. The origins of the first Gupta monarch were modest and were probably located in the western Gangetic plain. The first monarch took on the name of the first Maurya emperor—Chandragupta—and married a daughter of the Lichchhavi clan, a very distinguished lineage of North Bihar. Both these—taking the name Chandragupta and the marriage into an established family—are suggestive of the first Gupta monarch's endeavour to claim for himself a superior status and greater acceptability. In his coins, Chandragupta highlighted his Lichchhavi connections. He extended his kingdom to Prayaga and Magadha and took for himself the grandiose title maharajadhiraja (great king of kings). His son Samudra Gupta ascended the throne in 335 CE and claimed that he had been chosen by his father to be the successor.

The basic information about Samudra Gupta is known from what is called the Allahabad Pillar Inscription. The pillar is actually one of Ashoka's Pillar Edicts on which a eulogy on Samudra Gupta has been overwritten. This choice suggests one of two things. Samudra Gupta may have been trying to lay claims of continuity with Ashoka in terms of the extent of his empire. Or he may have been attempting the exact opposite: he was trying to demonstrate through his overwriting how different his policies were from Ashoka's. The ambition of Samudra Gupta was to establish a vast empire as extensive as that of the Mauryas. It would also be an empire that would be controlled from the capital. The principal source of his reign is the eulogy on the pillar, which raises questions regarding exaggerated claims and praise.

Samudra Gupta was succeeded by his son, Chandra Gupta II, who had a long reign from c. 375 CE to c. 415 CE. He was known for his chivalry and heroic qualities. It is possible that he was involved in a

Gold coins of Samudra Gupta. National Museum, New Delhi.

The coins of Samudra Gupta are unusual: there are representations of the king with his wife; another depicting him as a skilled royal archer; another coin with a powerful image of an animal next to the sacrificial staff portrays the king performing the Ashvamedha (a ritual involving horse sacrifice); and of the king relaxed, seated on a couch playing a stringed musical instrument (a lute or a lyre). The reverse side of the coin with the king playing a lyre has an image of Lakshmi, the goddess of wealth and well-being. These representations on tiny gold coins (of 20 millimetre diameter approx.) created the image of a strong, powerful ruler who was also a lover of music and poetry.

dispute over succession with his brother, Rama. The discovery of the coins of Rama Gupta seems to suggest this. Chandra Gupta II, once he ascended the throne, fought a major victorious campaign against the Sakas. The outcome was the annexation of western India which was commemorated by the issuing of silver coins. The security of the western border meant that the Guptas now controlled the ports and thus had access to the western trade. The western Deccan, once controlled by the Satavahanas, was ruled at this time by the Vakataka dynasty which had grown to be the dominant power in the region. The marriage between Chandra Gupta II's daughter, Prabhavatigupta, and the Vakataka king Rudrasena II, facilitated Gupta access to the Deccan but this did not mean a diminishing of the control of the Vakatakas. When Rudrasena II died five years into his reign, his wife became the regent and this cemented the Gupta–Vakataka ties. Chandra Gupta II took on the title of Vikramaditya (sun of prowess); he was known for his patronage of culture.

From the time of Kumara Gupta (c. 415–54 CE), the son and successor of Chandra Gupta II, through the next hundred years, the Huns—or the Hunas as they are called in Indian sources—loomed over the politics of northern India. A branch of the White Huns had taken over Bactria in the previous century and were pushing to cross the Hindu Kush. The later Guptas and their successors were not quite up to the task to resist the Huns but they were not utterly unsuccessful either because territory under the Guptas did not suffer the same fate as the Roman empire. The invasion of the Huns is another instance of the influence of Central Asia on the politics of northern India—the Huns followed the Sakas and the Kushanas, and the Turks would follow the Huns.

The decline of the Gupta empire cannot, however, be ascribed to the invasion of the Huns. While Skanda Gupta (whose last known date is 467 CE) fought the Huns—the mlechchha (or barbarians as they were called)—he was also plagued by domestic problems like faction fighting in his court and the defiance of feudatories. There also seemed to have been a fiscal crisis: the high-value Gupta coins were debased. After the death of Skanda Gupta, the central authority of the Guptas was a thing of the past—even the names and the order of his successors are uncertain. The final blow came at the end of the fifth century CE when the Huns descended into northern India, the erstwhile metropolitan area of the Guptas.

From the disappearance of the Gupta empire to the early seventh century, four kingdoms ruled over different parts of North India. Magadha was ruled by a dynasty called the Guptas—not to be linked to the Guptas of the Gupta empire—this was a minor line that coincidentally bore the same name. Kannauj was ruled by the Maukharis; Thanesar (north of Delhi) by the Pushyabhutis; and Valabhi (in Saurashtra) by the Maitrakas. The Maukharis expanded their dominion by ousting the Guptas from Magadha; they thus transformed themselves from tributary rulers to independent kings who styled themselves maharajadhiraja, supreme monarch, or the first amongst kings. The Pushyabhutis made a marriage alliance with the Maukharis and with the passing of the last of the latter dynasty, the two kingdoms were unified. The Maitrakas had been bureaucrats under the Guptas; they developed Valabhi as their capital and it became an important hub of commerce and learning. They continued to rule till the eighth century when their power began to be eroded by the attacks of the Arabs.

The Pushyabhuti dynasty acquired significance under Harshavardhana (conveniently referred to as Harsha) whose reign began in 606 CE. Harsha is probably the first important Indian monarch to have a biographer. *Harshacharita* was written by Banabhatta who was a friend of Harsha and a man of letters. Banabhatta, unwittingly, was creating a genre—the biographical eulogy; he was also setting a precedent as many subsequent kings had their biographies composed by courtiers. Sifted carefully, the *Harshacharita* does provide a chronological account of major events and thus provides clues to what was considered important at that time. Fortunately, we have another detailed account of Harsha and his times from the Chinese Buddhist monk Xuanzang who travelled across large parts of India.

View of chaitya halls and viharas, Ajanta, Maharashtra

Around the second century BCE, this horseshoe-shaped cliff (carved out by the Wagora River over millennia) was the chosen location for a large Buddhist establishment. Buddhist monks worked for centuries (second century BCE to fifth century CE) at this peaceful site to create chaityas (prayer halls) and viharas (monasteries). The rooms and halls of Ajanta were not built from the foundation upwards, like stone architecture, but cut out of the living rock. Therefore, the 'caves' of Ajanta are not really caves but monumental sculpted, rock-cut architecture. The walls, pillars, and ceilings of the prayer halls and living quarters for the monks were covered with sculptures and paintings. The volcanic rock of the Deccan Plateau, rich in minerals, provided vibrant colours for the paintings—ochre for red and yellow, basalt rock used for green, oil lamps provided black soot, lime for white, while blue from lapis lazuli may have been imported from Afghanistan.

Harsha ruled for forty-one years. In the course of his reign he moved his capital from Thanesar to Kannauj which was located in a rich agricultural tract and was free from any threats from the north-west. Kannauj also served as a bridgehead to the Gangetic plain, to the west and the south. Harsha reduced the rulers of

Jalandhar, Kashmir, Nepal, and Valabhi to tributary status but was unable to extend his control eastward where Shashanka, a king of Bengal, remained a hostile foe; he also did not succeed in making inroads into the Deccan. In fact, he suffered his most major military defeat in his encounter with Pulakeshin II, a Chalukya king of the western Deccan. Harsha was no ordinary king: he travelled around his kingdom and is said to have written three plays. The Chinese emperor Tai Tsung sent an embassy to Harsha's court in 643 CE so Harsha appears in Chinese sources. After Harsha's death, his kingdom fell apart into smaller kingdoms. The imperial structure that Harsha had established was eroded by the political and economic conditions of the time.

There is evidence that some towns declined but new urban centres also developed like Kannauj. In the Deccan, during the Vakataka era, Paunar grew as did Valabhi in western India. The latter was linked to the trade in the Arabian Sea which was flourishing. Indian ships were now regularly sailing across the Arabian Sea and the Indian Ocean. The more enterprising of the merchants were venturing out to Southeast Asia and as far as the China Sea. There is evidence of trading contacts with the east African seaboard. This trade and these contacts expanded, in spite of the prohibitions on travel over sea and coming into contact with the mlechchhas. Indian merchants were also making their presence felt in Central Asia. Sources of commerce were the raw materials from mines, plants, and animals that had been transformed by craftsmen. Gold was mined in Karnataka and then given very sophisticated shape by skilled craftsmen. The gold coins of the Guptas bear testimony to the high quality of the craftsmanship. Copper and iron continued to be mined and used to make household utensils. Ivory work was also prevalent.

Iron was being transformed into steel of a high quality as is borne out by the Iron Pillar which now stands in Mehrauli in Delhi and even today does not carry any evidence of rusting. On it there is an inscription which refers to a king called Chandra who is often identified as being Chandra Gupta II. In the Birmingham Museum in the United Kingdom there is a life-size copper statue of the Buddha; the statue was cast in two parts providing material and historical evidence of the mastery of metalwork during this period.

Painting of Padmapani, Cave No. 1, Ajanta, Maharashtra

Cave No. 1 is a vihara dated to the fifth century CE and contains some of the most famous paintings of Ajanta. The imposing hall has twenty pillars and fourteen residential cells where the monks slept. At the centre of the extreme end of the hall, the rock has been carved with a prayer niche with a life-size image of the seated Buddha. On either side of the prayer niche are large painted figures of the Bodhisattvas paying homage to the Buddha. The Bodhisattvas are compassionate beings who are said to have deferred their own attainment of nirvana to teach people the way of the Buddha. The Bodhisattva Avalokateshvara stands on the right and Padmapani to the left, their sheer size and distinct colours standing out against the dark background and the crowd of attendant figures. Padmapani holds a lotus or padma in his hand. His gentle expression, the softly modelled face, is framed by bow-like eyebrows and a high forehead. He is wearing an elaborate headdress, and an elegant pearl and sapphire necklace. The paintings of Ajanta influenced many early painting traditions from Sri Lanka to China.

Iron Pillar, Gupta period, Qutb Minar complex, Mehrauli, Delhi

The Iron Pillar (7.2 metres high, 40.6 centimetres in diameter, 3 tonnes in weight) was analysed and found to have been made of corrosion-resistant iron. It has a bell-shaped capital on top, above that must have been a capital with a figure of some significance. The earliest inscription on the pillar in Sanskrit uses the flowery poetic style of the Gupta era and mentions that this pillar was set up on a hill known as Vishnupada by the mighty king 'Chandra', identified as Chandra Gupta II.

Textiles of various kinds were manufactured in large quantities—silk, wool, various types of cotton-muslin, calico, and linen. These textiles were items of trade across India as well as in the Asian markets. The growth of trade suggests better communication and roads; the rivers, of course, served as convenient modes of transport of men and commodities. Spices, pepper, sandalwood, pearls, precious stones, perfumes, indigo, and herbs remained prominent export items. Horses were imported overland in large numbers from Iran and Bactria into Northwest India and by sea from Arabia into the western ports.

The Gupta age was famous for the advances it witnessed in the world of learning, literature, art, and architecture. Education and learning were, of course, confined to the elite and were carried out through Sanskrit. Learning followed the model of a guru teaching a group of disciples and was heavily dependent on memory. Apart from learning verses from the Vedas, grammar, rhetoric, logic, metaphysics, and composition (verse and prose) were part of the curriculum. These were considered part of traditional Sanskrit learning; to this was added astronomy, astrology, mathematics, and medicine (including veterinary sciences). Buddhist monasteries also contributed to learning first through the oral method and then moved to reading and writing. Monasteries were important repositories of manuscripts which were copied when they became brittle. Of all the centres of Buddhist learning, Nalanda was the most famous and it attracted scholars from all over India, China, and Southeast Asia.

Advances in astronomy were facilitated by contact with the culture of ancient Greece, which had by then spread to West Asia. Earlier studies focused on the moon, its cycles and seasons. During this period there was a shift to an emphasis on the planets and the solar system, and the development of a complex and more accurate calendar system. Ujjain, perhaps because it was on the prime Indian meridian, emerged as a centre for the study of astronomy. Around 499 CE, Aryabhata was the best-known astronomer and mathematician of the age. He calculated the value of pi to 3.1416 and the length of the solar year to 365.3586805 days. Both these calculations are impressive because they are very close to recent calculations. He explained eclipses as the shadow of the earth falling on the moon. This was a radical departure from the popular belief that during an eclipse the demon Rahu gobbled up the moon. Aryabhata described the earth as a sphere that rotated on its own axis. Varahamihira, a contemporary of Aryabhata, linked the study of astronomy with astrology. But there was also an effort, on the part of Aryabhata and his followers, to maintain a distinction between the two. What is important to highlight is that developments in astrology, astronomy, and mathematics were not carried out in isolation in India: they were the products of a continuous interaction between Indian and Arab astronomers and mathematicians. The works of Indian mathematicians and astronomers were studied in centres of learning located in places like Baghdad. A world of learning without boundaries was already developing. Arab scholars noted that the mathematical knowledge they had gained from India was richer than what they had learnt from the Greeks. Numerals that were to replace the Roman numerals were introduced by the Arabs who had learnt them from India. This is clear from the name Hindusa that the Arabs used to describe these numerals. Indians used the decimal system; they introduced the Arabs to algebra; and the earliest inscription using the zero dates to the seventh century CE.

In the field of Sanskrit creative writing in this period, the preeminent figure was the poet and dramatist Kalidasa. His long poem *Meghaduta* and his play *Shakuntala* came to be, and still are, regarded as classics. There were other writers too—Shudraka who wrote the play *Mrichchha-katika*, and Vishakhadatta whose famous play was *Mudrarakshasa*; Bharata also produced the famous treatise on dance, drama, and poetry called the *Natyashastra*. The *Panchatantra*, a book of fables, sought to educate a young prince in the ways of the world. There were developments in texts in Prakrit, especially concerning Jainism.

In the sphere of religious ideas and practices there were new developments. The most important of these were separate sects worshipping Shiva and Vishnu. Female deities, personifying shakti or power, emerged as the focus of new rites and rituals—these would later lead to a form of worship known as Tantrism. The religious sects produced a series of texts called the Puranas which fused myths, history, and rituals. The Puranas are difficult to date but some of them were written in this period. There were also changes in other non-orthodox sects like Jainism and Buddhism. As Buddhism spread into Central Asia, China, and Southeast Asia, it adopted and adjusted to local religious practices. This led to changes to the original message of the Buddha: one feature was the deification of the Buddha. Jainism underwent changes especially after the meeting of the Second Jaina Council held at Valabhi in the early sixth century. Here also the evolution of certain Jaina icons is noticeable.

The Buddha's first sermon, third–sixth centuries CE, Sarnath, Uttar Pradesh

In this celebrated sculpture of the Buddha seated in padmasana (lotus pose), the Buddha's hands are in the teaching gesture, the hair is pulled back into the ushnisha (topknot) that appears like a shell-like curl on top of his head. His body is firm and youthful, his clothes draped over one shoulder fall in a pattern of regular folds. The Buddha's gentle expression and bent head are framed by a large, decorated halo with two flying figures showering flowers over him. The halo symbolizes the attainment of enlightenment and the illuminating quality of his wisdom and teachings.

Growing trade and commerce, especially overseas trade, were not only carriers of goods but also of ideas. Religious ideas, especially Buddhist ideas, travelled across Asia during this period. All these features—in the economy, in politics, in art—made the Gupta age and the following epochs periods of extraordinary change and creativity.

The centuries that followed the breakdown of the Gupta empire in northern India witnessed significant developments south of the Vindhyas. South India, during this period, was evolving its own institutions and cultural traits and these have had an enduring legacy. Large kingdoms began to emerge in the region, and in the courts of these kingdoms there was a vibrant interaction between the local culture and the expanding culture based on Sanskrit learning and tradition. In the South Indian inscriptions of this period, the earlier ones tended to use only Tamil. Later there were inscriptions in Sanskrit and Prakrit along with Tamil. In the final period, the formulaic part (salutations and honorific titles) of the inscription was in Sanskrit, followed by the main body of the text in Tamil. Outside the Tamil country in South India, inscriptions used Sanskrit and Kannada. In the sphere of piety too there was coexistence of Vedic Brahmanism and forms of Tamil devotion. In the western Deccan, the kingdoms served as bridges and melting pots between the North and the South by making possible the circulation of ideas across both sides of the divide. This interaction notwithstanding, different styles, especially in architecture, began to emerge.

To form an idea of what was happening in South India, it is important to appreciate geography as a determining factor in the developments of the region. Two natural configurations have to be borne in mind. One, the rivers in the region flow from west to east. And two, South India is constituted by two distinct geographical entities: the western Deccan, a vast plateau enclosed by mountains (the Ghats) running along the western and eastern coasts; and the Tamil country, the rich and fertile plains south of Chennai. This division meant that the kingdoms in the west located in the plateau

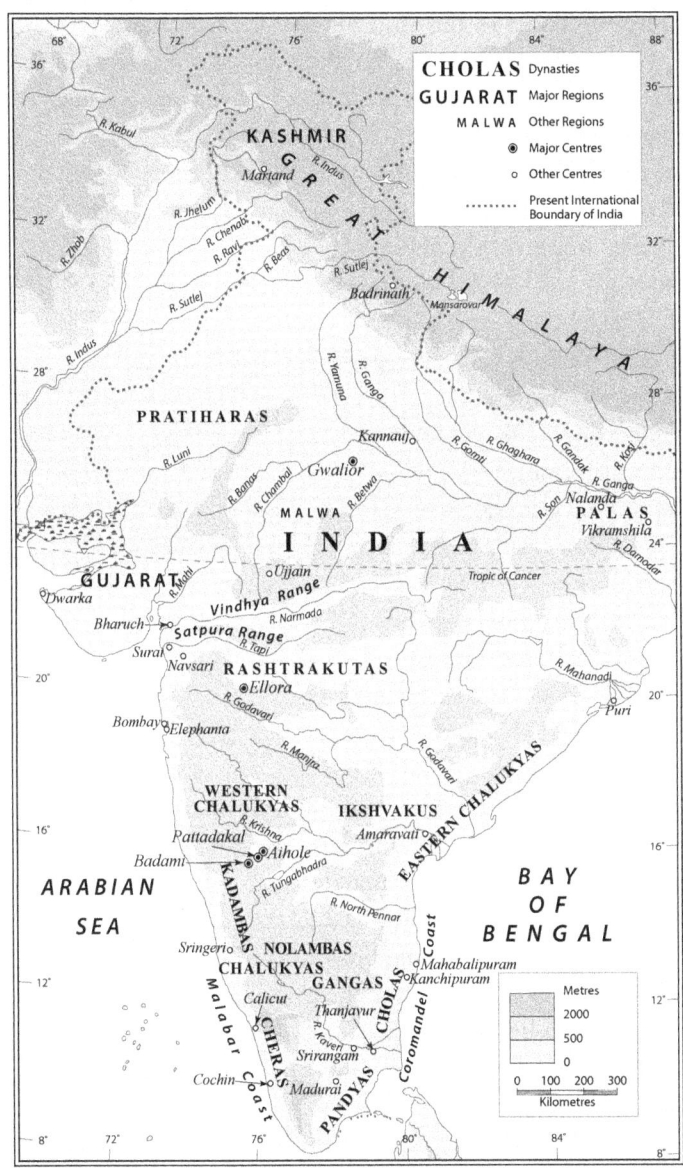

Kingdoms that rose after the breakdown of the Gupta empire

Not to scale. This map has been prepared in adherence to the 'Guidelines for acquiring and producing Geospatial Data and Geospatial Data Services including Maps' published vide DST F.No.SM/25/02/2020 (Part-I) dated 15th February, 2021

and the kingdoms in the east, the plains, both wanted to control the principal waterways, the Krishna and the Godavari. The land between the two rivers—the doab—was the site of long-lasting conflicts that were political and economic; and these conflicts were not related to which dynasty was ruling which region. Agriculture was confined to the coast, and the doab and these localities, around this time, had older Buddhist centres that facilitated trade. Kingdoms tended to be smaller, regional, and ruled over by powerful regional dynasties. This is one important difference between the polities of South India and those situated north of the Vindhyas.

The western Deccan, after the rule of the Vakatakas, was controlled by the Chalukyas from Badami. In the eastern Deccan towards the south, the Shalankayanas and later the eastern Chalukyas held sway. The Ikshvakus, from Nagarjunakonda and Dharanikota, ruled over the Krishna–Guntur area. Karnataka came to be divided between the Kadambas, Nolambas, and Gangas. Further south, various parts of the Tamil country were controlled by the Cheras, Cholas, and Pandyas. But their control was threatened by the Kalabhras, possibly a hill tribe who had settled in the plains and had extended their patronage to Buddhists and Jainas. Clan-based societies gradually gave way to kingship and the establishment of powerful dynasties. From around the middle of 500 CE over the next 300 years, the Chalukyas of Badami, the Pallavas of Kanchipuram, and the Pandyas of Madurai were in conflict over the control of the fertile plains.

The Chalukyas had strong links with the traders on the western seaboard and seaports. They also withstood incursions from the north when their king Pulakeshin II defeated Harsha at the Narmada. The deltas of the Krishna and the Godavari had been overrun by the Ikshvakus in the third century CE but they were defeated by the Pallavas who took over this region. The latter extended their rule southward by defeating the Kadamba rulers whose kingdom had been to the south of the Chalukya realm.

Dancing Natraj, late sixth century, Cave No. 1, Badami, Karnataka

Around 544 CE, the Chalukyas came to power in the Deccan and they chose Badami as their capital, as this river-fed region was fertile and protected by sandstone hills. The remains of the palace complex and temples at Badami provide a glimpse of the extraordinary talent of the artists of this period. The tradition of carving rock-cut shrines continued in Karnataka on the sandstone hillside. Cave No. 1 has at its entrance a rare and most energetic image of a sixteen-armed Shiva, the cosmic dancer, accompanied by musicians.

The Pallava kingdom was seen as being prosperous. The most important of the Pallava rulers was Mahendravarman I (600–630 CE) under whom the dynasty grew in strength; he was also a great patron of Tamil culture and was himself a notable dramatist and poet; he was the author of the play *Mattavilasa-prahasana* (The Delight of the Drunkards). He was the contemporary of Harshavardhana and Pulakeshin II. Mahendravarman was a patron of rock-cut temples: the temples at Mahabalipuram were built during his reign. He is said to have begun his life as a Jaina but later converted to Shaivism. He was also a great warrior king. His great adversary was Pulakeshin II and it was inevitable that two such powerful kings in the same territory would come into conflict. The Chalukya–Pallava wars continued, with the former getting the upper hand more often than not, especially under Pulakeshin II. The success of the latter was avenged by Narasimhavarman, the son of Mahendravarman, who captured the Chalukya capital. Around 655 CE, the Chalukyas under one of the sons of Pulakeshin II recovered some of the territories they had lost. The see-saw conflict continued as the armies of the two dynasties were equally matched.

In Kerala, in the deep south, and on the west coast, the Makotai kingdom ruled in the Periyar valley supported by Brahmin agricultural settlements in the fertile areas. But the real source of wealth in Kerala was maritime trade. Brahmins were late arrivals as migrants and they had to adjust and adapt to local cultures and customs. One outcome of this was the development of matrilineal societies.

There had been contacts with the east and west coasts of South India; these were strengthened because of the flourishing trade with West and East Asia. This trade reached the markets of Byzantium and was largely conducted by Arab traders, some of whom began to settle on the southern and western coasts. They were welcomed, patronized through land grants, and were allowed to practise their own religion as had been done with the Christian settlers earlier. The Mappilas or Malabar Muslims are descendants of these Arab settlers. The Muslim settlers along the west and southern coast adopted local practices and accepted customary law. It is important to underline that these Muslims, since they were primarily traders, were not interested either in political power or in conversions.

'Descent of the Ganga', mid-seventh century, Mahabalipuram, Tamil Nadu

Mahabalipuram or Mamallapuram was the port town of the Pallavas. The hard granite outcrop consists of a complex of early South Indian examples of Pallava monumental rock-cut architecture and shrines.

A massive sculptural panel identified as the 'Descent of the Ganga' is carved in high relief on two huge natural boulders and the cleft between them enabled rainwater to cascade down, and to cleverly simulate the story of how the river Ganga came down to earth. The river is symbolized by water-serpent deities. The upper level of the panel represents the sky with flying figures of gods converging to celebrate this extraordinary event. Shiva, on the left, offers the gift of the sacred river to the earth. Most Indian sculpture and painting have a universal composition containing the elements of nature; with the sky above, the earth below with human beings and water, and often humorous, enchanting observations of the natural world.

After Arab armies invaded Persia in the seventh century, there was a migration of Zoroastrians to India from the early eighth century onwards; they already had trading contacts with western India and many of them settled to the north of Mumbai and Gujarat. The

Arabs also invaded Sind in the eighth century and established themselves in parts of western India, but when they attempted to advance into Chalukya territory to gain control over the ports, they met with stiff resistance.

The Navsari Atash Behram (fire temple), Navsari, Gujarat

Escaping persecution in Persia, a small band of Zoroastrian followers landed in Gujarat, at Navsari, the place where the Parsis first settled, promising the ruler that they would amalgamate with the local community. They still speak Gujarati and have, over the centuries, contributed to every field—from science and industry to the arts in India. The fire temple or agiary consists of a hall, anteroom, and the sanctum, where the sacred eternal fire is kept burning perpetually, and is accessible only to the priest. The temple structure and façade is intentionally modest and undecorated. There are over 160 fire temples in India; forty of these are in Mumbai. However, sadly, this small but influential community is dwindling fast.

**Interior of the Paradesi Synagogue,
mid-eighteenth century, Kochi, Kerala**

Trade between India and the West began before the first century CE. Arab, Jewish, and Christian traders created small settlements and places of worship on the coasts of India. In Kochi, remains of the Jew Town consist of large warehouses once used for storage of spice and timber. Around the middle of the sixteenth century the Paradesi Synagogue was built (and renovated several times). Inside is a large hall paved with Chinese tiles and lit by chandeliers. In the centre is the pulpit and in the front is enshrined the holy tabernacle with scrolls of the Torah. A copperplate records that the local ruler made a grant permitting the Jews to trade with India. Unfortunately, over the centuries, the Jewish community in India has reduced considerably, due to migration.

This period witnessed the emergence of the Rashtrakuta kingdom. The rise of the Rashtrakutas was unfettered because of the absence of any intervention from the north and the declining powers of some of the kingdoms of the Deccan like the Pallavas. The Cholas,

Kailasanatha Temple, No. 16, mid-eighth century CE, Ellora, Maharashtra

Ellora in Maharashtra is a World Heritage Site with over thirty-four rock-cut shrines—twelve shrines of the Buddhist Mahayana sect in the south (sixth to eighth centuries CE), seventeen Hindu shrines to the north (sixth to ninth centuries CE), and five Jaina shrines (ninth century CE). It is interesting to note that these three different faiths lived and worked for over 300 years in one location. Kailasanatha Temple is entirely rock-cut, with no additional loose stone or parts. The temple is entered through an ornamental gateway that leads to a courtyard, a pillared mandapa or hall with a sloping roof and entrance porch. The free-standing temple in the centre was created by cutting three trenches to make a central block of the hill that sculptors carved from top to bottom to create two storeys, a typical pyramidal vimana of the South Indian style, a garbha griha, pillared rooms all profusely carved with sculptures of high quality.

the successors of the Pallavas, had not yet gained in strength and importance. The Rashtrakutas controlled large parts of the western coast and thus the trade with West Asia. They traded extensively with the Arabs and referred to them as Tajiks and appointed them as governors of administrative districts.

At the end of the first millennium CE, the pre-eminent political presence in South India, especially in Tamil Nadu, was the Chola dynasty. In the ninth century, the Pallavas could not successfully resist attacks from the Pandyas and their tributaries, the Cholas, who ruled the territory south of the Pallava realm. The Cholas built on the agrarian foundations of the Pallava kingdom and emerged as the dominant power in South India. The heart of their kingdom was Cholamandalam, around Tanjore (present-day Thanjavur), and up the eastern coast to what later came to be called the Coromandel. The pre-eminence of the Cholas grew not so much out of their political authority as from the cultural life under their rule. In religion, in social institutions, in sculpture, and in architecture, the Cholas set new standards of excellence and sophistication which became part of the living tradition of South India.

Apart from inland victories, the Cholas pushed their territorial limits to the eastern region and boasted that they had conquered lands along the river Ganga. A grand temple in Tamil Nadu memorializes this event and is called Gangaikonda Cholapuram (commemorating when the Ganga was brought to Chola country). In the tenth century, the Cholas under Rajaraja and his successor Rajendra Chola formed a powerful navy that established trade links and territorial rights in Sri Lanka, Maldives, the Malaya Peninsula, and neighbouring areas. The texts and inscriptions of the Chola period mention trade, and the export of spices and gems. The wealth from trade and conquest financed the construction of imperial temples in the Chola kingdom.

Sanskrit learning superseded Buddhist and Jaina education which had prevailed in peninsular India in the earlier part of this period. The Jainas had a tradition of Sanskrit religious literature but increasingly began to use Tamil; they set up educational institutions near Madurai and Kanchipuram and in Karnataka. They also lived as hermits in caves and the most notable of these was the one at Sittannavasal in Pudukkottai which has traces of very early beautiful murals. Buddhist learning was centred around monasteries located in the vicinity of Kanchipuram and between the Krishna and the Godavari. These monasteries in their time were as well known as the one at Nalanda. Brahmanical learning emanated from ghatikas and mathas (from the eighth century CE) which were initially meant only for the Brahmins. The mathas (or mutts) were centres of Brahmanical learning and of Puranic Hinduism; they were more than educational centres, they served as rest houses and feeding places. Many of these mathas still exist, and came to be associated with particular sects and some of them emerged as pilgrim centres. Through these institutions, the influence of Sanskrit spread and it became the court language. The rise of Sanskrit should not deflect attention from the importance of Tamil as the vehicle of lyric and epic poetry. *Shilappadikaram* and *Manimekalai*, two Tamil epic poems which represent a very special poetic style, are dated to the mid-first millennium CE.

There was a continuous interaction between the cultures of northern and southern India, and through this process there was adaptation and innovation as well.

One institution that gained in prominence through religious practices was the temple. Temples were maintained through grants of land, sometimes entire villages. The donors were very often individuals with royal lineages but merchants too made donations for temples. Brahmins were responsible for the rituals that were performed but members of other castes (including lower castes) carried out the subsidiary functions like playing music, lighting lamps, and so on. However, those castes who were considered unclean and outcastes—potters, tanners, and others—were not allowed entry into the temples. Temple construction increased through this period. One factor in this increase was greater engagement with devotional worship. Temples, especially when they grew out of royal donations, often served as an extension of the royal court and thus as a centre of power. Through the temples, the royal court could intervene in local affairs when it suited the interests of the monarch. There was thus a close interplay between royal and priestly power. Temples built

The gopurams and golden roof of the shrine of Srirangam, Tamil Nadu

The Srirangam Temple has grown to massive proportions since the time of its inception. The towering gopurams (gateways) of the temple complex dominate the skyline and act like a beacon drawing travelling pilgrims to the shrine. Annual temple festivals are accompanied with processions of the temple cart pulled by devotees, carrying the image of the deity; this act brings the community together.

on non-royal donations similarly served the interests of the elites and the wealthy. Important and large temples emerged as pilgrim centres which served as sites for markets and commerce and also for exchanges and interactions among various groups of people. Temples thus served not only an obvious religious purpose but also social and economic purposes.

Nataraja, eleventh century, Chola, Tamil Nadu

The Nataraja figure is a symbolic representation of Shiva, the cosmic dancer and creator. This bronze image, made using the lost wax process, is full of contained energy and movement, and yet retains in its metal hardness the soft textures of the wax from which it was made.

In one hand, Shiva holds a damaru (drum) symbolizing the source of all creation—rhythmic sound and the taal (or beat) of life. In the other hand, he holds a flame—the symbol of destruction. The third hand is raised in the mudra of abhaya (protection). The fourth hand points to Shiva's feet—trampling the dwarf figure Apasmara, the personification of ignorance.

The most important figure in the functioning of any temple was the Brahmin, who served to maintain the political status quo and to preserve the position and privileges of the local elite. Brahmin communities were settled in towns and villages and gifted land for their services. The pre-eminence of the Brahmins reaffirmed the caste system but certain changes and adaptations were noticeable. For example, a group called the Vellalar emerged; their economic functions covered a wide range of activities. In varna terms they were often equated with the Shudras but in terms of functions they were second in importance to the Brahmins. In the rural world, the Brahmins and the Vellalars managed the affairs of the temple.

The centuries following the decline of the Gupta dynasty in northern India are often neglected because they were not dominated by any one dynasty. There was a diffusion of political authority and many different ruling dynasties emerged all over the subcontinent. Urbanization and urban occupations thrived especially in South India. Trade links expanded within the subcontinent, across the seas and overland—Southeast Asia, China, West Asia, and the Mediterranean world. New forms of worship and devotion evolved. Temple architecture and other art and literary forms flourished, contributing to rich and varied cultural traditions.

· CHAPTER 9 ·

THE DELHI SULTANATE

c. 1206 CE–c. 1525 CE

From around 1000–1100 CE, North India again became the focus of major political developments. The core area of these developments shifted westward from Pataliputra initially to Kannauj and then more permanently to Delhi. Kannauj was the hub of routes going into the Gangetic plain and also of trading arteries moving southward and to the western seaboard. Kannauj thus became the site for strife as many regional political formations tried to establish control over it. Delhi, on the other hand, was at the receiving end of violent interventions originating from Central Asia which was coming under the influence of Islam.

The first invasion from the north-west came from a ruler of Ghazni, Mahmud. Ghazni, in Afghanistan, acquired importance from around the late tenth century under Sabuktigin, the Turkic slave commander who laid the foundations of the Ghaznavid dynasty in 977 CE. His ambitious son Mahmud decided to make Ghazni a major player in the politics of Central Asia and the Islamic world. He wanted to be known as the champion of Islam. From Mahmud's perch on the southern edge of the Hindu Kush, India appeared as the land of immense wealth. He carried out a series of raids and plundered Hindu temples to gain access to their wealth, but had no permanent interest or territorial ambitions in India.

The second burst of raids from the north-west came at the end of the twelfth century, and were carried out by Muhammad Ghuri. The political formations in Northwest India could not resist these raids, either because they were unprepared or because they were weak. Muhammad Ghuri, unlike Mahmud of Ghazni, was not a mere raider. He was looking to set up a kingdom that would yield revenue. In the late twelfth century, he annexed the upper Indus plains and Punjab.

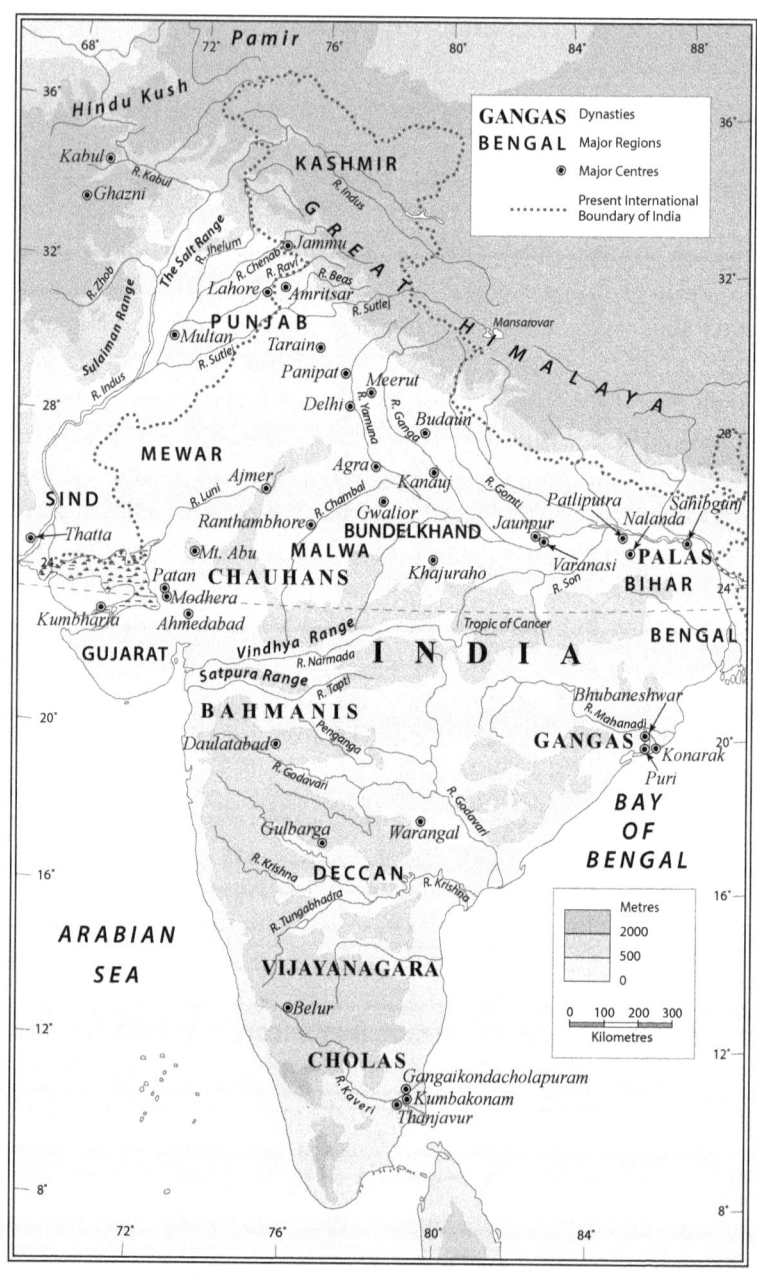

The Delhi Sultanate and other kingdoms

Not to scale. This map has been prepared in adherence to the 'Guidelines for acquiring and producing Geospatial Data and Geospatial Data Services including Maps' published vide DST F.No.SM/25/02/2020 (Part-I) dated 15th February, 2021

View of the Qutb Minar and Alai Darwaza, c. 1192–1210, Mehrauli, Delhi

Qutb-ud-din Aibak, the first sultan of Delhi, set about constructing the first stone mosque for prayer in Delhi called Quwwat ul-Islam (Might of Islam). On one side of the mosque, but not attached to it, is the Qutb Minar, a gigantic 72.5-metre-high free-standing tower that tapers as it reaches the top. It has five storeys (the last two storeys were later additions). The architect innovated a design that was not monotonous, the ground floor has pointed and circular flutings, the next level has rounded flutings, and the third is star-shaped. Each level is separated by ornate projecting balconies, with honeycomb-like supporting brackets and bands of geometric designs and low relief work of intricate calligraphic quotations from the Quran.

Ala-ud-din Khalji, who became the sultan in 1296, sought to enlarge the Qutb complex mosque and added the domed gateway entrance, Alai Darwaza, dressed with red sandstone and marble highlights. The pointed arches have a fringe of lotus buds and inlay work that set the trend of multiple-coloured stone façades with an Islamic design of stars and the use of older motifs like the lotus flower.

He gained control over Lahore and attacked the Rajput kingdoms that controlled the western Gangetic plain. In 1191, he was defeated by Prithviraj Chauhan at Tarain (present-day Taraori) located to the north of Delhi. Undaunted by the defeat, Muhammad Ghuri launched into another battle after strengthening himself with reinforcements. He defeated Prithviraj in the Second Battle of Tarain in 1192. This led to the capture of the capitals of the Rajput kingdoms; in these campaigns one of Muhammad's generals, Qutb-ud-din Aibak, played a leading role. Another general, Muhammad Bakhtiyar Khalji pushed further eastward and defeated the Sena king of Bengal. Muhammad Ghuri was murdered in 1206 but his successors retained his Indian possessions and harboured ambitions of ruling over northern India.

The successors of Muhammad Ghuri who decided to establish their sway over parts of North India were originally slaves. The most notable of these was Qutb-ud-din Aibak who established a sultanate in Delhi. Qutb-ud-din and his descendants severed their links with Ghazni and set up a self-governing dominion in and around Delhi. Their supremacy became evident under Iltutmish who was the sultan from 1210 to 1236. Through a series of military campaigns that Iltutmish carried out around 1215–16, he annexed the suburbs of Delhi, the Siwalik territories, Budaun, Awadh, and Banaras. These annexations formed the core of Iltutmish's sultanate; he consolidated his power over these and then moved against those who posed challenges to his authority especially in the area around Lahore in the north-west. The main threat here was Nasir al-din Qabacha, the governor of Multan. Iltutmish defeated Qabacha through a series of campaigns in 1227–28 and brought the Sindh provinces, most importantly Multan, under his command. Iltutmish also fought campaigns to establish his authority over Lakhnauti (present-day Gaur), Bihar, and Ranthambhore. These victories removed the main competitors to Iltutmish's power in North India, and in 1229, the caliph in Baghdad recognized Iltutmish as sultan. The latter did not depend only on military might to sustain his authority. He built up over time a sizeable body of loyal supporters recruited from immigrants from eastern Iran and from slaves, and gave them specific political responsibilities. Some of these subordinates were treated as free military commanders but Iltutmish retained extreme and final control over them. Through this process, Iltutmish integrated his conquests and consolidated his own position as sultan. He also set up urban centres which were connected by overland routes. It is important to underline that Iltutmish's attempt to create an independent sultanate based in Delhi and controlling large areas of North India was facilitated by the fact that the societies of eastern Iran and Afghanistan were subject to dislocation and destruction because of the campaigns of the Mongols, especially those of Genghis Khan. As a counterpoint to the Mongol threat, Iltutmish projected the Delhi Sultanate as a 'sanctuary of Islam'. This enabled him to secure the support of the ulama (Muslim clergy) for his rule.

After Iltutmish's death, the throne of Delhi passed to his descendants who reigned but did not rule. The idea of the Delhi Sultanate as a cohesive force survived this period of political uncertainty. Out of the looming political fragmentation emerged Ghiyas-ud-din Balban (whose original name was Ulugh Khan), a former slave who became a powerful ruler. Balban formed a stable coalition based on his supporters, many of whom had been important members of Iltutmish's court. Balban maintained this support base through a judicious distribution of honours and rewards. From around 1254, Balban began to consolidate his authority. One of the key steps he took to maintain and strengthen his position was to appoint some of his trusted lieutenants to establish a protective military circle around the capital, in Budaun, in Meerut, and in the west to command the ferries across the Beas. Balban himself commanded the areas adjoining Delhi and to its south-west. It was only after he had thus consolidated his position that he proclaimed himself sultan of Delhi and gave himself the title Ghiyas-ud-din Balban. It had been the view of many historians that in this period when the sultanate in Delhi was emerging as the centre of power, the source of the power was largely urban. Recent research, however, suggests that the military commanders were stepping out of their cantonments and making alliances with local chieftains and their supporters. The implications of such moves were dual-edged: on the one hand, they gave the power of the sultanate deeper roots but on the other they created opportunities for the military commanders to establish their own power bases which could serve to protect them against the authority of the sultan.

The reigns of Aibak and Iltutmish were periods of initial conquest and establishment of power. Balban's reign was not only a period of security and consolidation but also one of military, administrative, and financial expansion. Balban's work laid the foundations for further elevation of the sultanate's power under the Khaljis and the Tughluqs.

Ala-ud-din Khalji, who became the sultan in 1296, was an illiterate soldier. According to one important source, he had very little time for Islamic religious men. He was keen to place his ambitions and his politics above religious instructions. He repulsed Mongol invasions and made military and territorial advances against the Hindu chiefs in Rajasthan and in the Deccan. What enabled him to do this was the raising of a large and effective military army. This, in turn, was made possible by a series of market regulations that kept prices low in Delhi. The Moroccan traveller Ibn Battuta who reached the Delhi Sultanate around 1333, many years after Ala-ud-din Khalji's reign, noted that people looked back at his reign as a kind of golden age. When Ala-ud-din fell ill and died on 4 January 1316, the power of the Khaljis declined because of internal rivalry and power was taken over by one of his senior lieutenants, Ghazi Malik, who proclaimed himself Sultan Ghiyas-ud-din Tughluq and ruled from 1320 to 1324.

Of all the dynasties that ruled over the Delhi Sultanate, the Tughluq dynasty reigned the longest—for ninety-two years from 1320 to 1413. During the reign of the first Tughluq sultan some of the territories that the Khaljis had lost in their later years, Bengal in particular, were brought under the sway of the Sultanate. Warangal was annexed, as was much of the Pandyan kingdom of Ma'bar. Ghiyas-ud-din died unexpectedly when a newly constructed building collapsed on him.

He was succeeded by his eldest son and designated heir, Muhammad bin-Tughluq, who reigned from 1324 to 1351. Even though his succession was smooth, his rule was marked by a number of rebellions and disasters like plagues and famines. For the first eight to ten years of his rule, Muhammad bin-Tughluq was engaged in quelling rebellions that led to the loss of the territories his father had either regained or annexed. His power beyond the Vindhyas was threatened by the emergence of the kingdom of Vijayanagara. The last years of Muhammad bin-Tughluq's reign witnessed revolts by members of the military class in the Deccan and Gujarat. The rebellion in Gujarat was suppressed; but in the Deccan, the rebel leader Zafar Khan established the Bahmanid dynasty which ruled over an independent sultanate, and styled himself Sultan Ala al-din Hasan Bahman Shah. The best-known disaster of Muhammad bin-Tughluq's reign was his own creation. He decided to move his capital from Delhi to Daulatabad in the Deccan. The reasons behind the decision were sound. The new capital would be close to the newly conquered territories in the Deccan and would also be safe from Mongol raids. The execution of the scheme was clumsy and brutal, and resulted in suffering. Muhammad bin-Tughluq was a bundle of contradictions. He was a scholar and a philosopher but was prone to whims.

On Muhammad bin-Tughluq's death in 1351, the army commanders in Sindh and other important figures prevailed upon the late sultan's cousin, Firoz Shah, to ascend the throne. The latter accepted after some initial reluctance. Firoz Shah's reign was undistinguished. He lost the Deccan and the southern territories; he campaigned in Bengal with little success; and his only success was his victory over the Jams of Thatta in 1365–66. But Firoz Shah had the reputation of being a kind and merciful ruler and there are references to suggest that his reign was characterized by prosperity, justice, kindness, and security. The latter was shattered by the invasion of Timur from Central Asia in 1398. Timur came up to Delhi, which his troops sacked for several days. He campaigned east of the Yamuna going as far as Meerut. He finally withdrew westward in February 1398, attacking Jammu on the way.

Contrary to popular perceptions, Timur's invasion had been indiscriminate in its destruction—he attacked and killed Muslim nobles and Hindu chiefs. One principal reason behind Timur's swift success was the fact that he had at his disposal resources of revenue and manpower whereas sources of revenue of the Delhi Sultanate were dwindling. The declining revenues had an adverse impact on the military establishment under Firoz Shah with obvious implications for Timur's success.

The establishment, consolidation, and expansion of the Delhi Sultanate introduced a number of important facets and changes in the politics and society of North India. The rule of the sultans of Delhi added a new layer to Indian ethnic identities. It is convenient today to speak of the Delhi Sultanate as the beginning of 'Muslim rule' in India; and that this rule asserted itself on 'the Hindus'. This notion is misleading for the period when Indians were first encountering Islam. Neither the Muslims in India nor the Hindus in the first three or four hundred years after 1000 CE constituted a single homogenous religious community. The identities of people were determined by caste, professions, language, region, and religious sects. Thus, there were groups who identified themselves as Vaishnava or Shaiva or Shakta; just as other groups identified themselves as Buddhists and Jainas; and others as Sunni, Shia, Sufi, Bohra, Mappila, and so on. It is significant that in Sanskrit the traders and conquerors from the Arab world and Central Asia were not referred to by their religious faith but all of them had specific names. Thus the Arabs were called Tajiks and were differentiated from Turks who were called Turushka. The Turks and Afghans were also referred to as yavanas, a term originally used to refer to the Greeks. A more general term was mlechchha that not only denoted someone who was culturally alien but also someone who was outside caste society. So even a king or an untouchable could be a mlechchha. It is worth underlining that these terms had a long lineage of usage and were not created during the rule of the Delhi Sultanate. This would suggest that they were not considered complete outsiders but as participants in the making of life in North India.

The period of the Delhi Sultanate also initiated a new chapter in the Indian world of ideas and religious practices. Islam brought with it the messages of monotheism (belief in a single god) and equality. The latter had obvious attractions for those who were the victims of a hierarchical, caste-ridden society. Very often the carriers of these messages were a group of Islamic devotees called Sufis who believed that through a series of rigorous practices it was possible for every human being to feel the presence of God. They treated with contempt the material glitter of this world which they considered to be a den of immorality that needed to be transcended. The Sufis constituted the informal ranks of Muslim piety and had begun to arrive in India from around the 1220s. They formed communities of devotees around charismatic teachers (shaikhs) across North India. Because they were mobile, they not only took their own ideas to various places but were also able to observe and absorb local customs and forms of worship which were similar to their own. The court of the Delhi sultans was suspicious of the Sufis as they claimed mystical knowledge and a special relationship with God. The sultans could not, however, deny the popularity of the shaikhs. Thus, though the Sufis were carriers of influential religious ideas derived from Islam, they were not always in harmony with the prevailing political leadership.

At the heart of Sufi practices were the ideas of simplicity, piety, and devotion. These found and established affinities with the traditions of Bhakti that already existed in many parts of India from the era of the Guptas. Another common element in the Sufi and Bhakti traditions of piety was the emphasis on music. A remarkable outcome of this encounter was a series of social and religious movements from the fifteenth century onwards that fused together simplicity of worship, equality, devotion, and music. All these movements in their various ways challenged the dominance of caste and priestly orthodoxy. Guru Nanak (1469–1539), the founder of Sikhism, and the first of the ten Sikh Gurus, taught his followers that to transcend the everlasting cycle of birth and death, an individual would have to live in accordance with the will of God, the creator. Nanak's form of piety and worship did not involve austerities of any kind: there was no need for penances and pilgrimages, and no necessity for ritual-based formal worship in places like temples or mosques. Nanak's minimalist faith gained popularity, especially in Punjab, and this together with changing political and social circumstances made his successors give to Nanak's faith—Sikhism—more formal shape with designated centres of worship.

Harmandir Sahib (Golden Temple), sixteenth century, Amritsar, Punjab

The Harmandir Sahib, the sacred shrine of the Sikh community, was built in the sixteenth century. It is framed by high walls that block out the bustle and noise of the market outside. Within the Harmandir Sahib complex is a large man-made tank called the Amrit Sarovar or the ocean of eternal life. In the middle of the tank is the shrine, like a golden casket, floating on the serene waters. There are four stately gateways facing the four cardinal directions, open to members of all faiths and walks of life, echoing a passage from the Jaap Sahib prayer:

> The Almighty has no country, no traditional costume, no mark, no form, and favours no one in particular.
>
> The Almighty is present in every place, on every side, and in every corner, this universal love exists everywhere.

The arrival and the rule of the Delhi Sultanate brought to the forefront the question of how the sultans treated those subjects who did not share their faith. At one level, the treatment of non-Muslim subjects varied from sultan to sultan but a few general points can be made. In their coins and inscriptions all the Delhi sultans, bar one, styled themselves 'Father of the Victorious One'; the exception was Muhammad bin-Tughluq who styled himself 'The Warrior in the Path of God'. As victors, the sultans treated the vanquished as their subjects who were also not followers of Islam. These subjects could thus be open to plunder and the extortion of tribute. Many Hindus worked for the Delhi sultans. It is known, for example, that in the thirteenth century the sultanate was hugely in debt to Hindu bankers and brokers. Many of these bankers, the Multanis and Sahs in particular, were among the sultan's wealthiest and most important subjects. Moreover, the sultans carried out construction projects which required not only the labour of Hindus but also their architectural and engineering expertise. In the military sphere, the sultans maintained Hindu troops. Thus, diverse Hindu groups worked for the Delhi sultans who in their turn, following the Sharia, treated such people as 'protected peoples' (dhimmis) once they accepted the rule of the sultans. Such groups were supposed to pay the jizya (poll tax) but how exactly this tax was levied and collected is difficult to determine because of the paucity of evidence. It is highly unlikely that the jizya was collected uniformly from the entire Hindu population throughout the realm of the Delhi sultans. The sultanate did not have the administrative apparatus to handle the logistics of collection from a very large body of taxpayers. It is possible that the jizya did not exist as a separate tax but was subsumed under the land tax. Further, it is important to note that the jizya was a tax in lieu of military service. This meant that the large numbers of Hindus who were part of the armies of the sultanate would not have to pay the jizya. It is entirely possible that the collection of the poll tax was easier in urban centres and in fortified towns. The Delhi sultans exhibited remarkable tolerance towards Hindu religious practices; some of them permitted and contributed to the repair of temples that had been damaged by previous Muslim conquerors. It seems clear that the Delhi sultans did not approach the Hindu population as holy warriors but adopted a more nuanced and tactical approach which was dictated by their political circumstances. They were not hostile to Hindus per se but to troublemakers and rebels. Where Hindus were peaceful subjects and worked with the government, they were left alone and even rewarded. The Delhi sultans were not averse to using local craftsmen and the best manifestation of this use and adaptability was in the sphere of architecture.

Jama Masjid, seventeenth century, Delhi

Away from Delhi and the sway of the Delhi Sultanate, in central, eastern, and southern India, different styles of architecture and temple building were patronized under independent political formations. This artistic development can be best illustrated by three examples from southern, eastern, and central India.

Brihadeeshwara Temple and mandap, c. 1000 CE, Thanjavur, Tamil Nadu

Rajaraja I, the great Chola emperor who reigned from 985–1014, built the Brihadeeshwara Temple, that is considered today a classic example of the mature Dravida style of architecture. The rectangular plan of the temple is elevated on a high platform and base. The shikhara is made up of thirteen distinct receding tiers that create a sharp, pyramidal form, the hallmark of South Indian temples. The exterior wall of the temple has several examples of Chola stone sculptures of Shiva, to whom this temple is dedicated. By the thirteenth century, South Indian temples had become the heart of the city, the centre of the administrative, social, cultural, and economic life of the people. Around the temple's walled compound there were allocated spaces for markets for pilgrims, crafts centres, and residential areas for Brahmins and other communities.

Surya Mandir, Konark, Odisha (left, top). Lingaraj Temple, ninth to fourteenth century, Bhubaneswar, Odisha (left, bottom)

The eastern coast of India, Orissa (present-day Odisha), was ruled by the Eastern Ganga dynasty and during this period a number of important temples were built in Bhubaneswar, Puri, and Konark where the great Sun Temple or Surya Mandir was constructed by the seashore. These examples of eastern Indian temple architecture are unique in their form with the profusion of figurative art that features on the walls.

In Hindu mythology, the sun is said to travel through the sky and its arrival is heralded by gandharvas (flying musicians). The Konark Sun Temple was designed like a huge stone chariot that is being pulled through the sky by seven horses, representing the days of the week.

Kandariya Mahadev and Devi Temples, tenth to thirteenth century, Khajuraho, Madhya Pradesh

· CHAPTER 10 ·

REGIONAL KINGDOMS

c. 1200 CE–c. 1600 CE

As the Delhi Sultanate's political frontiers expanded eastward and southward from the fourteenth century, the institutions that the sultanate had implanted in North India, the court culture, scholarship, and aesthetics that they had displayed in architecture and through the circulation of Persian texts spread to different parts of India. Provincial centres of power, which replicated the practices of the Delhi Sultanate, emerged in various parts of India. Some of these centres were politically and culturally very significant.

Bengal was one of the earliest of such centres where provincial overlords tried to reproduce the cultural and political forms of the Delhi Sultanate. Before the invasion of Bakhtiyar Khalji, a chieftain under Muhammad Ghuri, Bengal had been ruled by the Pala dynasty (c. 750–1161), the Chandras (c. 825–1035), and the Senas (c. 1097–1223). Bakhtiyar Khalji defeated and overthrew the last Sena king, Lakshmana Sena, and established his own capital in Lakhnauti. Coins and new monuments built in the Islamic style proclaimed the arrival of new rulers with different sensibilities which were at variance from those of the local population.

Even though Bakhtiyar Khalji had declared himself in his coinage as a client of Muhammad Ghuri, subsequent governors of Bengal, sent out from Delhi, repeatedly asserted their independence. Bengal's distance from Delhi and the difficulties of overland communication in the delta facilitated such defiance. Successive Delhi sultans from the time of Iltutmish had to move against rebels in Bengal but the looming dangers of Mongol attacks did not allow them to stay in Bengal for long. During the reign of Muhammad bin-Tughluq, Bengal was brought under Delhi's control and was administered from three centres, all three in the delta: Lakhnauti (in the north-west), Satgaon (in the south-west),

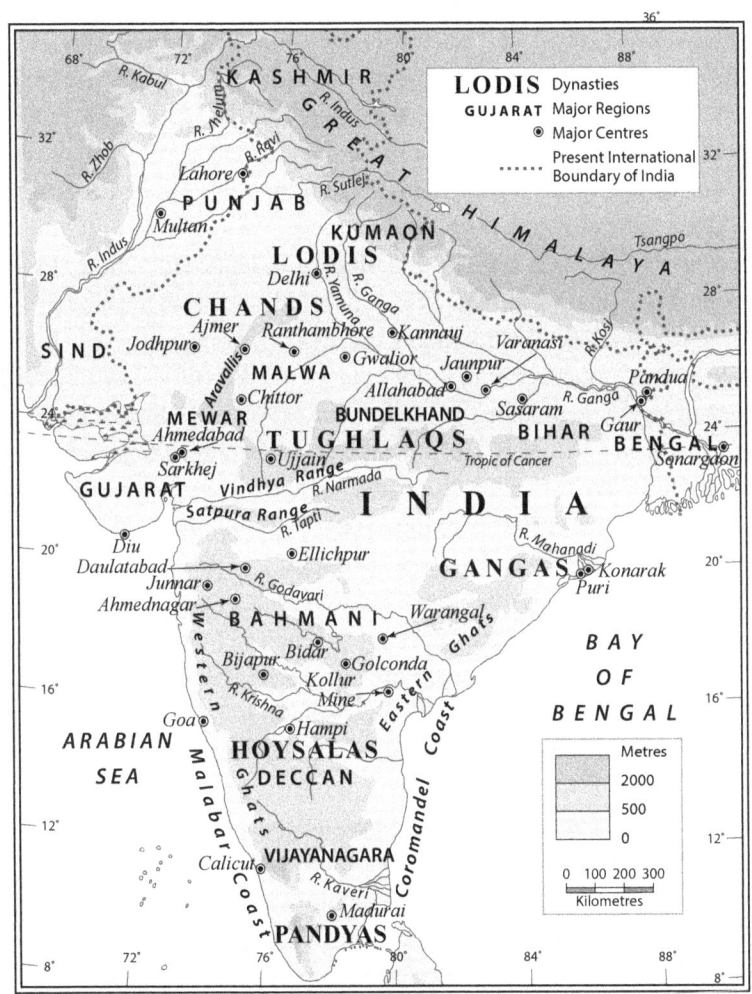

Vijayanagara, Bahmani, Golconda, and other regional kingdoms

Not to scale. This map has been prepared in adherence to the 'Guidelines for acquiring and producing Geospatial Data and Geospatial Data Services including Maps' published vide DST F.No.SM/25/02/2020 (Part-I) dated 15th February, 2021

and Sonargaon (in the east). The establishment of this control was brief as in 1338 Shams al-din Ilyas Shah, who had served under the governor, seized power and declared himself independent. He defeated his rivals, called himself sultan, and ruled over the entire delta until his death in 1357. Ilyas Shah, in a symbolic gesture to cut his links with the Delhi sultans, made Pandua, 30 kilometres away from Lakhnauti, his capital. In the 1350s, there were two unsuccessful attempts made by the Delhi sultan, Muhammad bin-Tughluq, to reconquer Bengal. The aftermath of these failures was that for two centuries, the Delhi sultans did not bother with Bengal. This long period of independence from Delhi enabled Bengal to fashion its own regional identity. Ilyas Shah's son and successor, Sikandar Shah, built in Pandua the Adina Mosque, which was bigger than any building that the sultans of Delhi had erected in their capital. It was a monumental statement of Sikandar Shah's imperial ambitions and also of Bengal's regional identity since the mosque did not replicate Delhi's architectural style. In its ornamentation and motifs the mosque adapted the traditions of the Palas and the Senas but in its imperial grandeur it harked back to the style of pre-Islamic Persia. It is significant that in the mosque's inscription, Sikandar Shah described himself as the most perfect among the kings of Arabia and Iran. The kings of South Asia, where he himself was located, did not merit a mention.

The Delhi Sultanate extended its political frontier into the Deccan and spread the influence of Persian culture. But this was followed by rebellions and the declaration of independence by groups and individuals leading to the establishment of two Deccani kingdoms. In the area south of the Krishna—territories that the Tughluqs ruled indirectly by collecting tributes from powerful chieftains—the five sons of the chieftain Sangama began to assert their independence by carving out principalities from the disintegrating Hoysala kingdom. Muhammad bin-Tughluq recognized these chieftains as amirs or commanders. But this form of governance began to end around 1336 when an obscure Telugu-speaking chieftain raised the flag of revolt in Warangal.

Dakhil Darwaza, Gaur, West Bengal

For a century or more, Lakhnauti was the capital of the sultanate in Bengal, and today the area straddles the West Bengal–Bangladesh border. The sultans built a citadel, many mosques, a royal palace, canals, and bridges. The Dakhil Darwaza was the entrance gate to the citadel known as Lakhnauti. Following the tradition of the earlier brick temples of West Bengal, the local artisans continued to use their skill in creating this massive gate with fired bricks, and also added arches to the structure. The gateway is 24 metres long and much of the structure has been destroyed over time.

This successful rebellion brought the curtain down on the sway of the sultanate over the eastern Deccan and also provided encouragement to rebellions across the Deccan plateau. The spirit of rebellion was explicit when Harihara—one of the five sons of the Sangama chieftain—described himself in 1339 as the 'Lord of East and West' in an obvious reference to his control over the large area lying between the Coromandel and Malabar. By the mid-1340s almost all of Karnataka had accepted the rule of the Sangamas. In 1346, all the sons of Sangama gathered in Sringeri (an important Shaiva centre of worship) to celebrate Harihara's dominance from east to west. This marked the inaugural moment for the formation of a new state—Vijayanagara. In 1347, it was declared that the principal

Platform of the royal palace, Hampi, Karnataka

The capital of the Vijayanagara kingdom stands on the southern bank of the Tungabhadra River. The remains of the capital are spread over 26 square kilometres, with temples—some still used for worship—royal palaces and apartments, and supplementary buildings, protected by massive fortification. All the buildings were built out of the local granite rock and interestingly the temples follow the Hindu temple plan and decorations, but in a few royal buildings like the so-called 'elephant stables', it is evident that local rulers were experimenting with the arch and domes, new engineering ideas from the north. The remains of the royal court platform and the walled enclosure of the Hazara Rama or Ramachandra temple have bands of horizontal relief panels with dancers, marching soldiers, horses, and elephants, a visual record perhaps, of the temple's annual festival and magnificence of medieval Hindu court pageantry.

deity of the dynasty would be Virupaksha, a form of Shiva. What is equally significant is that among the many titles the rulers adopted one was sultan. The kingdom of Vijayanagara would come to cover the entire southern half of the Deccan. The rule of the Vijayanagara sultans would pass through four dynasties—the Sangama being the first—and would last until the mid-1600s.

The power of the Vijayanagara rulers was evident in the enormous temple complexes that they constructed. These complexes had chariot streets, tanks, pillared halls, and columns. The most prominent and important of these complexes was near the southern bank of the Tungabhadra and the principal deities were the goddess Pampa and Virupaksha. In the twenty years between 1350 and 1370, the armies of Vijayanagara conquered large tracts of the fertile Tamil country. One consequence of this was the assimilation of classical Tamil architecture into the temples of Vijayanagara. The armies of Vijayanagara also marched into the deep south and conquered territories there. The kingdom thus came to be influenced by the beliefs and practices of diverse groups of people. The rulers of Vijayanagara stopped seeing their realm as a regional kingdom. They patronized various religious traditions and institutions—Shaiva, Vaishnava, Jaina, and Islamic. Especially prominent from the fifteenth century was their increasing patronage of Vishnu even as the importance of Virupaksha continued. From the late fifteenth century, when the Sangama house was overthrown by Saluva Narasimha (r. 1485–91), the worship of Vishnu acquired greater significance. The importance of Tirupati (in Andhra Pradesh), where Vishnu is worshipped as Venkatesvara, as a pilgrim centre can be dated from this period. Krishna Deva Raya, by far the most important of the Vijayanagara monarchs, made Venkatesvara at Tirupati his patron deity. Today this temple, one of most endowed religious centres in the world, owns land, and has built a university, several colleges, schools, and hospitals.

Virupaksha Temple, Hampi, Karnataka

The Vijayanagara kingdom is situated in an extraordinary landscape of hills and granite boulders dotted with rock-cut shrines, larger-than-life-size images of deities, and structural temples. The Virupaksha Temple follows the South Indian style of temple architecture. Surrounded by a walled enclosure, it is entered through a tall gopuram and is an important place of worship even today.

Agriculture obviously formed the economic foundation of the Vijayanagara empire but its importance was underlined by the resources the kings devoted to the construction of reservoirs to ensure water supply. These efforts could not however prevent severe droughts leading to famines in the fifteenth century—a period marked by a decline in agricultural production, fall in land revenue collection, and population contraction. This crisis was aggravated by the failure of the rulers to link the two distinct economic zones of the kingdom—the agrarian economy of the dry plateau and the commercialized economy of the Tamil coast. It is significant that in the very period when the agrarian economy was in a crisis, textile production around the Coromandel coast and the Kaveri delta was booming with increasing exports to Southeast Asia. The prosperity of the Coromandel coast fuelled the ambitions of local military commanders. This was the source of Saluva Narasimha's siezing of power from the Sangama dynasty. This began a sequence of violent attempts to capture the throne. Through this process in 1509, Krishna Deva Raya came to power and then carried out a series of successful military conquests that secured for the monarchy huge wealth that ended the economic crisis. In terms of the Vijayanagara kingdom's interaction with Muslim power in the Deccan, it is worth noting that in 1523 after his capture of Gulbarga (present-day Kalaburagi), the second capital city of the Bahmanis, Krishna Deva Raya styled himself 'the one who brings about the (re)establishment of Yavana [Turkish] rule'. It was a declaration of his dominance in the Deccan.

One of Krishna Deva Raya's trusted military commanders was Rama Raya (born 1484), a Telugu chieftain belonging to the Aravidu clan. The king gave his daughter in marriage to Rama Raya. Krishna Deva Raya had announced his half-brother, Achyuta Raya, to be his successor. After the death of Krishna Deva Raya, an attempt was made by Rama Raya to set aside the claims of Achyuta Raya and put the late king's infant son on the throne with Rama Raya himself as the regent. This scheme was foiled by the nobility but Rama Raya did succeed in securing for his kinsmen the key forts located in the kingdom's heartland. These served as the bases of Rama Raya's power which was further strengthened when he recruited 3,000 troops (all immigrants from Iran) who had been dismissed by Adil Shah I of Bijapur.

In the immediate aftermath of the death of Achyuta Raya in 1542, his young son claimed the throne but the regent tried to seize it through a violent coup. Rama Raya emerged as the focal point of the resistance to this coup. He marched into the capital at the head of a large army. In an astute move, Rama Raya did not make himself the king. He anointed Sadashiva, a sixteen-year-old nephew of Krishna Deva Raya, as the king in 1542. But after 1550, Sadashiva was a king only in name; he was not even allowed to appear in public. It was evident that all power was vested with Rama Raya who, to legitimize his position, associated himself and his family with the Chalukya dynasty who had ruled the Deccan plateau between 973 and 1183. Rama Raya carried out planned campaigns against the sultans that ruled the territories north of Vijayanagara. The outcome of these campaigns was to bring about a tactical unity among the rulers of the four northern sultanates—Ahmadnagar, Bijapur, Golconda, and Bidar. The armies gathered at Talikota, north of the river Krishna in December 1564, and then crossed the river to meet the huge Vijayanagara army just south of the river. Rama Raya was defeated and killed in the Battle of Talikota which brought about the end of the Vijayanagara empire.

North of the Krishna, an area that was under the direct rule of the Tughluqs, momentous events unfolded from around the late 1330s. Zafar Khan, a former officer of the Khaljis in the Deccan, raised the flag of revolt and briefly seized the forts of Gulbarga, Bidar, and Sagar. This started a series of anti-Tughluq uprisings north of the Krishna and, by 1345, Tughluq rule ceased to exist in the area. In 1347, Zafar Khan marched into the great mosque at Daulatabad, styled himself sultan and called himself Ala al-din Hasan Bahman Shah. The realm of the latter was spread over the entire northern Deccan and came to be called the Bahmani kingdom. Like the Vijayanagara kingdom, the rule of the Bahmani sultans covered areas inhabited by three different kinds of people with their varied cultures and speaking three different languages: Marathi, Telugu, and Kannada. The Bahmanis sought to legitimize their rule by seeking the blessings of a Sufi shaikh. Legend has it that Shaikh Nizam al-din Auliya, the great Sufi saint based in Delhi, had predicted that Zafar Khan would one day be a sultan. The more substantial blessing came, however, from a Deccan-based spiritual heir of Nizam al-din Auliya. This was Shaikh Zain al-din Shirazi, (who died in 1369) who through his blessings and actions legitimized the rule of the Bahmani sultans who made Gulbarga their capital.

The success of the Bahmani sultanate produced a peculiar kind of tension. It attracted ethnic Persians and Turks—referred to as Westerners—who arrived from across the Arabian Sea and came to occupy positions of influence. This came to be resented by the Deccani Muslims, descendants of North Indian immigrants, who had lived in the area from the 1320s. The Deccan was their home and they spoke the indigenous languages in addition to an early form of Hindavi called Dakani. The differences between the two groups were so pronounced that in Bidar's Hall of Public Audience, the Westerners in court stood on the right side of the throne, and the Deccanis to the left. The prime minister, Mahmud Gawan—himself a Westerner—attempted to minimize the tension by reducing the amount of land available to both groups and increasing the crown land. But Mahmud Gawan had to be frequently away from the capital to conduct military operations. Taking advantage of his absence, in 1481, the Deccanis hatched a conspiracy and persuaded the sultan, Zafar Khan, that Gawan was a traitor. The sultan had Gawan beheaded. This initiated the process of decline of the Bahmani kingdom which by the end of the fifteenth century had disintegrated into five separate sultanates.

The first sultanate to break away was Malik Ahmad, the founder of the Nizam Shahi dynasty of Ahmadnagar (1490–1636). He was the son of Nizam-ul-Mulk Malik Hasan Bahri who had been a steadfast Deccani. In 1486, Nizam-ul-Mulk Malik Hasan Bahri was assassinated and Malik Ahmad declared his independence in Junnar in Maharashtra where he had been governor. Malik Ahmad built a new capital, Ahmadnagar, which became a major centre of patronage in the Deccan. The process now replicated itself elsewhere in the Deccan. The governor of Berar, Fath Allah Imad al-Mulk (r. 1490–1504), declared his independence and established the Imad Shah sultanate (1490–1574) which had its capital at Ellichpur. In Bijapur, the governor Yusuf Adil Khan (r. 1490–1510), an immigrant

Tomb with tile inlay, Bahmani period, Bidar, Karnataka

The Bahmani kingdom first established their capital in Gulbarga and moved it to Bidar in 1425. Situated just 130 kilometres from Hyderabad, there are remains of the massive fort walls that protected the fortified palace complex of the Bahmani period. The Islamic tombs of this period carry large domes and were plastered and decorated with tilework in turquoise blue, yellow, and green, a continuation of the tradition inherited from its Persian origin.

from Ottoman Anatolia, declared his independence in 1490. In 1503, he declared Shiism (the religion of the followers of the Shia sect) the state religion of Bijapur but did not impose it on his subjects. His son and successor, Ismail (r. 1510–34), departed from his father's tolerant religious policies. He abjured all Deccani elements, employed only Westerners, and imitated the courtly customs of the Safavid dynasty in Persia. However, his son, Ibrahim Adil Shah I, identified himself with the Deccanis and embraced Sunni Islam, the faith of most of the Deccani Muslims. He also invoked the memory of the Chalukyas. Ibrahim's son and successor, Ali Adil Shah I (r. 1558–80), swung the pendulum back to Shiism though he was also a tolerant ruler and a formidable intellectual. In Bidar,

Golconda Fort, Hyderabad, Telangana

The Qutb Shahi dynasty of Iranian origin were Shia Muslims (like rulers of Persia and Turkey) who broke away from the Bahmani rulers to establish their independent sultanate. They chose a dramatic landscape with huge rock boulders and built Golconda, their capital. The enormous hilltop fort has three consecutive walls of fortification and eight gateways. Within the fort are arched palaces, courtrooms, the remains of the royal palace, and the grand Jami Masjid. At the end of the sixteenth century, the capital was moved to nearby Hyderabad, where the Shahis left their mark on several significant buildings.

the capital of the Bahmanis, the last Bahmani prime minister, Qasim Barid (d. 1505), finding himself isolated within a disintegrating sultanate established his own rule, the Barid Shahi dynasty. This turned out to be the weakest and the most ineffective of the five sultanates that emerged from the Bahmanis. Under the latter, the governor of eastern Deccan had been an Iranian immigrant, Sultan Quli (r. 1497–1543) who had the title Qutb al-Mulk. He asserted his independence and established the Qutb Shahi dynasty with its capital at Golconda. When Sultan Quli Qutb died in 1543, his son, Jamshid (r. 1543–50), blinded his elder brother and captured the throne. The younger brother, Ibrahim, fearing the same fate or worse, fled and took refuge in the court of Rama Raya. Upon Jamshid's death, a coalition of commanders invited Ibrahim back to Golconda to become the new king. The peak of the Qutb Shahi reign was the reign of Ibrahim and his successor Sultan Muhammad Quli Qutb Shah (r. 1580–1612). The latter established the city of Hyderabad around 1591. Under these two sultans, the wealth and prosperity of Golconda acquired legendary proportions.

Golconda diamond pendant

India was the first country and remained the only region in the world where diamonds were available until 1726, when the precious stone was discovered in Brazil. After this, India lost its predominant position as a diamond exporter. The diamonds that were brought to Golconda for polishing and setting in jewellery came to be called Golconda diamonds. Diamonds found in Kollur Mine in the Deccan produced legendary diamonds like the Koh-i-noor and the Hope Diamond that were coveted by the royalty of this region and the rulers of the world.

The phase between the rule of the Tughluqs and the rule of the Mughals, often neglected in Delhi-centric histories, was a very rich period whose centre was the Deccan. The achievements of these Deccani sultanates were substantial enough to attract the Mughals once they had established their power in North India in the sixteenth century.

The Malik-i-Maidan cannon, fifteenth century, Bijapur, Karnataka

Gunpowder was invented in China around the ninth century and was brought through trade to India and the rest of the world in the medieval period. The explosive power of gunpowder lay in the mixture of its ingredients; one of them was saltpetre. India became an important source for saltpetre, an important item of trade from medieval times through to the colonial period. The nature of gunpowder changed the face of warfare completely, both in its range and its destruction. This cannon, the world's largest bronze cast, was manufactured in Ahmadnagar. Like swords, shields, and guns of this period, these weapons of destruction were painstakingly embellished with fine relief work and delicate inlay in a variety of metals. The cannon was said to have been used during the Battle of Talikota.

· CHAPTER 11 ·

THE GREAT MUGHALS

1525 CE–1707 CE

Zahir-ud-din Muhammad, better known as Babur (1483–1530), was a proud descendant of Timur, the founder of the Timurid empire. Babur's father was the great-great-grandson of Timur and on his mother's side, he was descended from Genghis Khan but by fourteen generations. It is important to note that the Mughals, contrary to popular perceptions, never referred to themselves in ethnic terms. The term Mughal was the Persianized version of Mongol. European travellers to India in the seventeenth and eighteenth centuries began to use the term Mughal and this gained popularity among historians and in common parlance. Members of the Mughal dynasty referred to themselves as Gurganiyya (gurgan was derived from the Mongol kurugan or royal son-in-law) which underlined their descent from Timur and Genghis Khan. Gurgan was the title that Timur had adopted after his marriage to a Chingizid princess.

Babur, despite his best efforts and ambitions, lost his father's ancestral kingdom and set up base in Kabul. His control over Kabul and its surrounding areas was always vulnerable to attacks from the Uzbeks and so he decided to march across the Hindu Kush, cross the Indus, and descend on the plains of Punjab. In 1525, his small army encountered the very large army of Sultan Ibrahim Lodi at Panipat. Babur won the battle decisively at Panipat and marched to Delhi. Unlike Timur, he did not sack Delhi. On the contrary, he was kind to the inhabitants of the city. He sent his son Humayun to Agra, the Lodi capital, to gain control over the treasury. This by itself did not secure Babur's position. In the early sixteenth century, northern and western India were the sites for many contending martial lineages. One of the most prominent of these was the Sisodiyas in southern Rajasthan led by Rana Sanga. To strengthen his position, Babur defeated Rana

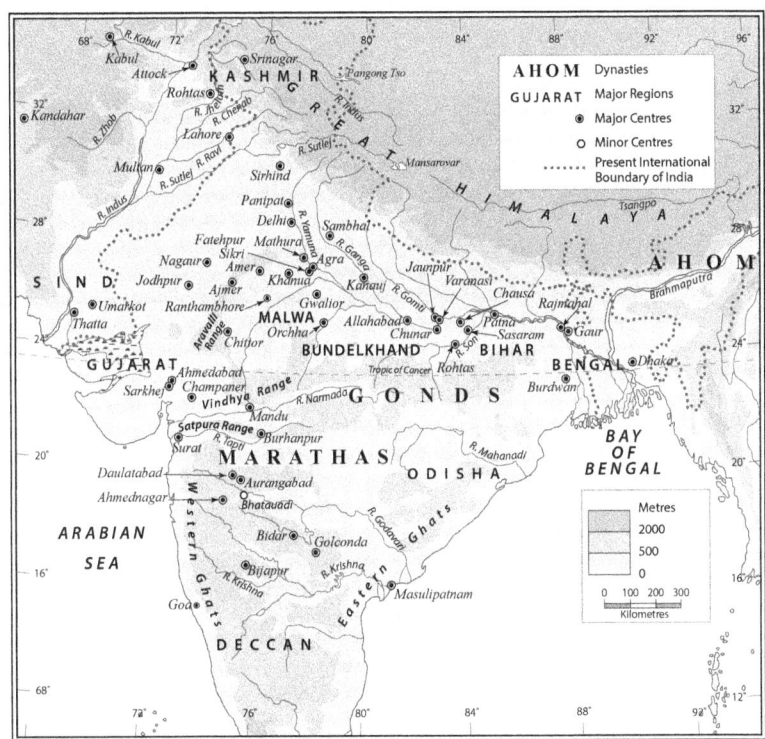

The Mughal empire

Not to scale. This map has been prepared in adherence to the 'Guidelines for acquiring and producing Geospatial Data and Geospatial Data Services including Maps' published vide DST F.No.SM/25/02/2020 (Part-I) dated 15th February, 2021

Folio of *Baburnama*, Persian, Nastaliq script, c. 1598

Babur, seated under an embroidered cloth tent, is surrounded by his courtiers and noblemen. He appears to be listening to a supplicant's plea, while around him is a scene packed with action; wrestlers have locked arms, an elephant fight is in progress, two camels have entwined their necks in battle, and the rams are banging their heads together. In the distance is a landscape of hills, rocks, and a fortress. Babur, it is said, was very impressed by the gardens and buildings built by his ancestor, Timur, in Samarkand, and designed gardens in his newly acquired territory.

Sanga in 1527 at Khanua. Babur was hugely outnumbered but he scored a decisive military victory. These victories, followed by the consolidation of his own position in a strip of territory stretching from eastern Afghanistan through central Punjab to the mid-Gangetic plain, convinced Babur that he could set up an empire in Hindustan and he invited his kinsmen and supporters in Kabul to join him in the project.

Babur ruled India, a place he did not particularly like, for only four years but he laid the foundations on which his descendants could build a grand empire. He modelled his court on Timurid practices, created a ruling structure manned by Mongols and Turks, and established enduring ties between India and the Persianate world. He built no major monuments except for mosques at Panipat, Sambhal, and Ayodhya but he laid out gardens wherever he could. He had a fine aesthetic sensibility and a sensitivity towards the natural world—both these were evident in abundance in an unfinished memoir, known as the *Baburnama*, that he left behind. Babur chose Humayun, his son, to be his successor. Humayun's reign was interrupted by a period of exile after he was defeated by the Afghan chieftain, Sher Khan (born Farid Khan in 1486 in Haryana). Sher Khan took the title Sher Shah Sur and established his base in western Bihar and from there he launched a military campaign in Bengal. By 1537, after a series of battles, regional alliances, and victories, he became the undisputed master of Bengal and the sultanate's prosperity. He raised an army of considerable size and challenged the supremacy of Humayun whom he defeated first at Chausa in 1539 and then again in Kannauj in 1540. Humayun had to flee. Sher Shah Sur became the sovereign of Hindustan and made Delhi his capital. He ruled till 1545 when he suffered an untimely and accidental death. But in his short reign, he took a number of significant steps: he established a system of surveying and measuring agricultural lands; this facilitated land revenue collection by making it predictable. He introduced a trimetallic currency based on the silver rupee which was complemented by the copper dam and the gold mohur. To strengthen the links of North India with Central Asia he created the Grand Trunk Road that linked Peshawar in western

Punjab to Bengal. He also undertook many architectural projects. After a fifteen-year hazardous exile, Humayun, with the help of the Safavid monarch, regained his dominance in Hindustan and established himself as the king. Humayun put in place certain court rituals—for example showing his face to the public at sunrise while seated in the jharokha (a raised platform) which his son and successor, Akbar, carried forward.

Humayun died in 1556, when his eldest son and successor (born in the years of Humayun's exile), Akbar, was only thirteen years old. He was put under the charge of a loyal Mughal nobleman, Bairam Khan. Even though Sher Shah Sur and his successors had been vanquished, the position of the Mughals was by no means free of challenges. The most important challenge came in 1556 from Hemu, a Hindu general, who had formally served the Afghan regime. He captured Delhi and declared himself king and the 'liberator' of Delhi. The Mughal army under Bairam Khan who used Akbar, all of fourteen years old, as the rallying point, met Hemu's army at Panipat. Akbar took part in the battle and even beheaded the defeated Hemu. The Second Battle of Panipat (November 1556) paved the way for the consolidation of Mughal rule in the Gangetic plain. The battle was a turning point in another way as well because with this victory Akbar began to assert his independence and removed himself from the control of Bairam Khan who was sent off on a pilgrimage to Mecca. Akbar recognized that he needed loyal supporters within the royal household. To this end he married one of Bairam's widows and brought into the household one of Bairam's sons, Khan-i Khanan, who would become one of the most influential noblemen in Akbar's court. Akbar also acknowledged that to rule effectively he had to form alliances with powerful martial lineages, especially the Rajputs, whose territories sprawled across the major trade artery connecting Delhi and Agra to the western seaboard. Akbar appointed many of the powerful chiefs to the Mughal imperial service and cemented the alliances by marrying the daughters of the chiefs. The alliances between the Mughals and the Rajput clans were particularly strong. Akbar allowed the chiefs to rule over their watans (hereditary possessions) so long as they acknowledged the supremacy of the Mughal emperor and offered tribute.

Humayun's Tomb, completed c. 1571, Delhi

The tomb of Mughal emperor Humayun was built by his son Akbar beside the Yamuna River. The large tomb stands on a high platform, in the centre of a six-by-six garden plan, with thirty-six divisions watered by canals and fountains, and is designed to look like the garden of paradise that awaits the faithful on Judgment Day. Within the octagonal building is the central octagonal chamber with a double-domed ceiling, and the tomb of Humayun. (In royal Mughal tombs the actual remains were kept in an underground chamber to prevent vandalism.) Around it in the eight smaller chambers, and on the spacious platform, there are later tombs of Mughal nobility, including that of Dara Shukoh, the eldest son of Shah Jahan.

From the modest tomb of Ghiyas-ud-din Tughluq (c. 1320–24), it took over 200 years of experimentation and generations of artisans to master building techniques to create this landmark that would serve as a model for later tombs, like the Taj Mahal, built sixty years later. The Mughals used familiar features—like the square or octagonal plans, arched openings, domed roof with a cluster of chattris (domed kiosks)—as earlier tombs but on a much grander scale. The entire tomb is faced in red sandstone on the exterior, the graceful lines of the arches and columns are accentuated in marble and other coloured stones to highlight its perfect architectural proportions.

Panch Mahal, Fatehpur Sikri, Agra

Emperor Akbar built the royal city of Fatehpur Sikri (commemorating his victory in Gujarat), that covered over 11 kilometres of natural sandstone ridge. The spacious fort and palaces were made of the local pinkish-red sandstone that gives them a rich, warm hue. The fort has enclosed courtyards with royal apartments, the grand Jami Masjid with the tomb of Salim Chishti, and courtrooms—the Diwan-i-Khas. Inspired by the architecture of the newly won territory of Gujarat, the Panch Mahal is a five-tiered palace, in which the top two floors are graded and carry a single open pavilion on top. The structures in the fort are an interesting experimentation of Hindu, Jaina, and Islamic architectural norms of ornately carved brackets, pillared halls, and domes, with intricate motifs. The pillared halls are open and breezy, suggesting that this palace was used as a pavilion for the royal family to enjoy the magnificent views.

There were other parts of India, however, that Akbar had to militarily conquer. What enabled Akbar to do this was a carefully organized administrative apparatus which was derived from the traditions established by the Timurids, the Mongols, and the Delhi Sultanate. According to this system, every Mughal nobleman/state servant was given a fixed rank called a mansab which was denoted by two numerical numbers—zat and sawar. The former indicated the individual's position in court and the latter the number of soldiers the individual was expected to maintain. The numbers could vary from 100 to 10,000. The state servants were thus called mansabdars. For the maintenance of the noblemen's standard of living and the soldiers they had to maintain, each mansabdar was paid a salary. Only in very rare cases was this salary paid in cash; it was usually paid through a land revenue assignment called jagir. Thus, every mansabdar was also a jagirdar. The jagirs were temporary; they could not be inherited and were transferable every few years. The mansabdari system was one of the pillars of the Mughal imperial structure. The mansabdars were drawn from different ethnic groups, the most important of which were the Turanis (those who came from Central Asia), the Iranis (from Persia), Afghanis, and Hindustanis. Akbar thus created an administrative bureaucracy that was loyal to the emperor, and he also created a pool of armed soldiers who could be called upon to fight for the emperor and, further, he solved, through the jagir system, the logistics of collecting land revenue in far-flung parts of his growing empire.

It is necessary to outline some features of Akbar's personality and his beliefs. In the strict, technical sense of the word, Akbar was illiterate and dyslexic but he was by no means uneducated. He had an amazing memory and was gifted with remarkable intelligence. He had an inquisitive mind, was eager to learn, and loved being in the company of learned men. In terms of his religious views, Akbar was an eclectic and innovative thinker. He was an absolute monarch but he was tolerant of the views of others. He was deeply compassionate and respectful to his elderly women relatives like his mother, Hamida Banu Begum, his aunt, Humayun's sister, Gulbadan, and his milk or foster mother, Maham Anaga. He took certain decisions that affected the lives of even ordinary women in his realm. In 1583, he introduced measures to ensure that sati did not occur unless it was voluntary on the part of the widow. He commented, 'It is a strange commentary on the magnanimity of men that they should seek their deliverance through the self-sacrifice of their wives.' Four years later, he allowed widows to remarry. It is worth noting that in these decisions he was foreshadowing the views of nineteenth-century reformers.

When Akbar died in 1605, he had consolidated the Mughal empire and he bequeathed to his son, Jahangir (r. 1605–27), a strong state with an efficient administrative apparatus.

Tomb of Akbar, Sikandra, Agra

Two tombs, that of Akbar's in Sikandra, and the tomb of Itimad-ud-Daulah (Jahangir's father-in-law) broke away from the domed, octagonal design format of tombs of the past. Akbar's tomb, similar to the Panch Mahal, has tiers supported by elaborately carved beams and pillars, rather than arches. Yet both these unusual tombs contributed new design elements for the making of the Taj Mahal, such as the minarets at the side of the building, cladding the building completely in white marble, and the intricate quality of the inlay work.

The tomb, like Humayun's Tomb, is set in a walled garden, entered through an enormous gateway, embellished with inlay in stones of many colours. The first three tiers of the tomb are graded and made of sandstone while the topmost floor opens into a square marble courtyard. The tomb of Akbar is situated in the middle, on a platform, with no dome to cover it, leaving it 'open to the sky' according to the orthodox tradition.

Shalimar Bagh, Srinagar, Kashmir

The garden, unlike the usage of the term today, was in Mughal times a bagh, an orchard. The Mughal court moved to Kashmir, away from their palaces, to avoid the summer heat of the plains. The entire royal household was set up in beautifully printed, embroidered cloth tents, lavishly furnished with carpets and cushions so that they could enjoy the summer surrounded by greenery under shady trees enveloped in the fragrance of summer flowers. This garden designed for Jahangir by his son Shah Jahan has five terraces, with tanks, fountains, and cascades running down to the next level. The lower three terraces were the more public spaces. The Diwan-i-Am (Hall of Audience) has a black marble throne, where the emperor-in-residence could meet top officials and visiting nobility. The upper terrace has a private space for the women of the royal household. The pavilion on the fourth terrace may have been used for banquets. It has an elegant, sloping roof supported by a row of six carved black marble pillars on each side and is set in a pool of water, echoing with the sound of playful fountains.

Jahangir and his son, Shah Jahan (1628–58), built and expanded on what Akbar had left behind. One indicator of the empire's growth and expansion, especially in the Deccan and in Bengal, was the fact that between 1580 and 1646 the revenue demand more than doubled.

Taj Mahal, c. 1634, Agra, Uttar Pradesh

Shah Jahan built the Taj Mahal (originally named Rauza-i-Munavvara, Illuminating Tomb), on the banks of the Yamuna River in Agra, for his favourite wife, Mumtaz Mahal, who died in 1631. This tomb had gardens on both banks, inspired by the garden and tomb of Emperor Humayun, Shah Jahan's great-grandfather.

The Taj Mahal stands at the northern end of an enclosed once private charbagh (garden) with a central channel that reflects the perfect symmetry of the building. The tomb, built on a high broad platform, has four tall, tapering, freestanding minarets that frame the building. To the west is a red sandstone mosque and on the right is a similar building giving the entire composition balance and visual harmony. The octagonal building is 72 metres high and carries a high drum that supports a well-proportioned dome above, with a long metal finial with a kalash, also a Hindu symbol of the water of eternity, at its apex. Within the building the central room contains the tombs of Mumtaz Mahal in the centre and Shah Jahan (at one side) encircled by a perforated marble screen, and like the tombs, has delicate pietra dura (hard stone) inlay work.

The magic of the Taj Mahal lies perhaps in its perfect symmetry and in the marble. The tomb is clad in white marble with the sky as the backdrop, making the building seem weightless and ephemeral. The crystalline white marble of the building changes colour throughout the day as it reflects the pink hues of sunrise, the fiery orange of the sunset, and the luminosity of the full moon night.

Mughal Emperor Shah Jahan in the marriage procession of his eldest son, Dara Shukoh, 1740–50, tempera on paper

This painting of Shah Jahan's favourite son Dara Shukoh's wedding procession is set in the night, and the dark sky explodes with myriad colours. The manicured and elegantly adorned marching horses, the fashionable outfits of the royal family, the fireworks in the background, and the musicians and dancers in the foreground speak of joyful times, before the horror of accession rivalry begins to cloud the future.

There was one particular development in the reign of Jahangir which is somewhat unique in the annals of the Mughals. This was the rise to dominance of Jahangir's wife, Nur Jahan. She was the daughter of a Persian nobleman who, like many other noblemen from Persia and Central Asia, had left his homeland with his family around 1577 to seek his fortune in Al Hind, as India was known. Large parts of North India were then ruled by Akbar. Nur Jahan or Mehr un-Nisa, as she was called before she became an empress, was in fact born as the caravan made its way from Persia to India. Ghiyas Beg, Mehr un-Nisa's father, through family connections, made himself part of Akbar's court. Mehr un-Nisa was married to Ali Quli Khan, a Mughal mansabdar who was posted in Bengal. Life in a remote province as a young and intelligent woman shaped Mehr un-Nisa. She was free from the confines of life in a harem and thus could train herself in certain skills which were considered 'masculine' in the Mughal world. She learnt how to shoot, to hunt, to practise the art of poetry, and most importantly she could observe the ways of politics in the Mughal empire. After her husband's death, Mehr un-Nisa was moved to the harem in the Mughal capital. The first two great Mughals—Babur and his son Humayun—had been camp emperors, moving from place to place and ruling from large tents rather than from forts and palaces. It was Akbar who began the practice of ruling from a fixed court and of having the Mughal women live together in a specially protected part of the fort or the palace called the harem. This did not necessarily mean that all women of the harem became passive onlookers to the play of politics and power that surrounded the persona of the Mughal emperor and the way he ruled. In *Empress: The Astonishing Reign of Nur Jahan*, the historian Ruby Lal has shown that there were some very powerful women in the harem and they could influence decision-making in critical matters. It was in this somewhat unique ambience of the harem that Mehr un-Nisa found herself and it was here, with her remarkable qualities, that she attracted the attention of Emperor Jahangir.

Fountains of Nishad Bagh, Srinagar, Kashmir

Asaf Khan, brother of Nur Jahan, laid out this garden. The gardens of Srinagar were constructed on the gentle slopes surrounding the Dal Lake, enabling the construction of gravity-based movement of water in channels, fountains, and cascades. The Mughals introduced several non-Indian trees and plants and added local varieties of fruit trees. Sadly much of the plants seen today are those brought to India during the British colonial period, rather than the flowers referred to in the poetry and paintings of this era.

Aurangzeb ascended the throne in 1658 through a bloody war of succession in which he imprisoned his father and killed his eldest brother and heir apparent Dara Shukoh. He ruled for nearly fifty years, out of which he spent half fighting the Marathas and the sultanates in the Deccan. It was a war that he knew he could not win but he pursued the war because he needed territories. The resources of the empire were running dry and so more revenue was needed.

The most controversial aspect of Aurangzeb's monarchy was his religious views and their impact on policies. Generations of historians have portrayed him as a Muslim zealot. He was a pious and a puritanical Muslim and liked to portray himself as one. But his policies were directed by hard-nosed realities. There were periods in his life in which he had to emphasize his Islamic piety to win over the orthodox elements within the nobility. He did this during the war of succession when he was fighting Dara Shukoh who was of an eclectic bent of mind. Similarly, he imposed the jizya in 1579 just prior to his full-blown invasion of the Deccan when he not only needed greater resources but also needed the Muslims to rally behind him when he was about to undertake a major political and military initiative. His personal religious views did not prevent him from appointing a large number of Hindu mansabdars. Under Shah Jahan, Hindus constituted 22 per cent of the mansabdars holding a rank of 1,000 zat and more. Under Aurangzeb, this number had gone up to 32 per cent. Aurangzeb was also very generous in making revenue-free land grants to non-Islamic religious establishments. The best testimony to his attitudes was evident in a comment made on a petition that a Sunni be appointed to a post. An obviously irate emperor wrote, 'What connection have earthly affairs with religion? And what right have administrative works to meddle with bigotry? *"For you is your religion and for me is mine"* [Quran 109:6]. If this rule [suggested by the petitioner] were established, it would be my duty to extirpate all the [Hindu] Rajahs and their followers. Wise men disapprove of the removal from the office of able officers.'

The Mughal empire, under its first six emperors, brought large parts of India under a single, centralized administrative machinery. The extent of their dominion was in many ways the principal source of their weakness. They did not possess the resources to sustain their empire. That they did for nearly 200 years was an amazing feat. The great Mughals ruled in a grand style as befitted their elevated position. They left behind magnificent monuments; they were patrons of art, music, and scholarship. The making of the Mughal empire took 200 years but its breakdown took less than five decades. Chapter 13 will look at that process of decline and fall.

Aurangzeb's Tomb, Khuldabad, Maharashtra

Aurangzeb was critical of his father Shah Jahan's lavish lifestyle, the building of extravagant building projects, and that he had inherited empty royal coffers. He chose to live in accordance with Islamic teaching and his simple grave stands in the dargah of Shaikh Burhan al-din in Khuldabad near Aurangabad. The grave, open to the canopy of the sky, has few embellishments, in direct contrast to the opulence of his father's final resting place in the Taj Mahal.

· CHAPTER 12 ·

INFLUENCE OF ISLAM

c. 1400 CE–c. 1750 CE

Conventional wisdom sees India's encounter with Islam and the Persianate world as being a hostile one. That this was not the case is best illustrated through the life of the Mughal prince Dara Shukoh.

Dara Shukoh was born in 1615 during the reign of his grandfather Jahangir. As he was growing up, Dara Shukoh witnessed the uncertainties and the intrigues of the Mughal court. In fact, in the aftermath of Khurram's (Jahangir's son, Dara Shukoh's father, better known as Shah Jahan) failed rebellion against Jahangir, Dara Shukoh and his younger brother Aurangzeb had to be sent to Jahangir as hostages to guarantee Khurram's obedience. Thus, Dara Shukoh knew, when he was the obvious heir apparent to Shah Jahan, that his path to the Peacock Throne (which Shah Jahan made for himself) would not necessarily be smooth. Dara Shukoh's eyes were not focused on the throne. He was drawn more towards philosophical–religious ideas of various kinds. He did not lead a military campaign until he was nearly forty, when he was sent by his father to conquer Kandahar. This was highly unusual for a Mughal prince—who all won their spurs in battle as young men, often in their teens. Dara Shukoh's campaign in Kandahar ended in failure.

That Dara Shukoh would eventually lose the succession struggle through a military encounter was an outcome that was foretold. He tried to fashion himself as a philosopher-king. The first part of the portmanteau attracted Dara Shukoh; it was also the one in which he was better trained and more successful. He became a Qadiri Sufi under the training of Miyan Mir and Mulla Shah. His interests were not confined to Sufism and its practices. He turned to Hindu religious figures and drew on Indic traditions. Dara Shukoh had many meetings and discussions with thinkers and practitioners of different religious traditions. He himself was a devout and pious man and spoke of having experienced visions in which he had felt the presence of divinity.

Dara Shukoh in his religious and philosophical pursuits was continuing a Mughal tradition. His father, grandfather, and, more importantly his great-grandfather, had in their own times sought the company and the counsel of Sufis, mystics, and Hindu holy men. Dara had an enduring engagement with Indic texts and had some of them translated. The Mughals encouraged the translation of works that had existed in Indian culture and tradition. It was one way for them to assert imperial authority. To translate a text that had been read and cultivated in India far longer than one's ancestors was to establish deeper roots in Indian soil. Thus, Dara Shukoh inherited and used a tradition of fashioning political authority—asceticism and piety—that monarchs in India had used for a very long time.

One aspect of the coming of Islam that has generated an enormous amount controversy and emotion is the view that Muslims carried out forcible conversions of non-Muslim peoples in India. That there was conversion is undeniable and obvious. Without conversions India could not have had a Muslim population. The problem lies with the word 'forcible'. There is no evidence to believe that all Muslims or Muslim rulers were Islamic zealots who went around imposing their beliefs on their subjects. The very fact that Muslim rulers employed large numbers of non-Muslims and even appointed them to very high positions is testimony to this fact. There were many reasons why individuals and groups converted to Islam. One was the perception among certain sections of the population that by converting to the religion of the rulers they stood a better chance of getting employment and protection. There was also the attraction of the message of Islam based as it was on equality of all human beings. Those who were at the lowest rungs of the caste system and were thus victims of it were attracted by this message of equality and converted to Islam in the expectation of a better life. In certain parts of India, there was a noticeable propensity among the lower castes to embrace Islam. In certain cases, more complex processes were at work. These can be illustrated through the research of historian Richard M. Eaton by what happened in Bengal and how it came to have a large Muslim population.

Female pilgrims at the dargah of Moin-ud-din Chishti, Ajmer, Rajasthan

Moin-ud-din Chishti, founder of the Chishti mystic Sufi order, emphasized in his philosophic teachings the ideas of asceticism, love of God, and humanity. He came to Ajmer from Persia in the year 1192 and died in 1236. The dargah where he was buried was built by Emperor Humayun. Jahanara, the daughter of Mughal emperor Shah Jahan, is said to have established a prayer room especially for his female followers. The shrine still welcomes followers of other faiths, echoing the teachings of Oneness.

Bengal, as is well-known, is criss-crossed by powerful rivers that have sustained the economy and the society of the region. The course of these rivers was always changing; as one channel silted up a river found another course. In the 1570s, for example, the Ganga had bifurcated near present-day Malda into two channels—

one flowing southward towards what is now Kolkata and the other flowing eastward towards Dacca (present-day Dhaka). Within a hundred years, the eastern channel had become far more important. This development in the riverine system had the inevitable consequence of pushing eastward the centre of civilization and culture of Bengal. One outcome of this eastward shift was that in this fertile terrain pioneering groups began to clear forests to bring virgin land under the plough for more wet rice cultivation, the agricultural staple in Bengal. Rice production increased to unprecedented levels and rice was being exported to ports around the Bay of Bengal and even Southeast Asia. Around the same time, Mughal power, headquartered in Dacca, was establishing itself in Bengal. Also, European trading companies were becoming active in the trading world of Bengal and connecting the latter to the world economy. These changes—riverine, political, and economic—coincided geographically and chronologically with the first recorded presence of a Bengali Muslim peasantry. Foreign travellers noted in the late sixteenth century that in places near Chittagong in the south-east of present-day Bangladesh and near Narayanganj the people in the villages were nearly all Muslims. In Noakhali too (in the eastern corner of Bangladesh) there were Muslim communities. What is worthy of note is that in the eastern delta, before the advent of Mughal rule, the population of the area was not an integral part of the Hindu social and religious order. The implication of this is that when Islam arrived in this region there was no transition from Hinduism to Islam. The people of this area—fishermen, hunters, slash-and-burn agriculturists—worshipped various different local and forest deities like Manasa and Chandi. These people took to Islam. In contrast, in the western delta where the Hindu socio-religious order was more strongly entrenched, Islam did not penetrate to any noticeable extent even though Islam as the religion of the rulers had been present in the western delta from the fourteenth century.

Parvathy Baul, Sacred Spirit Annual Festival 2017, Nagaur, Rajasthan

Parvathy Baul is a well-known practitioner, performer, and teacher of the Baul tradition which originated in Bengal. She sings, dances swinging her matted locks, and simultaneously plays a traditional instrument, the ektara (small, single-stringed instrument) or the duggie (drum). Baul singers are wandering minstrels who go from village to village taking their message to the remotest regions; they perform for the community, who offer them food and shelter.

The arrival of Islam in India brought a new momentum. One part of it was violent conquests that brought with them a new political discourse that was accepted and used even by non-Muslim rulers. The other part was less obvious and more enduring, creating new forms of devotion, aesthetic sensibilities, and even the extension and organization of agriculture. Through these influences, Islam became an integral part of the diversity of Indian history and culture.

· CHAPTER 13 ·

CENTURY OF TRANSITION

1707 CE–c. 1800 CE

In 1707, the year of Aurangzeb's death, the Mughal empire had reached its largest geographical extent. Its frontiers extended from Kabul to Bengal and even parts of Assam; from the foothills of the Himalaya to the deep south. The sprawling empire, as Aurangzeb was shrewd enough to recognize, was in the throes of a structural and economic crisis.

The ultimate victims of this crisis were the peasants, whose growing exploitation led to their discontent. From the last years of the seventeenth century and into the eighteenth, Delhi and its surrounding areas saw a series of peasant revolts led by the Jats, Sikhs, and Satnamis. These revolts spread into the Maratha territories. The situation was aggravated by the fact that Aurangzeb was followed by a series of monarchs who were either incompetent or frivolous or both. They were clueless about the crisis that faced them and about ruling. The actual process of disintegration began when powerful Mughal noblemen declared their autonomy from Delhi by carving out independent principalities for themselves.

One of the first of the Mughal subahs (provinces) to declare independence was Bengal under Murshid Quli Khan, who was the governor of the province from 1713–27. He was a very successful governor who reformed the administrative system and increased the collection of land revenue. Murshid Quli entrusted large zamindars (landholders) with the responsibility of collecting land revenue; in the process he eliminated small and middling zamindars. His measures received widespread support and this allowed him to work independently of Delhi which was then under a number of worthless monarchs. What is important to note, however, is that Murshid Quli continued to transfer the Bengal land revenue to

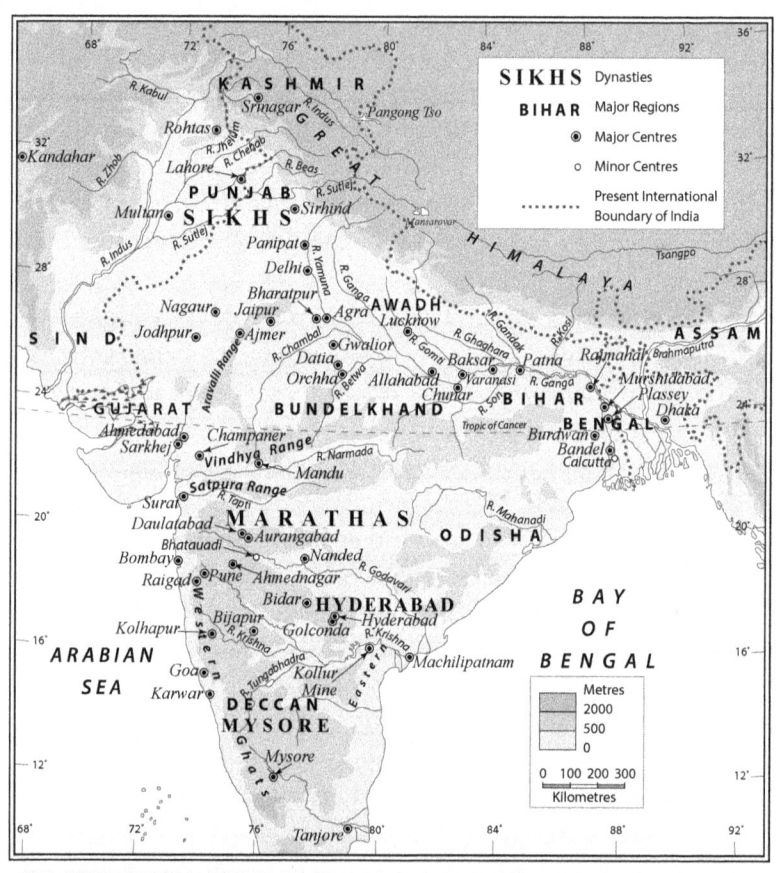

Kingdoms that rose after the decline of the Mughal empire

Not to scale. This map has been prepared in adherence to the 'Guidelines for acquiring and producing Geospatial Data and Geospatial Data Services including Maps' published vide DST F.No.SM/25/02/2020 (Part-I) dated 15th February, 2021

the imperial exchequer in Delhi. The transfer of this huge amount was made possible by the banking house of Jagat Seth which had established itself in Murshidabad (the capital of Murshid Quli Khan) in the seventeenth century. The presence of these banking facilities also made possible the payment of land revenues by large zamindars. The system set up by Murshid Quli Khan was carried on by his successors and this ensured the prosperity of Bengal—both in agriculture and manufacturing in the first half of the eighteenth century. But the system began to fall apart largely under external pressure from the late 1750s as we shall see in a subsequent chapter.

The Kathgola Palace, Murshidabad, West Bengal

Several Jain families from Rajasthan, rose to prominence and power when they became the bankers (seths) and financiers of the nawabs of Murshidabad. The Jagat Seth family forged close ties with the British and conspired to overthrow Nawab Siraj-ud-daulah, for which they were later punished. Murshidabad lost its eminence when the treasury and banking centre was moved to Calcutta. These palaces are Indian imitations of European buildings, with hybrid plasterwork and stucco decoration. Many are now museums.

In 1724, a very powerful Mughal mansabdar, Chin Qilich Khan, was given the title Nizam-ul-mulk and made the governor of the Deccan. He was utterly frustrated by the factionalism and the ineffectiveness of the Mughal court and began consolidating his own position in Hyderabad and its surrounding areas. He asserted his autonomy by setting up his own administration. He suppressed local rebellions to consolidate his authority. The rulers of this principality—Nizam-ul-mulk and his successors—had to contend with inroads from the growing power of the Marathas across the Deccan plateau and also from the powerful state emerging in Mysore (present-day Mysuru). People from different faiths from the Deccan and North India performed administrative tasks. In spite of the external threats the principality of Hyderabad faced, and the consequent sense of instability, there was prosperity. But growing pressure from the Marathas and from Mysore made the ruler sign a treaty with the English East India Company (EIC) in 1759 which ensured an influential British presence—in the position of the Resident, British troops, and concession of territory to the British—in Hyderabad.

Almost replicating what happened in Hyderabad, Saadat Khan, another powerful Mughal nobleman, refused the imperial order transferring him to Malwa from Awadh in 1722 and declared himself the independent ruler of Awadh based in Lucknow. From this time, Awadh emerged as a flourishing principality sprawling across the heart of North India. It was one of the areas in North India where economic growth was very noticeable in the eighteenth century. The new state that was established in Awadh by Saadat Khan was strengthened by his successors, especially Safdar Jang (1739–54). The state was maintained through a fine balance between the ruler (called the nawab) in Lucknow and powerful taluqdars who controlled the countryside especially in the collection of land revenue. Trade flourished in Awadh, making it one of the more prosperous areas in North India.

Charminar, Hyderabad, Telangana

This landmark gateway to the old city of Hyderabad was built by Sultan Quli Qutb Shah between 1591–1612 to provide employment after a deadly plague. It has a staircase leading to the upper storeys. It has a huge archway guarded by four minarets 56 metres high—such arches are usually found in mosques. Nearby is a crowded bazaar, with numerous lanes each assigned with shops that sell one item—the lane for glass bangles, clothes, metalware, and so on. Beyond the bazaar is the Chowmahalla Palace of the nizam of Hyderabad that has been recently restored to showcase the fabled wealth of this family.

Maharashtra had never been successfully subjugated by the Mughals in spite of the best efforts of Aurangzeb. The great leader of the Marathas, Shivaji, had declared his independence from the Mughals and had proclaimed himself king in 1674. He wanted to establish swarajya in the Maratha desh and styled himself explicitly as a Hindu monarch. One of the titles that he gave himself was haindava-dharmoddarakla (protector of the Hindu faith). His support base was from the deshmukhs (landed families). He was a military strategist and extremely courageous. His activities and military raids did not give a moment's peace to the Bijapur sultanate and to Aurangzeb. A period of instability followed after Shivaji's death in 1680. This ended with the emergence of a succession of Chitpavan Brahmin prime ministers (peshwas) who served and advised the Maratha regent Shahu from 1713–61. The first of these peshwas was Balaji Vishwanath who ended the period of trouble and instability through his shrewd handling of finances. Under his son Baji Rao I, the activities and the military strategy of the Marathas took a new and dramatic turn. With the support of some young warlords—Malhar Rao Holkar and Ranoji Sindhia in particular—Baji Rao I argued that the only way to strengthen the position of the Marathas in the given circumstances of the eighteenth century was to move outside the Maratha desh, both eastward across the Deccan and northward into the Mughal heartland. He put forward the dream to young and ambitious Maratha warriors of taking the Maratha cavalry to Attock on the Indus. To this end, he created a cavalry-based army that was capable of swift raids. He captured Malwa, Gujarat, and Bundelkhand which formed the southern points that were under direct Mughal control. He moved as far north as Delhi and in 1739 the Marathas entered Delhi. This expansion continued under his successor Balaji Baji Rao who, however, changed the character of the Maratha army from a mobile force to an army that was camp-based and therefore slow on the move. Maratha expansion northward was thwarted by the defeat of the massive Maratha army in the Third Battle of Panipat (1761) at the hands of the Afghan king Ahmad Shah Abdali. This expansion northward for thirty years from the 1730s was sustained by the levy of taxes called chauth and sardeshmukhi over large parts of the Deccan.

Safdar Jang's Tomb, New Delhi

Safdar Jang was the nephew of Saadat Khan, the nawab of Awadh. He lived in Delhi and served in the court of Muhammad Shah. He died in 1754 and was buried in Delhi. The tomb is set in an enormous garden with orchards and fountains in the favoured style of the Mughals. It was made of red sandstone and is similar to Humayun's Tomb, yet its elongated form, pointed onion-shaped dome, and painted stucco decorations lack the elegance of the older imperial style.

In Mysore, developments followed a somewhat different trajectory. Mysore, originally under the Vijayanagara empire, became autonomous in the seventeenth century and had powerful military commanders. Haider Ali, rising from the ranks, was one such commander and, in 1761, through a coup took control over the state. He modernized the army, was strict in maintaining financial discipline, and succeeded in defeating the British in a number of military encounters. Under his son, Tipu Sultan, who took over from his father in 1782, Mysore became more than just a powerful military state. Tipu established centralized control over the administration and over the revenues of the state. Under him the state became a critical player in various kinds of economic activities.

He extended cultivation by reclaiming wastelands and introduced commercial crops like sugar cane, silk, and timber for military and commercial use. He initiated irrigation works under state ownership and also set up gun foundries and saltpetre factories under state ownership. He set up state trading houses along the west coast and in Madras, Pondicherry, Hyderabad, and even in Muscat. The state itself engaged in the trade of valuable commodities like sandalwood, silk, spices, coconut, rice, sulphur, and elephants. He established state monopoly over foreign trade and had the central treasury fund the building of seagoing vessels. Tipu's multifaceted projects made him a monarch—he gave himself the title of padshah—who was in many ways similar to absolute monarchs of Europe whose power was based on wealth brought in by trade. His growing power and independence in South India made a conflict with the expanding British power in the eighteenth century inevitable but this is a theme of a later chapter.

Daria Daulat Bagh, Tipu Sultan's Summer Palace, Srirangapatna, Mysuru, Karnataka

Mural of the Battle of Pollilur in 1780 when Haider Ali defeated the EIC forces

Tipu Sultan built a walled enclosure for the Daria Daulat Bagh (Garden of the Wealth of the Seas) around his wooden summer palace. The wide veranda around the Summer Palace, as it is now referred to, is animated with paintings of marching, warring armies of the French and the British. The painting offers a wealth of information on battle formations, the composition of the armies with horses, elephants, foot soldiers, the uniforms of the various players, and the military band that accompanied them. The battle scenes are vivid and dramatic, depicting victory and defeat. There are several paintings of Tipu Sultan and his courageous father, Haider Ali, leading their men into battle.

In the seventeenth and eighteenth centuries, Sikhism came to acquire political dimensions and the Sikhs became a major political force in the Punjab. The strength of Sikhism was its egalitarian appeal and the development of certain institutions such as the langar and sangat that helped to forge a sense of community. This community increasingly came under pressure from Mughal expansion and economic exploitation in the late seventeenth century. The Sikhs decided to resist this pressure through a series of militant uprisings.

In 1699, Guru Gobind Singh, the tenth guru from Nanak, formed the Khalsa brotherhood. Through this, not only did the guru assume control but also strengthened the bonds within the Sikh community and enabled it to resist Mughal oppression. One crucial dimension of the Khalsa was its militarization and this became more evident after the death of Guru Gobind Singh when leadership was assumed by Banda Bahadur. In 1709–10, Banda Bahadur led an uprising and began to collect revenue, defying Mughal authority, in parts of Punjab. He appointed his own officers and minted his own coins. Banda became the embodiment of Sikh resistance to Mughal rule. He was captured by the Mughals and executed in 1716. This only aggravated the situation. The Sikhs using Amritsar as their base continued to exert their authority over large parts of Punjab in spite of attacks from Nadir Shah who came from Persia and the Afghans from the north-west. By 1765, Sikh rule in Punjab was an undeniable reality. That year the Sikhs declared their sovereignty and struck their own coins in Lahore.

South of Punjab, the transformation of peasant resistance into a political formation was noticeable in the case of the Jats based out of Bharatpur. The process began under Churaman Jat (1695–1721), the leader of a militant peasant group of Jats living in the environs of Delhi and Mathura, which resisted Mughal oppression. The first rebellion in 1699 was so powerful and militant that Aurangzeb himself led the expedition to suppress it. But Churaman continued with his hit-and-run raids and Aurangzeb's successors had no option but to yield to the demands of the Jats. Under Badan Singh, the nephew of Churaman, the Jats consolidated their position and increased the area under their control between the Yamuna and Rajasthan.

This chapter has drawn attention to the bigger principalities that were established in defiance of the Mughal empire. There were smaller ones as well: Afghan principalities in Farrukhabad and Rohilkhand in North India and the kingdom of Travancore in Kerala. The collapse of the Mughal empire and the speed at which it happened—less than two decades after the death of Aurangzeb—made many historians describe the first half of the eighteenth century as a period of decline and chaos.

Many British historians wrote of the eighteenth century in such terms and then went on to argue that it was from this state of chaos that British rule rescued India by restoring peace and stability. Many Indian historians also depicted the eighteenth century as a period of decline but they did not buy into the second part of the argument that the British historians had put forward. In the view of the Indian historians, the activities of the British in India in the eighteenth century had only added to the chaos and the decline. There is no doubt that under a succession of weak and ineffective emperors—emperors only in name—Delhi had lost most of its former grandeur especially after it had been raided by the Marathas and sacked by Nadir Shah in 1739–40. Most recent historians have looked at the eighteenth century from a different perspective by shifting the focus away from Delhi and Agra. In their view, after the Mughal empire began to disintegrate as a centralizing force, India did not descend into chaos and economic decline. On the contrary in large parts of India, trade and economic activity continued to flourish under strong rulers. The most notable of these areas were Bengal, Awadh, Mysore, the Maratha Confederacy, and Hyderabad. There is an additional and important point. It was precisely because of the existence and importance of these successor states to the Mughal empire that the British had to conquer India region by region and not in one fell swoop. There was no British conquest of India but there were British conquests of India spread over more than half a century. This is the theme of the next chapter.

· CHAPTER 14 ·

THE ARRIVAL OF EUROPEAN TRADING COMPANIES AND BRITISH CONQUESTS

c. 1490 CE–1856 CE

The Portuguese were the first Europeans to arrive on the western coast of India—more precisely Malabar—in the late 1490s. Vasco da Gama's ships cast anchor off Calicut (present-day Kozhikode) in 1498. The Portuguese came to India with the explicit mission to find Christians and spices. To secure the latter, they aimed at an armed domination of the maritime trade of the Indian Ocean. They were partially successful in this because they had naval superiority over Asian ships, and so could set up a few key outposts on land as their bases of operation. One of the earliest of these Portuguese bases was secured by the capture of Goa from the sultan of Bijapur, Ismail Adil Shah, in 1510 by Afonso de Albuquerque.

To Goa was quickly added Diu and a series of fortified settlements in the Coromandel, Chittagong, and Hooghly. This maritime empire acquired the name of Estado da India. The trade of the Portuguese in India concentrated on pepper and spices. They did not hesitate to use coercive methods to secure their monopoly over these commodities. One such coercive method was the cartaz system by which every Indian ship sailing to a port not reserved by the Portuguese for their own trade had to buy one of these passes from the viceroy of Goa to avoid the confiscation of its cargo. One consequence of this was that at the end of the sixteenth century very few Indian ships could sail to east Africa, to the Far East, and the Spice Islands.

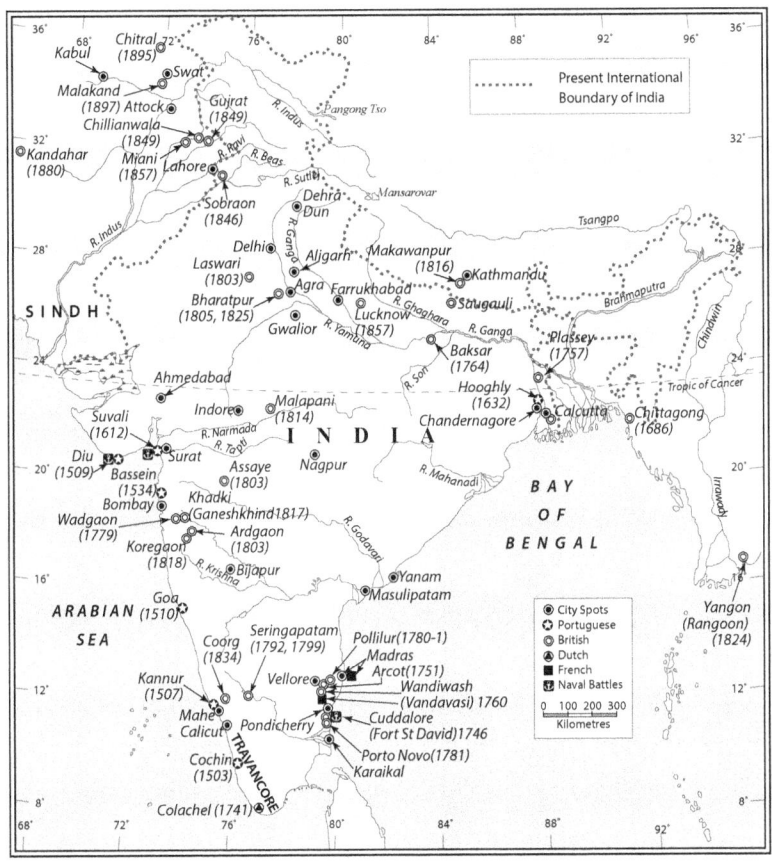

300 years of European battles and engagements across the subcontinent

Not to scale. This map has been prepared in adherence to the 'Guidelines for acquiring and producing Geospatial Data and Geospatial Data Services including Maps' published vide DST F.No.SM/25/02/2020 (Part-I) dated 15th February, 2021.

The success of the Portuguese maritime enterprise in the Indian Ocean produced many imitators. One of these was the Vereenigde Oost-Indische Compagnie (VOC) or United East India Company of the Netherlands.

The Dutch had initially directed their ships to the Indonesian archipelago where they would not face too much competition from the Portuguese. But they discovered that the economy of many of the islands did not have enough cash available for trading. To overcome this, the Dutch began to buy cotton textiles from India for which there was a demand among the islanders. Indian cotton textiles thus became an item of barter to secure spices. The Dutch obtained these textiles from the Coromandel coast and from Gujarat. Masulipatam (present-day Machlipatnam) in the Coromandel and Surat in Gujarat became strongholds of Dutch trade in India. The Dutch were soon to discover that there was a European demand for Indian cotton textiles. This altered not only the pattern of their trade but also that of the English East India Company—fashioned as a joint stock company—that had been formed in 1600.

A very late entrant into this emerging trading world were the French. The first organized attempt on the part of the French to enter the Indian trade was the formation in 1664 of the Compagnie Française des Indes Orientales. The French faced serious competition from the Dutch and the English but by the beginning of the eighteenth century their trade had expanded and they had settlements in Pondicherry and in Chandernagore (present-day Chandannagar) on the Hooghly. In fact, in the eighteenth century the right bank of the Hooghly (coming downstream) was dotted with settlements of European trading companies—the Portuguese in Bandel, the Dutch in Chinsurah, the Danes in Serampore, and the French in Chandernagore. Only the English were on the left bank (in what was to become Calcutta); but this had happened when they had been forced to flee in 1690 from their original settlement in Bengal in the port town of Hooghly.

Statue of Dupleix, Puducherry

The French East India company was founded in 1644 and established factories and warehouses along the west and east coast of India, including Pondicherry. In 1742, a war broke out between competing countries Britain and France, over trade routes to Asia and America. The British captured French ships off the Indian coast and the French retaliated. Dupleix marched into Madras and occupied Fort St George in 1746. After the battle a settlement was made and Madras was returned to the British. This statue of Dupleix was erected in Pondicherry to honour this French colonial hero.

It is necessary now to turn to the English East India Company (EIC) in some detail since its activities shaped the future history of India. This company began its operation under a royal charter granted by Elizabeth I. The charter gave the Company the monopoly to trade in Asian waters. The monopoly meant that nobody, corporate or individual, in England, save the East India Company could trade in the vast stretch of land and water from the Cape of Good Hope to the South China Sea. This monopoly, as we shall see, was always a fragile one and the EIC for its own reasons preferred it that way. The fortunes of the EIC took a dramatic turn in 1717. That year it was granted a farman (royal order) by the Mughal emperor Farrukhsiyar. This farman was the outcome of an English delegation headed by John Surman to the Mughal court in 1717. According to the farman, all goods carried by the Company in the subah of Bengal were to be free from customs duties. The goods, in other words, were covered by a dastak (free pass). The farman also contained other important concessions to the Company—the rent of thirty-eight villages adjacent to Calcutta; and the permission to use the royal mint for minting coins out of its imported bullion (bars of gold). The dastak became the bone of contention between the nawab of Bengal and the Company. The latter claimed that the free pass included the private trade of the Company's servants, whereas the nawab argued that it covered only the trade of the Company. In spite of protests from successive nawabs of Bengal, especially Alivardi Khan, the Company continued its operations according to its own baseless interpretation of the farman. The EIC was, as the nawabs pointed out, defrauding the exchequer of valuable revenue as the Company's servants were refusing to pay duties by claiming their goods were covered by the dastak. After 1717, the boom in the Company's trade in Bengal was based on its refusal to pay the nawab his legitimate dues which all other merchants, foreign and Indian, were paying. Siraj-ud-daulah, who became the nawab in 1756, decided to put an end to this situation by sacking Calcutta. For Siraj-ud-daulah, the Company was defrauding his exchequer by misinterpreting the farman, and further he believed that the Company, by building a fort, Fort William, in Calcutta was defying his sovereignty. His sacking of Calcutta set in motion a chain of momentous events that would go down in the annals of history.

Having sacked Calcutta, Siraj-ud-daulah went back to Murshidabad. The Company sent up reinforcements from Madras under a maverick young man called Robert Clive. Clive resumed trading operations from Calcutta but more importantly began to hatch a conspiracy to topple Siraj-ud-daulah and put in his place a puppet nawab. This was not difficult to do as Siraj-ud-daulah had made many enemies because of his volatile temper. Clive held out the promise to Siraj-ud-daulah's commander-in-chief, Mir Jafar, that he would be made the nawab if he took no part in the military encounter between the Company and Siraj-ud-daulah. That encounter took place on 23 June 1757 in the village of Plassey, downstream from Murshidabad. It was not much of a battle with Mir Jafar standing by. Siraj-ud-daulah was defeated and killed and Mir Jafar was made nawab. The Company's troops entered Murshidabad and plundered it. Soldiers and officials, including Clive, garnered fortunes through this looting. This looting and plunder in Bengal continued right through Mir Jafar's nawabi and this period came to be known as 'the shaking of the pagoda tree'.

Siraj-ud-daulah's tomb, Khushbagh, Murshidabad, West Bengal

Siraj-ud-daulah (meaning Light of the State) was the nawab of Bengal; with his death, and the end of his reign, Bengal came under the administrative control of the EIC and thus began the commencement of foreign rule in India. His single-storeyed grave is set in a garden named Khushbagh (garden of happiness); the building has a flat roof, with five elegant arches leading to the chamber with the grave. Within the garden complex, and standing opposite the tomb, is a modest three-domed mosque for prayer. It was customary to build a mosque near a royal grave for regular prayers for the deceased and for those who came to honour the dead.

Officials and factors of the EIC went back to England with huge sums of money, pursued an ostentatious lifestyle and came to be known as 'nabobs'—thus a new word was added to the English language. Even Mir Jafar found this situation unacceptable and when he protested he was replaced by his son-in-law, Mir Qasim.

Mir Qasim, contrary to the Company's expectations, did not prove to be a puppet nawab. He won the support of the Indian merchants in Bengal and of the large zamindars; he formed an alliance with Shuja-ud-daula, the nawab of Awadh, and with Shah Alam, the then Mughal emperor who retained a symbolic importance. The armies of this alliance met the Company's troops at Baksar in 1764. The Battle of Baksar was a genuine battle, unlike Plassey, and the outcome was touch and go throughout the day. The Company's troops finally won. On the basis of their victory, in 1765 the Company extracted two concessions, one each from the nawab of Awadh and the Mughal emperor. They got the nawab of Awadh to agree to the opening up of Awadh to British traders and the stationing of a British garrison under a Resident in Lucknow. The concession from the Mughal emperor was momentous. The latter agreed to grant the Company the right to collect revenue in Bengal. It began to use this revenue to finance its own purchases to be sent to Europe. This meant that the Company no longer spent any of its own money to carry out its trading operations. This placed the Company in a unique position as a trading company. It also enhanced the Company's effective control over Bengal. It used this control to maximize the land revenue demand since this would serve to increase its investment. This uncontrolled increase led to a devastating famine in Bengal in 1770.

In South India, especially in the Carnatic, the Company was engaged in a series of military encounters with the French. These were reflections of Anglo-French rivalry in Europe—the War of Austrian Succession (1740–48) and the Seven Years War (1756–63). The Company also began to interfere in local politics by embroiling itself in succession struggles in Hyderabad and the Carnatic. In so doing the Company succeeded in placing their own candidates on the thrones of these principalities. The more serious engagements were those with Mysore under Haider Ali and Tipu Sultan. The former's kingdom stretched all the way from the river Krishna in the north to Malabar in the west. This meant that his presence and his ambitions threatened the Company's position in Madras. Haider Ali made his intentions clear by making an alliance with the Marathas and attacking Arcot in 1767. This conflict, known as the First Anglo-Mysore War, lasted for two years and ended with the Company suffering serious losses and being forced to agree to a treaty. Both sides knew that this would not be a lasting peace. Haider Ali's control over Malabar was a major hindrance to the Company's trading interests as Malabar was a source for pepper. To make matters worse, Haider was also openly negotiating for support from the French. Haider mounted an offensive against the Company in the Carnatic with a huge army supported by 100 guns. He won major victories and devastated the countryside. Haider's death in 1782 marked a pause in the conflict and both sides signed the Treaty of Mangalore.

Tipu Sultan, Haider's son and heir, followed pro-French trade policies which made the Company very apprehensive. The EIC faced pressure from private traders to resolve the conflict with Mysore. Tipu's intention was to curtail the Company's trade in South India. He put an embargo in 1785 on the export of pepper, sandalwood, and cardamom from his kingdom; in 1788 he passed an order banning any commercial transactions with English traders. The Company would not, of course, accept this. This was the context of the Third and the Fourth Anglo-Mysore wars. Neither of these two wars went in favour of Tipu. In the Third Anglo-Mysore War he was surprised by a night attack led by Lord Cornwallis on his capital, Seringapatam. This resulted in Tipu being forced to accept the harsh terms of the Treaty of Seringapatam (1792) by which he had to yield half of his kingdom to the Company. The curtain fell on Tipu's ambitions when the Company's troops, driven by the imperial ambitions of the new governor general Lord Wellesley, overran Mysore in 1798. Tipu died defending his capital in 1799. The Company was now the master of a substantial part of the Deccan.

Tipu's tomb, Srirangapatna, Karnataka

Seringapatam (present-day Srirangapatna) was the river island capital of Haider Ali and his son Tipu Sultan. The Marathas attacked the capital in the eighteenth century but Haider Ali managed to ward them off. The greater threat came from British forces, and so Tipu Sultan forged an alliance with the French to secure his lands. A simple sign within the fort marks the spot where Tipu Sultan fell in battle and died in 1799, trying to preserve his territory in southern India from foreign rule.

The power of the Marathas suffered a severe setback with their defeat in the Third Battle of Panipat, 1761, at the hands of Ahmad Shah Abdali. In the years after Panipat, the court in Poona (present-day Pune) was caught up in intrigues and split into factions or groups with different interests. From around 1770, Maratha power revived under the leadership of Mahadaji Sindhia. Around this time, the Company was firmly entrenched in Bengal and was spreading its tentacles into Awadh. The directors of the Company were pushing for a more aggressive policy towards the Marathas because the territories that they controlled were rich in cotton—raw and finished—which was vital for the Company's trade. Another factor was French mercenaries arriving in India and joining the Maratha army. The First Anglo-Maratha War (1775–82) did not bring tangible gains to either side. But in the 1790s when the two most important Maratha warlords, the Holkars and the Sindhias, were locked in combat, Lord Wellesley decided to move. His argument was that the French were poised to set up a mini state on the banks of the Yamuna and the British needed to protect themselves against such a possibility. He pressured the nawab of Awadh to cede a large chunk of territory between the Ganga and the Yamuna. He argued that this was necessary to create a buffer to protect Awadh against a possible Maratha–French attack. It is important to underline that Awadh by the end of the eighteenth century had become an important hub of British trade. Wellesley was driven by economic and strategic interests. Having secured the position of the British in the Gangetic plain, Wellesley was ready to take on the Marathas. The military encounter with the Marathas—the Second Anglo-Maratha War (1803–05) happened in two separate locations. In the Deccan, Arthur Wellesley (Lord Wellesley's brother and the future duke of Wellington) defeated Sindhia's army at Assaye. Up in North India, Lord Lake defeated the bulk of the Maratha army in successive battles (August–September 1803) at Koil, Aligarh, and most decisively at Laswari. Given these victories, the Mughal emperor, Shah Alam, had no option but to seek British protection.

The British were now in control of the Mughal capital. The final blow to the languishing Maratha power was rendered when Holkar was defeated in 1818. The British could now claim that they had an empire in India.

There were two territories that the British still had not militarily conquered. One was Awadh which they controlled and had encircled; the other was Punjab. In the early nineteenth century, Ranjit Singh had emerged as the leader of the Sikh power in Punjab. Initially, the British were not keen to antagonize Ranjit Singh since he served as a convenient buffer for any invasion from Afghanistan. This situation began to change when in 1808 a number of Sikh military units, from south of the Sutlej, approached the Company for protection against Ranjit Singh. This was followed by the Treaty of Amritsar (1809) and the creation of a British protectorate south of the Sutlej. The trans-Sutlej areas remained under Ranjit Singh and he expanded his dominion by occupying Jammu in 1812, Attock the next year, and Multan and Kashmir in 1818 and 1819 respectively. The death of Ranjit Singh in 1839 completely altered the politics of the region for two reasons. One was the hostility between various Sikh leaders and the other was the growing fear of a Russian invasion via Afghanistan. The latter factor made the British decide to militarily intervene and annex Punjab. This resulted in two bloody wars against the Sikhs: one in the mid-1840s and the other in 1849. The result of the two Anglo-Sikh wars was the subjugation of the Sikhs and the British occupation of Punjab.

Beginning with Plassey, the British, operating through the EIC, had conquered India region by region. The few principalities that they did not conquer through violence, they either brought under their mastery through what was called the Subsidiary Alliance by which an Indian ruler was allowed nominally to rule his kingdom so long as he recognized the authority of the British, or the British annexed these kingdoms on the pretext of misgovernment or by arguing that the ruling lineage had lapsed in the absence of a biological male heir.

Memorial of the Battle of Plassey, West Bengal

Madras had been the centre of the East India Company's activities in the seventeenth century. After the British won the Battle of Plassey on 23 June 1757, the EIC moved its headquarters from Madras to Calcutta, and Clive became the governor of Bengal in 1765. This memorial was erected, with a tall obelisk set in a small cordoned off garden, to mark the site of the Battle of Plassey, as it stands today, just off the road from Kolkata to Murshidabad.

· CHAPTER 15 ·

INDIA AND THE WORLD

c. 3000 BCE–c. 1800 CE

It is a common misconception that India's cultural developments were entirely self-contained and isolated from the rest of the world till the time the European trading companies arrived on Indian shores. It is undeniable that the arrival of these trading companies, especially the English East India Company, marked a turning point with momentous and far-reaching consequences for India's history. However, right through India's long past, there had been a rich interaction between different parts of the world and various regions of India with their diverse cultural traditions. Some of these encounters have been touched upon in the preceding chapters. Here, we will tie in the more significant moments of India's exchanges with other parts of the world.

Going back to the Harappan Culture, it is clear that trade networks linked different sites of this culture to the Mesopotamian world and to areas in the Persian Gulf. This trade, entirely based on barter since coinage was unknown in this period, was composed of the exchange of raw materials and finished products. Various parts of the Harappan Culture zone—Baluchistan, Sind, Rajasthan, Punjab, and Gujarat—were linked through routes. There existed a coastal route that connected sites like Lothal in Gujarat to sites such as Sutkagen Dor on the Makran coast. Goods and artefacts were transported on tracks (track marks have been discovered) on pack animals. Some Harappan objects like ivory dice, silver seals, spearheads, ladles, and so on have been found in south Turkmenistan. The discovery of a Harappan seal with the Harappan script in Altyn Depe is the most definite evidence of the connections that existed with this region and the Harappan zone. Similarly, archaeologists in Iran have discovered remains of Harappa-related artefacts. There is strong evidence that

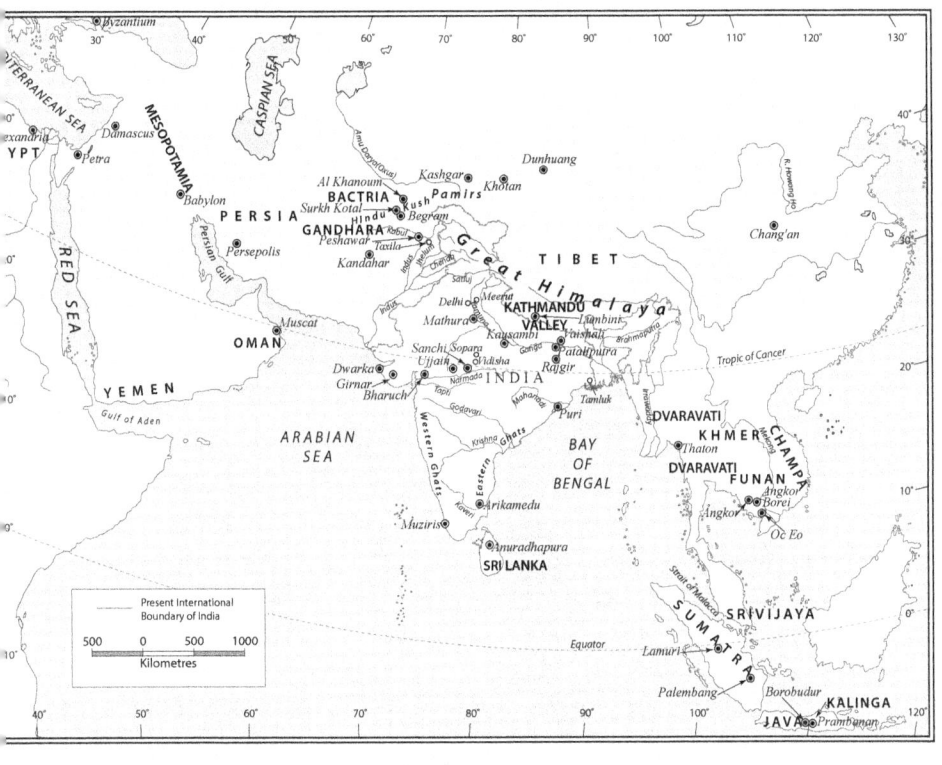

India and the world

Not to scale. This map has been prepared in adherence to the 'Guidelines for acquiring and producing Geospatial Data and Geospatial Data Services including Maps' published vide DST F.No.SM/25/02/2020 (Part-I) dated 15th February, 2021

Boudanath Stupa, Kathmandu Valley, Nepal

the people of the Harappan civilization were trading with the Oman peninsula. Two main overland routes—one going through northern Afghanistan, North Iran, Turkmenistan, and Mesopotamia, and a southern route that went through Jalalabad and Ur—linked the Harappan zone. Even though there is not enough evidence to write about this trade in great detail, there is enough to suggest that this exchange was not negligible. It is important to emphasize that trade involves not just the exchange of commodities but also the active engagement of people who were on the move carrying ideas, beliefs, languages, practices, and so on. This must have made for a rich interaction about which we know precious little.

Monks and ascetics belonging to different sects and beliefs were very significant in the transmission of ideas. Ascetics immersed in the profound wisdom of the Upanishads and others belonging to different dissenting sects were the carriers of philosophical ideas, as were Buddhist monks and scholars. It is well known that travellers from Southeast Asia and China visited India at different points of

Ship, Borobudur, Java, Indonesia

time and spent many months and years here. They were not only the bearers of the message of the Buddha but were very often the preservers of old Buddhist texts. Thus, knowledge and wisdom originating in India moved across geographies. Such movements of ideas were often enmeshed with trade. Arab traders on the western coast of India carried with them some of the truly original findings of Indian scientists and mathematicians.

This was how the concept of zero, the numerals, the decimal system, the numerical value of pi, and the mathematical system of algebra became a part of the global system of knowledge. Some of the discoveries and calculations of Indian scientists in the domain of astronomy were also fundamental contributions which, unfortunately, because of the dominance of Western science, have not received the recognition they deserve.

A remarkable example is Aryabhata—the astronomer and mathematician of the fifth century, whose work in astronomy and the field of trigonometry was original and foundational; he had also proposed the daily motion of the earth and a theory of gravity to explain why objects are not flung off the earth as it rotates. This was later to be elaborated by Brahmagupta in the sixth century. This corpus of knowledge travelling with Arab traders and sailors reached the city of Constantinople (present-day Istanbul), a major centre of learning and trade and from there moved to Venice, and thus contributed to the making of the world of European learning associated with the Renaissance. In the ancient world there was a great deal of give and take and reciprocal learning. India was an integral and important constituent of such interchanges of goods and ideas. There was a general acknowledgement of what the Syrian bishop Severus Sebokht said in 662 CE: 'There are also others who know something.'

An interesting facet of India's achievements in the world of astronomy and mathematics was the attention scholars devoted to the development of calendars. Calendars were important initially because they marked out days and periods of rituals, worship, and even of harvests. In spite of the links of calendars with religious functions,

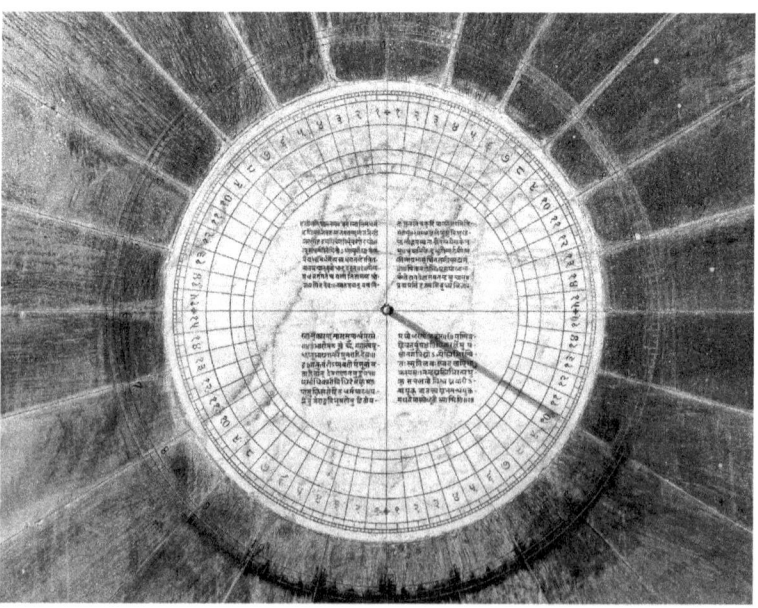

Detail from the Jantar Mantar, eighteenth century, Jaipur (left)

There are more than thirty indigenous calendar systems used in India, and several more were added from other countries—the Gregorian or ('Christian' or 'Western') calendar, the Hijri (or Islamic) calendar system, the Buddhist calendar system (followed for traditional and ritual purposes), and the Parsi (Zoroastrian or Jewish) calendar. Likewise, the Tamil calendar is prevalent among the Tamil community, and the Kollavarsham calendar is used in Kerala.

The two main systems used in India are both lunar–solar (moon–sun) based. The Vikrama calendar started from the Vikrama Samvat era, founded by Vikramaditya, signifying his coronation in 56 BCE. Its zero year is taken as 56 BCE, according to the Western Gregorian calendar. The Saka (or Shalivahana) calendar started from the Saka Samvat era, founded by Gautamiputra Satakarni (or Shalivahana) in 78 CE to celebrate his victory against the Sakas. The main difference in the two systems is the observance of the New Year. The Vikrama calendar starts its year with the month of Baisakh (April) while the Saka calendar begins the New Year on the first day of Chaitra (March).

Both calendars count one year of twelve lunar months, with twelve full cycles of the phases of the moon. The difference between the lunar year of 354 days and solar year of 365 days was resolved in the Indian calendar by adding an extra month every thirty months.

This system of integrating the lunar and solar cycles makes the Indian calendar unique and more accurate than others in predicting agricultural seasons, so critical for the economy of India. Each month is divided into two paksha or pakhwaaraa—a bright half when the new moon grows to full moon (Shukla Paksha) and a dark half when it wanes back to no moon (Krishna Paksha). These moon phases and seasons determine the best period for sowing, harvesting, fishing, and festivities.

the former cannot be established without the knowledge of astronomy and mathematics. In this context, it is worth noting that many calendrical systems were used by Indians. The Nobel Prize-winning Indian economist and philosopher Amartya Sen, in 'India Through Its Calendars', an essay on Indian calendars, noted by way of *Whitaker's Almanack* seven principal 'Indian eras'. According to these the year 2000 in the Gregorian calendar translates as:

- year 6001 in the Kaliyuga calendar;
- year 2544 in the Buddha Nirvana calendar;
- year 2057 in the Vikram Samvat calendar;
- year 1922 in the Saka calendar;
- year 1921 (shown in terms of five-year cycles) of the Vedanga Jyotisa calendar;
- year 1407 in the Bengali San calendar; and
- year 1176 in the Kollam calendar.

There were other calendars as well, like the Jaina, Islamic, and Parsi calendars, and many of the above are still in use. The presence and practice of these various calendrical systems clearly demonstrate the level of sophistication that was present among Indian scientists. The latter had arrived at the calculation of 365 days to the year and also made adjustments by adding a leap month. Varahamihira in the sixth century made the computation that the year consisted of 365.25875 days and this was only very marginally wrong. These computations travelled and were appropriated into the body of Western knowledge.

The coming of Islam strengthened India's links with West and Central Asia. India became part of the Persianate world. A good illustration of India's integration into the Persianate world is the career of the Iranian scholar and polymath Alberuni born in Central Asia in 973 CE. His first visit to India was with the plundering army of Mahmud of Ghazni. He chose to be engaged with India and all things Indian. He wrote in the early eleventh century a text in Arabic called *Tarikh al-hind* (The History of India). This work was built on Alberuni's formidable intellectual attainments. He had learnt and mastered Sanskrit and read Indian texts on mathematics, sciences, literature, religion, and philosophy. He had conversed with many experts of the time and had closely observed social customs and conventions. His book is thus a unique blend of Indian and Arabic scholarship. But he was astute and objective enough to note the differences between the people of India and the inhabitants of his own world. He wrote: 'In all manners and usages, [the Indians] differ from us to such a degree as to frighten their children with us,

Tomb of Mirza Ghalib, Nizam-ud-din, New Delhi

The language called Urdu is closely related to Hindi (and Sanskrit), and uses a similar grammatical system. Many of the words used in Urdu are drawn from Persian and Arabic vocabulary. Urdu is a hybrid language and is said to have originated as a language of the camp that acted as a bridge between the speakers of Hindi, Arabic, and Persian. The script adopted for this language is drawn from the Perso-Arabic script while Hindi is written in the Devnagari script.

Urdu is a poet's language and the first poet to use Urdu (then called Hindavi) was Amir Khusrau (1253–1325) to compose poetry, folk songs, and couplets. Another poet who wrote famous ghazals and is equally revered today is Mirza Ghalib (1797–1869). In the Nizam-ud-din area in Delhi, the tombs of both these well-known poets lie in close proximity.

our dress, and our ways and customs, and as to declare us to be the devil's breed, and our doings as the very opposite of all that is good and proper. By the by, we must confess, in order to be just, that a similar depreciation of foreigners not only prevails among us and [the Indians] but is common to all nations towards each other.'

Alberuni was not the only scholar from the Arabic world to be interested in India though he was by far the most remarkable.

Pepper vine

Pepper is indigenous to southern India and grows especially well on the Malabar coast. It can be said that pepper is the most traded spice in the history of the world. The pepper vine yields peppercorns that are green and hang in clusters—these turn black when dried. Pepper was in great demand in ancient times and was annually exported by sea and land to distant parts—the Roman empire, Egypt, and Mesopotamia. Pepper was a luxury item then and came to be referred to as black gold, as it brought great wealth to merchants and only the rich could afford to savour this spice. Its value lay in its use as a spice and seasoning, often used to camouflage the smell and taste of rotting game meat in an era when there was no means of refrigeration.

Brahmagupta's Sanskrit treatise on astronomy had been translated into Arabic, as had several works on science, philosophy, and medicine. It is important to note that unwittingly perhaps Alberuni was following in the footsteps of Chinese travellers, Faxian and Xuanzang who had visited India in the fifth and seventh centuries CE respectively to study Buddhism. They had spent many years in India and left behind detailed accounts of what they had observed and experienced. In the seventeenth century, just as the European trading companies were beginning their operations in India, an Italian Jesuit, Roberto de Nobili (not in any way connected with the trading companies), visited South India and mastered Tamil and Sanskrit. His linguistic abilities enabled him to produce texts in Latin and Tamil on Indian intellectual debates and discussions. The French Jesuit Jean François Pons wrote a grammar of Sanskrit in Latin and also sent back a collection of original manuscripts to Europe.

Indigo, Tamil Nadu

Traces of indigo dye on cloth and in paintings suggest that it was a luxury item known to the subcontinent from the early centuries of the Christian era. The *Indigofera tinctoria* plant is found naturally and cultivated in India. The process to obtain the blue dye is tedious and labour intensive and requires the leaves to be soaked in water, and fermented; then the solution has to be left to oxidize and dry. The powder is then boiled, filtered, and pressed into cakes. The powder is used in different proportions to produce an array of blues—from royal midnight blue to pale shades of blue smoke. Indigo is also called 'magic blue' as the fabric changes colour from yellow, green to blue as the air oxidizes the dye. The colour bleeds, as this dye does not bind with cloth, making it difficult to stabilize and fix to the cloth. However indigo dyed, printed, and painted fabrics are magical as the rich colour changes with washing and ageing.

The expansion of the economy in the sixteenth and seventeenth centuries, both in terms of agricultural productivity and manufacturing, made India a very prosperous country which is what attracted the European trading companies in the first place. Indian cotton cloth, especially of the fine variety, silk, spices, and other commercial crops like indigo and natural resources like saltpetre made India a very lucrative destination for European buyers. The growth of the economy had also produced a strong economic infrastructure—banking, insurance, transport—which facilitated trade both inland and overseas. The strength and spread of this infrastructure is best exemplified by the activities of the house of Jagat Seth (translated as bankers to the world) which had its headquarters in Murshidabad in Bengal but whose letters of credit (or hundis as they were called) had currency all over India and as far as Tashkent.

India's entry into the Persianate world also provided new vistas for forms of art and architecture.

· CHAPTER 16 ·

THE NORTHEAST UP TO THE COMING OF BRITISH RULE

c. 1200 CE–c. 1850

The term 'north-east' in its simple lexicographical sense indicates a direction—and raises the question north-east of what? The answer to the question in the case of Indian history and culture is simple: north-east of the Gangetic plain and peninsular India. But the term cannot be restricted, in the case of India, to merely its dictionary meaning. Northeast India—or in shorthand just the Northeast—has come to denote histories and cultures that are distinct from those of the Indian heartland.

As things stand today, the Northeast consists of seven separate states—Arunachal Pradesh, Assam, Manipur, Meghalaya, Mizoram, Nagaland, and Tripura. Each of these states has its distinctive culture and history. But in the past, before the Indian republic fashioned these seven states, this vast geographical territory was referred to as Assam which harked back to the land of Kamrup, which stretched from the eastern points of the Brahmaputra valley to the river Karatoya. In the early thirteenth century, Kamrup, already in ruins, saw the arrival of the Turko-Afghans from Bengal, and the Ahom settlers from Upper Burma. From this period to the coming of the British in the late eighteenth and early nineteenth centuries, this area did not see any centralized ruling structure. Political authority was fragmented—tribal state formations, and non-tribal and armed landed sections of the population known as Bhuyan or Bhaumik exercised power. The dominance of the Bhuyan was concentrated in the western and central parts of the region.

One of the more important tribal formations was that of the Ahoms. They used the plough and made their own village settlements and established their authority over other tribal villages. The Ahoms

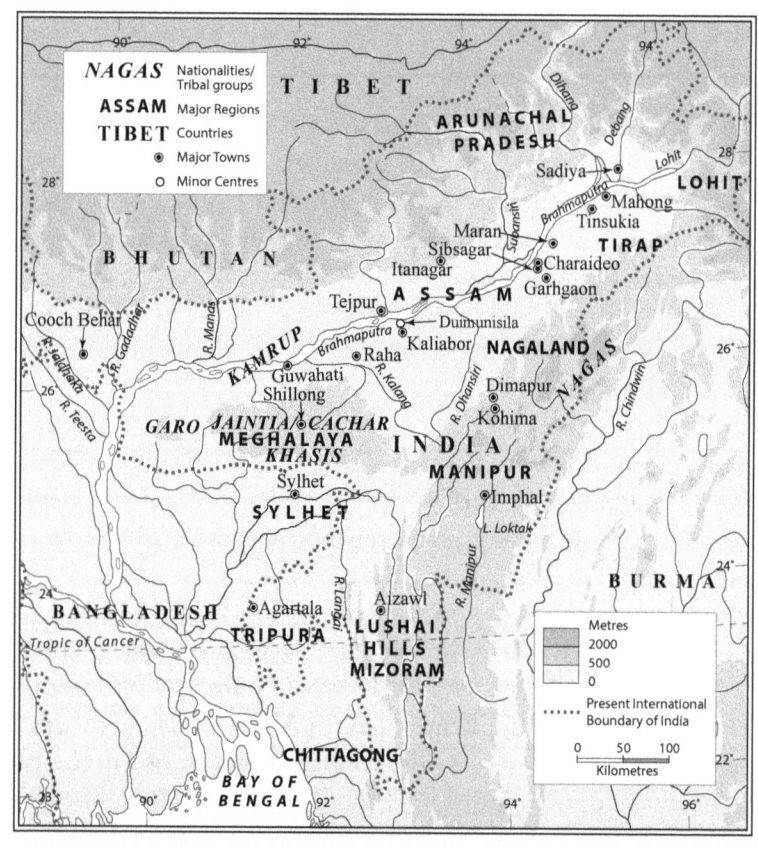

The Northeast region of India

Not to scale. This map has been prepared in adherence to the 'Guidelines for acquiring and producing Geospatial Data and Geospatial Data Services including Maps' published vide DST F.No.SM/25/02/2020 (Part-I) dated 15th February, 2021

were ruled by a king chosen from the royal clan; the king allocated domains to the nobility but the king could also be removed by the council of great nobles. The system was thus based on loyalty and service. The two other major tribal formations—the Chutiyas and the Kacharis—were either subjugated or pushed back to the southwest by the Ahoms who also pushed westward at the cost of the Bhuyans. These were processes that occurred in the sixteenth century. Another tribal state formation was that of the Koch which during the sixteenth century established its power in the western part of the region from the Karatoya to the Barnadi. In 1562, the Koch were powerful enough to march to the Ahom capital of Garhgaon and sack it. But the power of the Koch dissipated when the kingdom split into the Koch-Bihar and the Koch-Hajo. The latter overlapped with the western part of what is today known as Assam. In the Khasi Hills there emerged in the fifteenth century the state of Jaintia.

Under the dispensation of the Koch and the Ahoms, the Bhuyans were absorbed into the official class and formed an elite. They could attain this status because of their knowledge of the scriptures, measurements, and arithmetic, and their ability to use arms. The Bhuyans were mostly high-caste migrants from North India who wielded considerable local political authority. Some of them were Muslims. Their power base was control over land and over armed tenants whom they could mobilize. Sometimes they formed partnerships against a common enemy. The Bhuyans were very often pioneers in land reclamation and in dyke-building activities for water control. The Koch-Hajo areas were subjugated by the Mughals but this was not permanent. The Ahoms in 1682 annexed the Koch-Hajo areas. This meant that Ahom control extended right up to the Manas River. The conflict between the Ahoms and the Mughals opened up the region to external influences. In economic terms, since the Ahoms knew the use of the plough, there was a shift among the tribal populations they subjugated to permanent cultivation.

The use of the plough and the prevailing ecology facilitated wet rice cultivation. This is not to say that hunting and fishing and other tribal occupations disappeared in a geography where forests and swamps were prominent. Increasingly, however, the rice economy gained in importance.

Under the Ahoms, the militia (regular members of the civil population trained to serve as a military force) played a crucial role in the extension of rice cultivation by reclaiming land, settling the population, and building embankments as safeguards against floods. The land was also carefully levelled. An observer in the second half of the seventeenth century wrote, referring to the lands the Ahoms controlled: 'In this country they make the surface of the field and gardens so level that the eyes cannot find the least elevation in it up to the extreme horizons.'

During the course of the sixteenth century, the Vaishnava movement became very popular in the region and by 1700 there were around 1,000 monasteries (sutra). The latter also enhanced the process of land reclamation and extension of cultivation. The monks sought for themselves exemption from obligatory military service to the state. There was a period when the Ahom state attempted to suppress the monasteries and force the monks to join labour camps to build roads and embankments. But this was a passing phase. By the late seventeenth and eighteenth centuries, the Ahom state was making revenue-free grants of wastelands to the monasteries. Originally, the militia system was not very coercive but from the reign of Pratap Singha (1603–41), coercion became an integral part of the militia. The entire male population, with the exception of serfs, priests, and those of noble birth, within the age group of fifteen to sixty, was expected to be part of the militia. The system was organized in such a fashion that at any given point of time one-fourth to one-third of the militia was available for work. In the Koch and Kachari kingdoms and also in the neighbouring kingdoms of Jaintia and Manipur a somewhat similar system operated.

The Mughals imposed their rule on the Koch territories towards the close of the sixteenth century. This brought about significant changes in those areas and also in the adjacent Ahom kingdom. The most important of these changes was the greater role of money since the Mughals demanded revenue in cash. The cash revenue demand provided a boost to trade. Equally significant was the fact that following the Mughal model, the Ahoms initiated a detailed land survey operation between 1681 and 1751. Such a survey enabled the identification of taxable wet rice lands and the exploration of the possibilities of expanding the tax base. By the end of the sixteenth century but ever so slowly, there were signs of a land market emerging especially in the western parts of the region.

Villages were by no means self-sufficient. Salt came from the surrounding hills and from coastal Bengal. Varying ecological conditions meant that certain villages specialized in certain types of crops like cotton, sugar cane, lac, silk, and mustard seeds. Elephant tusks, buffalo horns, incense, and iron were procured from the foothills and the hills from where they were transported. There is evidence of long-distance trade—riverine and sea—with boats carrying pepper, incense, nutmeg, ginger, etc. This trade was a popular theme in sixteenth-century Assamese literature. Needless to add, these trading networks and flows increased from the late sixteenth century.

During the Mughal period, Mughal–Ahom trade increased but the trade surplus was generally in favour of Mughal India. This would suggest that the bullion that was coming into India from Europe from the seventeenth century did not have much of an impact on the economy of the Ahom kingdom. It is safe to arrive at the conclusion that this region was not a trade-rich economy.

The limited nature of trade meant that division of labour was also limited. Weaving, oil-crushing, rice-pounding, basketmaking, and a number of other crafts were largely carried out within the households. No specific castes were attached to these occupations. Even at the risk of stating the obvious, it needs to be said that this was a timber-rich region and therefore the art of carpentry was highly developed. There existed at Garhgaon a timber palace that had been built in one year by 12,000 workmen; it had very intricate and sophisticated woodwork. It needs to be mentioned that the Mughals were impressed by the war boats built in this region because they were easy to manoeuvre. Technology in general was simple except in metalworking even at the village blacksmith level.

Little or no population data is available till 1872. It is assumed that from the sixteenth to the eighteenth centuries there was a rise in population because of the expansion of rice cultivation. This assumption is supported by the attempts made by the state and the Vaishnava monasteries at setting up new villages in remote parts. This period also witnessed migration into the region and the adoption of various labour-intensive cultivation methods. In an area of land abundance, low urbanization, and a functioning natural economy, the population could be classified into three broad groups. One, a privileged aristocracy that had no obligation to offer any kind of manual service; two, the peasantry, including fishermen and artisans—by far the largest section of the population—who were required to render manual service or pay tax in cash or kind; and three, the servile class of slaves, serfs, and bondsmen—these people did not serve the state but their masters. The privileged aristocracy included a large spiritual group who received revenue-free grants from the state.

Life was simple and there was an ecological balance between human beings and nature. The population suffered from frequent floods; the area was earthquake-prone but earthquakes were not as frequent as floods. What is noticeable is the absence of devastating famines.

The British conquest and rule of Bengal between 1757 and 1765 brought the East India Company and its officials into direct contact with the kingdoms of Manipur, Jaintia, Cachar, and Assam as well as with those tribes who lived in the neighbouring hills. The nature of the economies of these areas did not immediately attract the attention of the British administrators. But this changed dramatically with the Burmese invasion (1817–24) of Manipur, Assam, and the Cachar plains. The British had to intervene to defend these territories. But in a Bengali proclamation the British announced: 'We have not come here to quench our thirst for the conquest of your kingdom but to destroy our enemies, interested as we are to protect ourselves.' The Burmese were defeated and were forced to surrender their claims over the territories they had invaded by the Treaty of Yandabo (1826). Between 1826 and the early 1840s, the kingdoms of Jaintia, Cachar, Assam, along with their dependencies and the independent tribal states in the Khasi hills, were all annexed by the British. In the second half of the nineteenth century, the North Cachar Hills, the land inhabited by the Nagas and of the Lushais (Mizos), were all annexed and brought under British control. There are two points to be noted here. This long drawn-out process of annexation was not without resistance from the tribal population and, equally importantly, the boundaries of British power in Northeast India were always in flux, never cast in stone.

As noted earlier, there had been a rise in population between the sixteenth and eighteenth centuries. This rise was halted and reversed in the five decades following 1770. There was a devastating civil war between 1770 and 1809 during which half the population was wiped out. This process of depopulation was aggravated by the Burmese invasion. The census of 1826 that followed the British annexation of Ahom territories yielded a population count of 0.7 to 0.8 million. And then, in the census of 1872, the population of the same area was seen to be less than 1.5 million. The destruction and loss of lives caused by the civil war and the Burmese invasion allowed the British conquerors to project themselves as saviours of the people from chaos and oppression and as protectors from invaders from the east. The irony, of course, was that the British themselves were invaders. It did not take long for the people to realize that the new masters were more interested in extortion and exploitation than in the welfare of those over whom they ruled.

Battle of Kohima War Cemetery, Kohima, Nagaland

Kohima, the capital of Nagaland, was built by the British. The state of Nagaland shares a long border on the eastern side with Myanmar. The War Cemetery at Kohima commemorates a significant location and event of Indian history. It was here in April 1944 during World War II that British and Indian forces halted the advance of Japanese troops from entering India from Burma. The plaque on the memorial carries the enduring epitaph seen above.

Tea garden, Kaziranga, Assam

Tea is the most popular and widely consumed beverage in the world. This cash crop has had a profound impact on the ecology of the Northeast, Darjeeling in West Bengal, and parts of southern India. Tea plantations were created by destroying ancient natural forests and the habitat of indigenous species of plants and animals. The destruction of old forest trees led to erosion and the deterioration of the soil. The loss of fertility and ability to replenish nutrients naturally resulted in a complete dependence on synthetic fertilizers and chemicals. This in turn contaminated the waterbodies, affecting humans and animals who depend on them. The price paid for a cup of tea, in ecological terms, is extremely high.

British exploitation in the Northeast, particularly in Assam, acquired a distinctive character through the introduction of large tea plantations. Tea production on a commercial basis began in Assam in the early 1840s. From 935 hectares in 1841 the acreage under tea increased to 8,000 in 1859 and for the same period the output had grown from 13 tonnes to more than 450 tonnes. The pioneer in this enterprise was the Assam Company. By the end of the 1850s, other companies, all British-owned, had joined the race to grow more tea and make more profits. The links between the tea companies and the government were strong. Facing labour shortages, the planter community lobbied the government to increase the land revenue demand so that peasants, unable to meet the higher rates, would opt to work for wages on the tea plantations. Thus was created what a historian has aptly called the 'planter raj' that lorded over and tyrannized the entire people of the region.

· CHAPTER 17 ·

CONSOLIDATION OF BRITISH RULE

1765–1856

As the British conquered and annexed different parts of India, they were faced with the difficult question of administering and governing these territories. In the late eighteenth and early nineteenth centuries, at the heart of the question of governance was the collection of land revenue—how much to collect, how to collect, from whom to collect, and so on. These questions confronted the officials of the EIC first in Bengal where as we have seen from 1765 land revenue came to serve as the Company's investment. The relentless thrust to maximize the collection of land revenue resulted in the famine of 1770 which devastated the rural world of Bengal. As a consequence, cultivation declined and the collection of land revenue plummeted. This alarmed the shareholders of the EIC, many of whom were influential in British politics, and they drew the attention of the House of Commons to what was happening in Bengal. From the early 1770s, the British government began to intervene decisively in the Company's handling of its territories in India. The first milestone in this process was the passing of the Regulating Act in 1773.

By the Regulating Act, the first step was taken to establish the control of the House of Commons over Indian affairs. By the Act, the head of the Bengal government was redesignated as the governor general and it became mandatory for the EIC to submit all despatches from India to parliament. The next step in establishing the control of the British government came in 1786 with the passing of Pitt's India Act. The latter created the Board of Control over and above the Court of Directors of the EIC. The Board of Control became the most important decision-making body on Indian matters. It was further decided that the royal charter which the EIC had been granted in 1600 would come up for periodic renewal beginning from

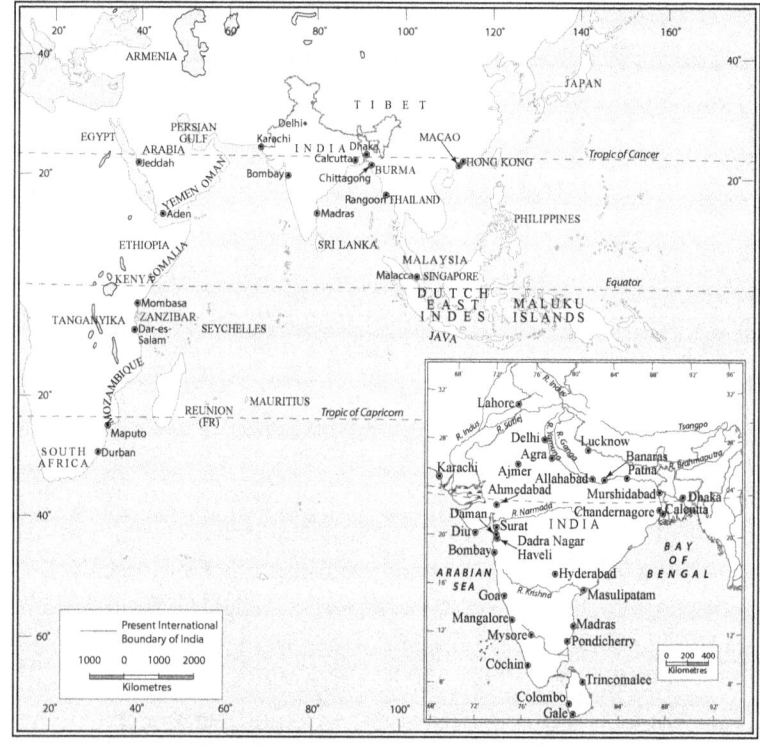

Extent of British rule across the Indian Ocean and Asia

Inset: Extent of British rule in the Indian subcontinent

Not to scale. This map has been prepared in adherence to the 'Guidelines for acquiring and producing Geospatial Data and Geospatial Data Services including Maps' published vide DST F.No.SM/25/02/2020 (Part-I) dated 15th February, 2021

1793. Thus there were the Charter Acts of 1793, 1813, 1833, and 1853 which clipped the wings of the EIC in stages. The shift from regulating to control needs to be underlined as this is the indicator that the distinction between the rule of EIC in India and British rule in India became blurred, and over time, irrelevant.

The Asiatic Society, Mumbai, Maharashtra

Classic Greek architecture, much admired by the British, was used to inspire the plan and elevation of this building in Bombay, as it did in other towns; Government House, Calcutta, Hyderabad, and Mysore. The Town Hall complex built in Calcutta, in 1820, included British government offices, a library, and the Asiatic Society museum with branches in other towns. Interest in understanding India's past, her mineral and natural wealth began at the turn of the eighteenth century for the purpose of commerce and trade. This later led to more serious scholarship, research, and the documentation of India's history, the study of birds, animals, trees, and plants.

The actual consolidation of British rule occurred through the implementation of land revenue policies across India, beginning with Bengal. In the late eighteenth century, the two principal concerns of British policymakers were security of land revenue

Golghar, 1786, Patna, Bihar

One of the strangest buildings erected by the British was constructed in 1786 by John Garstin of the Bengal Engineers. It was designed to store grain and worked like a silo—grain was put in through a hole on the top and retrieved from the base. The granary was shaped like a beehive or an upside-down cone, its walls are 3.5 metres thick and over 28 metres high. The structure has no ornamentation, but a spiral ramp on the outside enabled workers to lift sacks of grain to the top to be poured into the granary. On the side of the building is a carved inscription that states that the granary was ordered by the governor general in 1784 for the 'Perpetual Prevention of Famine in these Provinces'. Unfortunately, the building never served its purpose.

and a reliable collection agency. These two concerns were addressed through the Permanent Settlement of 1793 introduced by Lord Cornwallis. Through this, the land revenue of Bengal was fixed forever and the zamindars of Bengal were made responsible for the collection and payment of land revenue and they were also made owners of their landed estates. The expectation was that the security of property and an unchanging land revenue demand would transform the zamindars into improving landlords similar to those in England in the same period. The land revenue was fixed at 90 per cent of the rentals. This proved to be too high and many of the zamindars were unable to meet the demand by the sunset of 31 March annually—the Sunset Law as it was called. The failure to pay resulted in the government seizing the estate and putting it up for auction. By the 1820s, it was clear that the Permanent Settlement had failed to meet its original expectations.

In the Madras presidency, Thomas Munro introduced a land revenue system that was very different from the Permanent Settlement. This came to be known as the raiyatwari system because Munro decided to do away with intermediaries like zamindars and settle directly with the raiyats—the cultivators of the soil. In practical terms, this was a complicated operation that involved making a detailed survey of each field, calculating the yield and converting it into cash, which in turn involved finding out the price and finally required finding the cultivator of each field and recording his name and making him responsible for paying the land revenue. Such data proved difficult to obtain and often land revenue officials made vague and arbitrary recordings of this information. According to the principles laid down by Munro, raiyats of 'dry' land—unirrigated land or land irrigated by private wells—were to pay one half of the gross produce; 'wet' land—land produced by public waterworks—were to pay three-fifths of the gross produce; and land producing high value crops—designated as 'garden'—had even higher rates imposed on them. In reality, the land revenue demand was pitched so high that the raiyat managed to keep only one-fifth of the crop, sometimes even less.

In the late 1820s—the period in between the land revenue settlements in Bengal and Madras and the land revenue settlements in Western India and North India—British policies and attitudes underwent a radical shift. The policy of non-intervention in the socio-religious and cultural practices of India was set aside and administrators were seized by the project of improvement and an agenda of reform. This zeal emanated from developments in Britain. The defeat of Napoleon and the emergence of England as the 'workshop of the world' after the Industrial Revolution had given to the British a sense of superiority. This produced a new aggressive attitude which the French, who adopted it later, called la mission civilisatrice. India was to be reformed in the image of Britain. The physical distance separating the East and the West was now complemented by a mental distance separating the two and this distance was sought to be annihilated by the discoveries of science, by commercial exchanges, and by transplanting English laws and English education on to India.

Interior of Dr Bhau Daji Lad Museum, Mumbai

The Dr Bhau Daji Lad Museum, originally named the Victoria and Albert Museum, opened in 1872 and was the first museum in the city of Bombay. In 1851, the Great Exhibition had been held in London, and thousands of Londoners thronged to see the extraordinary crafts created by skilled Indian artisans. Duplicates from this exhibition were exhibited in this museum to serve as a 'showroom', a sampling of the industrial arts and crafts of India, to enhance the export trade in these valuable products. The building and galleries were restored and opened to the public in 2008 and it is being run professionally as a museum with a variety of activities for the community and especially for children.

The shift in policy had strong economic reasons. The Industrial

Revolution in Britain brought about a fundamental change in the economic relationship of India with Britain. From a provider of manufactured goods that supplied the trade of the East India Company, India came to be looked upon as a supplier of raw materials and as a vast market to be conquered and exploited for the benefit of British industries and the British economy. To ensure this new economic relationship, political power in India had to be used to create the necessary conditions of law and order and policies had to be directed towards creating a class of people in India who would buy British goods and support the new and emerging empire.

The era of reform was inaugurated in 1828 with the arrival of Lord William Bentinck in Calcutta as the new governor general of India. But even earlier there had been disapproving voices aimed at the language policies followed by the Company. In 1792, Charles Grant, later to become a member of the Court of Directors, had proposed in a tract that English rather than the vernaculars should become the medium of instruction in India and that language alone would provide a gateway to reason for the Indians and civilize them. The Charter Act of 1813 stipulated that a sum of ₹100,000 each year should be set aside for 'the revival and improvement of literature and the encouragement of the learned natives of India, and for the introduction and promotion of a knowledge of the sciences among the inhabitants of the British territories of India.' Already with the reforming zeal of Bentinck nearly two decades away, the emphasis on the sciences is clear although nothing came of this stipulation in the Act. The point about introducing the sciences was even more forcefully made by none other than James Mill who in 1819 had been appointed assistant examiner for the Court of Directors of the East India Company. In 1824, in a despatch, Mill wrote that the 'great end should not have been to teach Hindoo learning, but useful learning.'

British land revenue officials set about in West and North India not only to do away with all intermediaries, by whatever name they were known in their localities, and settle with the raiyats but also to calculate the net produce which would form the basis of the land

St. Stephen's Church and graveyard, 1831, Ooty, Tamil Nadu

In 1799, the British defeated Tipu Sultan and they took over his lands and property. This English church in Ooty (present-day Udhagamandalam) is said to have been built with valuable timber ransacked from Tipu's palace. This church tells many stories: of how the British took over the properties of defeated Indian rulers, the idea of the 'hill station resort' where the British elite could spend the hot summer months in the cooler climes of Shimla, Mussoorie, Dalhousie, Darjeeling, Ooty, and others. Another aspect is the type of buildings to be found in these British hill stations: imposing administrative structures, railway stations, churches and graveyards, summer cottages, and country clubs, all infused with nostalgia for their home country and quite alien to the Indian landscape. The cottages had gardens to which were introduced English vegetables, fruits like strawberries, and trees and flowers that were brought by ship from Britain. In an attempt to recreate their home on Indian soil and introduce their language and culture, colonial roots were planted deep into India. Its lasting impact can be seen in every aspect of contemporary Indian life.

tax. Land revenue settlements were made for thirty years to provide security for cultivators. In many parts of North India, British officials were also surprised to discover that contrary to their assumptions, land was not tilled or owned by individual peasants but by a brotherhood of peasants (bhaichara). Given these different patterns of landholding and cultivation in North India, land revenue officials separated villages as mahals (areas) and settled the land revenue according to mahals. Thus the land revenue settlements in North India were described as mahalwari settlements.

That the land revenue demand had been pitched too high was acknowledged by the government when in 1855 through the Saharanpur Regulations it was laid down that the land revenue demand would not exceed 55 per cent of the gross produce. It is worth underlining that even under these regulations, the state claimed more than half of what the peasant produced. This proved to be a terrible burden on the peasantry and often drove them to debt. There was another factor that aggravated peasant indebtedness. The land revenue was collected in quarterly qists (instalments); these qists were determined according to the state's financial calendar running from 1 April to 31 March and took no account of the harvest calendar (the cycle of tilling, planting, and harvesting). This absence of synchronization between the financial calendar and the fasli (harvest) calendar meant that the revenue demands were made when the peasants most needed cash or were short of cash. Under the circumstances, peasants were forced to borrow to meet the land revenue demand. Through this process, indebtedness and the moneylender became common in the rural world.

The changes in the British economy outlined above—the Industrial Revolution—meant that by the 1820s, Britain had become the most important manufacturing country in the world. Britain was thus no longer buying manufactured products (like cotton textiles) from India but was buying raw materials (like raw cotton) to supply the cotton mills of Manchester. Britain also needed expanding markets to sell the ever-increasing products of the cotton mills. Here, Britain's Indian possessions served as invaluable captive markets. Manchester cotton cloth flooded the Indian market adversely affecting India's handicraft cotton production. Many artisans could not cope with this competition, lost their markets, and had either to give up their occupations or drastically shrink their production. The livelihoods of artisans were threatened and many of them had no other alternative but to fall back on agriculture. This dramatically altered the land–man ratio and increased the pressure on land. This pressure was not unrelated to the series of famines that threatened different parts of rural India at various points of time in the second half of the nineteenth century.

The British for their own administrative conveniences established in India administrative and judicial systems; they also set up educational institutions—including three universities in Calcutta, Madras, and Bombay—to introduce English and Western learning so that a Westernized elite would be produced in India; they also pioneered social reforms. But all these—the so-called White Man's Burden—existed to support what was at the heart of the British empire in India—wealth making for the white man, the creation of markets, and the swift and efficient extraction of raw materials from India. British rule in India was consolidated to facilitate the rapid growth of the British economy and the British empire.

· CHAPTER 18 ·

INDIAN RESPONSE AND RESISTANCE

c. 1800–1857

An earlier chapter has noted the shift that occurred in British policy towards India—the move from non-interference to an active involvement in the project to reform Indian society so that the latter would be on the track of modernity. The British chose two vehicles to drive their reform project—education and the enactment of laws to change social practices. Bengal, because it had been the first to come under British control, felt the initial impact of this project and was the pioneer in responding to the new policies.

The announcement in the Charter Act of 1813 that a sum of money was being set aside to promote education in India made some important Indians in Calcutta get together to establish an educational institution in the city which would impart Western education to the sons of the rich and privileged in Calcutta. The idea was first put forward by a Scotsman, David Hare, who had settled in Calcutta as a watchmaker and had also set up a school. He did this in a meeting of like-minded people in the house of Rammohun Roy; the individuals present at the meeting thought this was a good idea. Hare secured the assistance and cooperation of the government and out of this was born in January 1817 the Hindu College. The primary aim of Hindu College was 'the tuition of the sons of respectable Hindoos in the English and Indian language, and in the literature and science of Europe and Asia'. This was the first educational institution of this kind; it was born out of the initiative and funding of private individuals and the government. In 1855, it became the Presidency College which was run and financed by the government. Similar institutions were also set up in Bombay and Madras. While noting the pioneering role of Hindu College, its restrictive character should

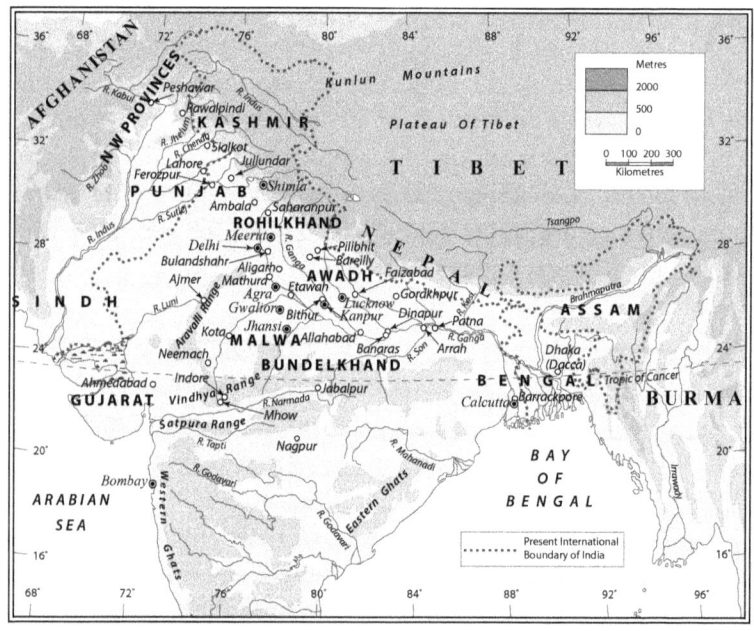

Centres of revolt

Not to scale. This map has been prepared in adherence to the 'Guidelines for acquiring and producing Geospatial Data and Geospatial Data Services including Maps' published vide DST F.No.SM/25/02/2020 (Part-I) dated 15th February, 2021

also be highlighted. It was meant solely for upper-caste Hindus. Families who sent their sons to study there wanted an education that would enable their sons to get lower-level government jobs. They most certainly did not want the students of Hindu College to adopt Western attitudes and styles of living.

Portrait of Rammohun Roy, 1774–1833, painted by Rembrandt Peale in 1833

The name of Rammohun Roy has already appeared in passing. A little more needs to be said about him since he was the moving force behind the first legislation to transform social and religious practices in India. He was born in rural Bengal to a prosperous Brahmin family. He learnt Sanskrit, Arabic, Persian, and (after 1805) English; and, of course, he was fluent in his mother tongue, Bengali. Very little is known of his early life.

Around 1815, Rammohun moved to Calcutta. He was already quite wealthy, having acquired wealth through trade and moneylending. He was also an owner of landed property. In Calcutta, Rammohun cultivated a group of like-minded people and began to campaign, through various pieces of writing, against orthodox Hindu religious and social practices—idol worship, priestcraft, rituals, and the position of women. This earned him some notoriety among the orthodox in Calcutta. The most notable outcome of his campaign was the law in 1829 to abolish the practice of sati (the immolation of the widow on the funeral pyre of her dead husband). Rammohun described sati as a form of murder and accused the proponents of sati to be utterly lacking in humanity and compassion. He persuaded the government led by the governor general, Lord

William Bentinck, that this practice had no sanction in the Hindu scriptures. Bentinck was convinced that Indian society needed to be reformed and 'civilized' and so he seized upon the proposal of Rammohun and passed the law to abolish sati—a milestone legislation in India's journey to modernity. Rammohun died in Britain in 1833 (he is buried in Bristol) where he had travelled at the behest of the Mughal emperor, Akbar II, to present the latter's case to the British monarch and the public.

The policy to reform Indian society through legislation was significantly advanced by the passing in 1855 of the Hindu Widow Remarriage Act which removed restrictions on widows to remarry. This law was made possible by the efforts of Ishwarchandra Vidyasagar (1820–91), a Brahmin pundit and educator who was a pioneer in the sphere of female education in Bengal. Moved by the plight of widows in Bengal, Vidyasagar began a campaign to free widows from the shackles imposed on them. He made a detailed study of the scriptures and on the basis of this he convinced the government of the day that the scriptures did not forbid widow remarriage. His work prepared the ground for this legislation. In spite of the Act, widow remarriage did not catch on but Vidyasagar had created a legacy for the future.

Individuals like Rammohun and Vidyasagar worked closely with British administrators to change some aspects of Hindu society. But this was not the only response to the arrival and consolidation of British rule. From its very inception, British rule, as it spread to different parts of India, encountered resistance not only from deposed rulers and princes but also from the common people. The late eighteenth and early nineteenth centuries were marked by peasant insurgencies across India. These resistances acquired a mass and dramatic dimension in the Revolt of 1857.

On the afternoon of 10 May 1857, the sepoys in Meerut rose in open mutiny. It is difficult, of course, to pinpoint when and how the mutiny began. From all existing accounts it seems that in the late afternoon, around 5 o'clock, there was an outcry in the Sudder

Bazaar that European troops were coming to deprive the native regiments of their arms and ammunition. The sepoys who were in the bazaar rushed back to their lines. They rushed to the Bell of Arms, broke it open, and opened fire. They shot and killed a British officer. The sepoys from the cavalry rushed from the parade ground to the jail and broke it open. As a group of sepoys from the cavalry passed through the city, they called on the people to join them in a war of religion. The mutiny did not remain one for very long. It became an outbreak as the defiance and the violence moved from the barracks to the bazaar. As the news of the mutiny spread, crowds of the ordinary people of Meerut, especially those belonging to the lower castes, 'the bazaar mobs', according to British observers, joined the outbreak and entered the bungalow area, where the white population lived. Plunder, arson, and murder followed. The targets were clearly defined: Europeans, all that the Europeans owned, and the symbols of European power. Thus, the bungalows were the first to be burnt and the Europeans found in them or those trying to escape were killed. Gender and age were no bar to the killings. During the night, the rebels were strengthened by bands of villagers coming in from the surrounding villages. The mutiny had become a general uprising as the destruction was no longer in the hands of a disgruntled soldiery. Sepoys and the common people had merged in a rebellion. It is easy to assume that the destruction and the violence were mindless and the plunder was the product of greed. Such an assessment overlooks one simple but significant fact: sometime during the evening, as the mayhem raged in Meerut, the rebels had cut the telegraph line to Delhi and Agra. The telegraph was, of course, the symbol of British rule and an alien way of life. It was also the quickest way to communicate news and to ask for reinforcements. By cutting the telegraph line, the rebels ensured that their next object of attack could not be revealed.

'Repulse of a sortie on the Delhi Ridge', 1857, from 'The Campaign in India 1857-58', a series of twenty-six lithographs by William Simpson, E. Walker, and others

Soldiers armed with muskets fixed with bayonets and swords charge at sepoys.

As night fell on Meerut, a group of sepoys sped southward to Delhi. The sepoys from Meerut arrived at Lal Qila (Red Fort), the seat of the Mughal emperor, Bahadur Shah II, early in the morning of 11 May. The palace was already awake as it was the month of Ramadan. Bahadur Shah was an emperor only in name. He had been stripped of his powers and lived off a pension provided by the British. He took refuge in music and poetry. Yet he enjoyed the charisma associated with the name of the Mughal badshah. The mutineers from Meerut entered the Mughal capital through the eastern end, crossing the Yamuna by the Bridge of Boats. The sepoys rode up beneath the windows of the king's apartments and appealed to him, 'Dohai badshah (Help O King), we pray for assistance in our fight for the faith.' Another group of sepoys from Meerut entered the city and started plundering the European quarters in Daryaganj.

The sepoys soon started attacking and killing any European that they saw. The sepoys on guard at the palace showed their defiance by refusing to close the palace gates and by firing their guns in the courtyard of the Diwan-i-Khas. This brought the king out to meet them. Surrounded by militant sepoys, Bahadur Shah agreed to be the leader of the uprising which had begun in Meerut. Thus the rebellion acquired the sanction and stamp of authority which was distinct from the British. It had acquired legitimacy.

'Capture of the King of Delhi by Captain William Hodson', illustration from *The History of the Indian Mutiny* by Charles Ball

The Mughal emperor, Bahadur Shah II, and his two sons were captured on 20 September 1857 by William Raikes Hodson, a leader of the British Light Cavalry (1821–58).

Outside the Red Fort, in the city, the insurgency had not waited for any official sanction. The mutineers joined by the common people of Delhi proceeded to plunder, to destroy, and to kill. The violence was directed at all things British and at Britons. The city and its populace went over to the rebellion. The Britons who survived took refuge on the Ridge, 3 kilometres north of the city.

The fall of Delhi had a remarkable impact on the cantonments all over North India. Between 10 and 14 May, there were no outbreaks of violence. But once the news of the fall of Delhi had travelled down the Gangetic valley, the garrisons of North India raised the flag of revolt. The fall of Delhi was interpreted as the breakdown of British authority. As early as end-May 1857, Henry Lawrence in Lucknow had perceived the importance of Delhi in the way events were unfolding. He wrote to the secretary of the governor general: 'Tranquillity cannot be much longer maintained unless Delhi is speedily captured.' By the beginning of June 1857, every single garrison in North India had risen in mutiny, killed the white population, destroyed and plundered property owned by the Europeans, and they had been joined by villagers of the surrounding areas. In that summer, a British officer declared, British rule had fallen like a 'house of cards'.

The rebels also won military victories against the British. The most significant of these was at the Battle of Chinhat (just outside Lucknow) at the end of June. Such victories and the physical annihilation of so many Britons engendered the perception that the rule of the white man was over. There was also the fear that the British would return and try to re-establish their authority. In the various locations of the revolt, the rebels, just as they had done in Delhi, rallied around the pre-British rulers and leaders of that area. Under these leaders, the rebels began to set up administrative structures and processes to continue the rebellion and to prepare to fight the British when they returned. Thus, the rebellion was not a mindless campaign of destruction.

A glimpse of what the rebels aimed to achieve and why they had taken to arms and violence can be had from the few ishtahars (proclamations) that the rebel leadership issued. Some common themes emerge from a study of the proclamations. The rebels were convinced that the British were deliberately following policies to despoil the caste and religion of all Indians. It was a common belief among the sepoys that the cartridges of the new Enfield rifle were

Mutiny Memorial, 1863, New Delhi

The Ridge of the Aravalli Range provided a hilly elevation to the north of Delhi and was witness to the rebellion. On 11 May 1857, the shocked and wounded British survivors gathered near Flagstaff Tower hoping for safety, but were massacred. A ripple effect spread across North India as the insurgency gathered momentum, with the fall of Delhi.

This memorial was erected in 1863 in the memory of those who lost their lives here. The tower was erected on a high platform that narrows gradually after each floor till it reaches the spire at the top. An internal winding staircase provides access to views of the city from the top floor. The Gothic design of this memorial tower makes it look like a dislodged church steeple.

greased with the fat of cows and pigs; that the flour that was given to them as rations was mixed with the bone dust of cows and pigs. They wrote in the ishtahars about how the British were interfering with Indian customs and social practices, how the British were reforming a familiar way of life, how they were treating Indians and all things Indian with contempt, how they were deposing kings, princes, taluqdars, and so on. Every aspect of British policy came in for attack. It was thus the duty of all Indians, the ishtahars said, irrespective of their caste and religion to fight the British. Hindus and Muslims should join the war against the British and defeat them. All of them appealed to Hindus and Muslims and emphasized the necessity of unitedly fighting the British. What was invariably invoked was the pre-British Hindu–Muslim coexistence—'as brethren to each other'—within the Mughal imperial framework.

St. James' Church, Delhi

The earliest church to be built in Delhi was consecrated in 1835, and sponsored by Colonel James Skinner, a Scottish military officer who served under the Sindhias; his unit was called Skinner's Light Horse. The church was probably designed by engineers, and has a dominant dome, raised high on a drum base. The dome is supported by the cross-shaped building below. The arms of the cross have entrances with four Ionic pillars supporting a sloping roof, ending with a triangular pediment, in the classic Greek style. The interior of the church is simple with pillars and medallions. The church was witness to intense battles during the uprising in Delhi. It has been restored and renovated a few decades ago and is still in use.

The idea of a united fight against the British was enacted on the ground: witness the British failure to raise the Hindu population of Bareilly against the Muslims in 1857. One British officer recorded: '[the Chief Commissioner] had authorized the sum of Rs.50,000/- to be expended in an attempt to raise the Hindoo population of Bareilly against the Mahommedan rebels...the attempt was quite unsuccessful and has been abandoned.' The most telling and poignant instance of this unity was the hailing of Birjis Qadr (the twelve-year-old-son of Wajid Ali Shah, the deposed king of Awadh, who had been made the king of Awadh after the revolt) by the rebel sepoys as our Kanhaiya (Krishna). In many ways, 1857 was the peak of Hindu–Muslim unity in North India. The rebel leadership promised, through the ishtahars, that it would restore life to what it had been before the disruption caused by British rule.

The British counter-attack was not slow in coming. Forces from Punjab moved in to take over Delhi. Two other armies moved from Calcutta and Poona to suppress the rebellion in North and Central India. These armies were bestowed with unprecedented powers: they could punish—and execution was the only punishment—without even the semblance of a trial. Any adult Indian male in the Gangetic plain was seen as a rebel and strung up from the nearest tree. Villages and crops were burnt. Vengeance knew no limits. Through such measures, the British reconquered North India and re-established their authority. But this authority was given a different character.

In August 1858, the East India Company was disbanded and Queen Victoria became the ruler of India. In other words, the rule of the Company was set aside and the British government took over the reins of administering India. India thus formally became a part of the British empire. The manner of restoring authority—through military might—and status of the Crown gave to the British a greater sense of their own superiority. They had won against all odds and this proved their superiority. The Indians were an inferior and barbaric lot because they had failed to recognize and accept the gifts of civilization that had been offered to them. Racial superiority and intolerance became even more embedded among the British in India. The policymakers also realized that Hindu–Muslim unity, if allowed to continue, would remain a threat to British rule. To divide and rule became a watchword of British policy. The post-1857 years also saw the growth of the idea that British rule in India was there to stay. The British cultivated what one historian has called 'the illusion of permanence'. One British prime minister articulated this illusion memorably when he wrote in 1872 to the then viceroy in India: 'when we go, if we are ever to go'. The illusion proved to be remarkably short-lived.

· CHAPTER 19 ·

RISE OF INDIAN NATIONALISM

c. 1870–1947

The years between the restoration of British authority immediately after the Revolt of 1857 and 1905 marked the height of British rule in India. From 1905, shadows began to lengthen across an empire over which it was believed the sun would never set. As noted at the end of the previous chapter, during these years British rulers pursued policies of racial superiority and arrogance. They believed that they had a right to rule India because they had militarily conquered the country.

This sense of superiority had some material basis since Britain dominated the world in trade and manufacturing, and India—often described as the jewel in the Crown—had a critical place in the system of imperial dominance. The British laid out a railway system in India to facilitate the export of raw materials from the country; the railways brought great profit to British investors and manufacturers but made little or no contribution to India's economic growth. All essential items required to build the railways were imported into India and British companies were encouraged to invest in Indian railways by a guaranteed system of returns. The British pursued a policy of forced commercialization through which Indian cultivators were made to grow cash crops like cotton and jute needed in British factories; and to cultivate opium and indigo which sold at high prices in international markets. Indian agriculture served British imperial interests and this led to a decline in food production. The large bulk of British capital was invested in 'white settler' colonies. There was no serious effort made to promote industrialization in India. One consequence of this was greater pressure on land and the rural economy was trapped in a vicious cycle of debt and a growing landless labouring class. Famines became a common feature in many parts of rural India. It was estimated that between 1854 and 1901, 29 million people had died of starvation. In 1900, the annual per capita income was £2 or ₹30 (in 1901, Britain, by contrast, had a per capita income of £52). This level of per capita income made India one of the poorest countries in the world.

Interior of Victoria Terminus, Mumbai, Maharashtra

In 1534, a chain of islands on the west coast of India was handed over by the local nawab to the Portuguese in exchange for assistance to fend off Mughal advances. In 1662, Charles II married Catherine of Braganza of Portugal and the islands became part of her dowry. The royal British islands were rented out to the EIC for a small sum and soon grew into a prosperous port and town called Bombay. Mosques, temples, synagogues, Parsi fire temples, and churches like the Afghan Church (1847), colleges, and schools were built on these islands.

In 1878, Frederick William Stevens conceived the iconic Victoria Terminus railway station in the Gothic Victorian style with arched doorways and windows in different coloured stones. A huge vaulted interior made of steel and cement and stained-glass windows made it look like a cathedral rather than a railway station. Stations and the railway system developed across India by the British served trade and the movement of administrators, military personnel, and equipment. Today, millions of commuters use this station.

Contrary to the expectations of the British, it was the Western-educated intelligentsia that became more important and vocal as the nineteenth century came to its end. It was a small group numbering about 50,000 in 1885. They had been educated in the educational institutions that the British had set up or had helped to establish, especially the three universities of Calcutta, Bombay, and Madras. Students of these institutions, educated in English and Western learning, discovered that they could not aspire to any government jobs above that of clerks. The higher ranks of the bureaucracy—members of the Indian Civil Service (ICS), the 'heaven-born', as they were called, were open theoretically to the Indians but in practice it was almost impossible because the ICS examinations were held in London and there were age restrictions. These students also encountered other facets of the reality. In their classrooms and the books that they read they had learnt of the virtues of liberty, equality, and democracy. In the real world, they discovered as a shock to their innocence that none of these existed in India under British rule in which the British saw themselves to be superior to all Indians. These students had been taught to study history and when they turned to study India's past, they were appalled to discover that India's past had been misrepresented to them. India, they found through their own scholarship and study, had a glorious past—in terms of culture and politics—a past that Indians could be proud of. This sense of pride formed the basis of a new kind of identity—'we have a history of our own'—the first feeble step from servility to an assertion of independence. This new consciousness was buttressed by the knowledge that the British economically exploited India—India's poverty and backwardness were a direct consequence of Britain's exploitation of India. Writers like Dadabhai Naoroji and Romesh Chandra Dutt in their books presented in detail the exploitative dimensions of British rule in India. They argued that there was taking place a 'drain of wealth' from India to Britain. The latter prospered at the cost of India's economic backwardness and poverty.

The Western-educated intelligentsia was gathering an arsenal of ammunition which they would soon direct against British rule. The process began gradually and gently with sections of the intelligentsia forming local and provincial associations to put forward various grievances and demands to the government. But the realization dawned that their aims and aspirations would be better served if there was one united all-India organization. Thus was born the Indian National Congress (INC) which met for the first time in the winter of 1885. For many years, the INC was nothing more than a gathering of Westernized Indian elites who pleaded with the government to pay heed to their views. The INC in its early years served in the words of one historian as 'her Majesty's loyal opposition'. It did not articulate any demand for independence from British rule but urged the government to allow educated Indians some role in administration. It also argued to reduce the drain of wealth from India to Britain. The INC's aims and methods were moderate: no confrontation, no mobilization of the masses. It wanted to persuade the British in India to stop being 'un-British', and bring to India the gifts of governance which were practised in Britain.

Photograph of the first Indian National Congress meeting in 1885, Mumbai

On 28 December 1885, social reformers, journalists, and lawyers congregated for the first session of the Indian National Congress at Gokuldas Tejpal Sanskrit College, Bombay.

Events brought about by British policymakers dramatically altered the nature of moderate politics and resulted in the slow and gradual emergence of nationalism in India. The British announced in 1904 that the province of Bengal would be partitioned between eastern and western Bengal. The official reason given was that in terms of physical size and population the province of Bengal was proving difficult to administer. The nationalist intelligentsia in Bengal and in other parts of India did not fall for this explanation. They interpreted the move as a deliberate attempt to divide the Hindus and Muslims of Bengal since eastern Bengal had a Muslim majority and western Bengal was largely inhabited by Hindus. Further, the intelligentsia argued that by this policy of divide and rule, the British aimed to nip nationalism in the bud. It needs to be highlighted that the suspicions and interpretations of the intelligentsia were absolutely spot on since the study of archival documents by historians have revealed that dividing the people of Bengal and undermining nationalism were indeed what the British wanted to do. For example, the home secretary in two notes (dated 7 February and 6 December 1904) wrote: 'Bengal united is a power; Bengal divided will pull in different ways. That is perfectly true and is one of the merits of the scheme....' The intelligentsia was not willing to allow this policy to go through without protest. The policy of dividing achieved its exact opposite.

The intelligentsia organized a protest movement against the partition plan. They mobilized the common people of Bengal and moved away in many significant ways from the prevailing moderate ways of the Indian National Congress. The movement grew to embrace different forms of political agitation—mass demonstrations, hartals (general strikes), boycott, and political violence through the bomb and the pistol. The movement also witnessed a cultural flowering in Bengal and this cultural dimension was used in very innovative ways to mobilize the people.

Amba Vilas Palace, 1912, Mysuru, Karnataka

The palace is built in the Indo-Saracenic style, with a mixture of features taken from Hindu temples, such as the brackets and ornamentation, and Islamic and Gothic architecture—with arches and domes. It was originally built in wood that was destroyed in a fire and replaced by this stone and masonry structure in 1912.

The palace, like many of its kind in this period, is built around several inner courtyards, protected from the public gaze by a domineering façade on all four sides. The tall walls are punctured by ornate arched windows and balconies with prominent towers. The interiors also reflect a haphazard jumble of styles and forms from different countries and sensibilities: enormous chandeliers from the Czech Republic, tiles from England, stone and wooden carvings by traditional artisans from Rajasthan and Karnataka—all jostling for attention and comment.

The palace was the official residence of the Wadiyar maharajas of Mysore state, and the present descendant of this family lives in a portion of it. The rest of the palace has been converted into a museum open to the public who may view the vast estate, dotted with temples, and see the paintings, royal costumes, and art collections of the Mysore royal family.

One of the key features of the movement was the call to boycott all foreign commodities and practices and to use things that were Indian. Hence, the name by which the movement is known: the Swadeshi Movement. One of the persons at the very forefront of the movement in its early phase was Bengal's pre-eminent literary figure—Rabindranath Tagore. On Partition Day—16 October 1905, a day on which Calcutta observed a hartal—a gathering of people that included many famous persons went to the riverbank with Tagore at the forefront and started the day with a dip in the Ganga. After this bath in the Ganga they tied rakhis on each other's wrists. Tagore was later to recall that he tied rakhis on the wrists of whoever he met, even policemen were not exempted. On the same day, he was present at two very large meetings. One of his major contributions was the patriotic songs that he composed during this period. Among these were 'Amar Sonar Bangla' (My Golden Bengal) which became the national anthem of Bangladesh from the moment of its birth; and 'Jadi tor dak shune keu na ashe ekla cholo re' (If no one listens to your call, walk alone) which became one of Gandhi's favourite songs. As Ezra Pound was to say later, 'Tagore has sung Bengal into a nation.' Tagore lent his active support to build a national fund and on the very first day of the launch of the fund ₹30,000 was raised.

The call of the Swadeshi Movement included the boycott of government-run educational institutions, but the principal arena of the boycott was that of foreign cloth and here the movement faced its main hurdle. Foreign cloth was cheaper than cloth made in India and was of a more standardized quality. Poor people preferred to buy and use the foreign cloth and thus sellers (retailers and wholesalers) refused to respond to the call of boycott. When this happened, swadeshi campaigners resorted to violence: first by picketing the shops and when this did not work, by sabotaging the supply lines (sinking boats that carried the commodities into the rural world) and setting fire to shops. This is how threat and coercion entered the Swadeshi Movement. In 1908, Tagore wrote: 'We could not bear the delay involved in gradually winning the consent of the people.

We became busy in showing the English the consequences of their actions.' He enumerated the ways through which this coercion was deployed on those who defied the boycott call—from the threat that their forefathers would rot in hell, to the stoppage of essential services like the barber, the washerman, etc., to the burning of houses to the beating up of people on the roads. The main victims of such acts were those that belonged to the lower classes whose interests and advantages the movement had sought to suppress. Rabindranath emphasized that the use of force had divided the people when the aim of the movement had been to unite the people in a patriotic movement. Force had alienated large sections of the common people. He wrote: 'To enforce unity by strangling a person can hardly be called unity.' Rabindranath called for going back to the people and an abandoning of arrogance and pride and a cultivation of namrata—humility and grace. His growing disillusionment made him turn away from the Swadeshi Movement and focus on village reconstruction.

Rabindranath Tagore with members of the All-Union Society of Cultural Relations with Foreign Countries, USSR, 1930

Lutyens's working sketch for the new capital in Delhi

After the announcement in 1911, King George V chose two British architects, Edwin Lutyens and Herbert Baker, to design the capital of the British empire in Delhi. The architects' first task was to find an appropriate space for the British capital on a land already crowded with remains of older cities, along the banks of the Yamuna River. On the outskirts of the old city they finally located Raisina Hill that provided a prominent vantage point for the construction of the viceroy's residence. They began preparing the design for the capital, laid out with a geometric pattern branching out from Raisina Hill. This architectural drawing by Lutyens for the Viceroy's Residence shows an early concept for the grand residence they planned to build.

The failure to reach out to the people on any enduring basis made some young men turn to bombing and assassination. This turn to violence, which happened at the end of the Swadeshi Movement, around 1907–08, was followed by swift repression. The government in order to curb the protests and the first display of mass nationalism used arrests, preventive detention, deportation, and press censorship.

By 1909, the movement had begun to die down. But there was a general recognition, even at the level of King George V, that the partition of Bengal had not been a wise and tactical move. The king wanted to revoke the partition, and wanted to do so at a coronation durbar, which he was determined to have in India.

One important fallout of the Swadeshi Movement was the decision to shift the capital of the British empire in India from Calcutta to Delhi. The former city was emerging as the nerve centre of Indian nationalism and the British thought it wise to shift the capital to Delhi where a new capital city was to be built.

Towards the end of the same year, Mohandas Karamchand Gandhi composed a text of about 30,000 words on a ship coming back to India from London. This was the *Hind Swaraj*, written in Gujarati, between 13 and 22 November 1909. Gandhi wrote in the Preface: 'I have written because I could not restrain myself.' It was apparent that the ideas in the book had been incubating in his mind for a long time since the manuscript had very few revisions or deletions. Even though Gandhi was still based in South Africa, where he was famous for having pioneered a new form of peaceful and passive resistance against racial discrimination directed at Indians, and was still immersed in the political struggle there, the *Hind Swaraj* was about India and was addressed to Indians. It was first published in December 1909 in two successive issues of the *Indian Opinion*. When it was printed as a book in January 1910, the Bombay government confiscated copies of the book; in March 1910, Gandhi published an English translation that he had dictated. The English translation was called *Indian Home Rule*. It is the only work of Gandhi's that he himself translated.

The *Hind Swaraj* presents two interrelated themes. One is a critique of Western civilization and why it should be rejected by Indians. The second consists of a programme to build a new India that is free from the influences of Western civilization. It is important to bear in mind that the text was composed at a time when the Indian National Congress had been in existence for nearly a quarter of a century and was claiming to speak for India and Indians. The term swaraj had already entered the vocabulary of Indian nationalist leaders, many of whom had been involved during 1905–07 in the first mass protests against British rule and its unfairness. Freedom from British rule and exploitation no longer appeared like a distant dream. Gandhi was trying to define what kind of freedom this should be. He equated Western civilization with industrialism and rejected industrial society as immoral. Now that there was a movement growing in India to attain swaraj, Gandhi said it would be incomplete to define swaraj as merely political freedom from British rule. India would never achieve complete swaraj if British rule ended but British institutions and influences remained. Such a situation would produce conditions for what Gandhi called 'English rule without the Englishman'. He argued that to achieve swaraj in its truest sense, India and Indians would have to reject every single facet of British rule. Gandhi argued that there were large parts of India which were uncontaminated by the influence of modernity and Western civilization. These were the villages that lay in the deep interior of India: this was the real India which had been functioning in the same manner for thousands of years. In these villages, he said, individuals lived and functioned not on the basis of individual self-interest as individuals did in the West, but on the basis of interests that would benefit everyone. India would have to be built from these villages and, therefore, on foundations that were radically different from those that formed the basis of modern/Western civilization. Based on the ideas laid out by him in the *Hind Swaraj*, Gandhi began working among the peasants by organizing satyagrahas in Champaran in North Bihar and in Kheda in Gujarat. This was Gandhi's first involvement in political activity in India.

In February 1919, events propelled Gandhi from the local and the provincial to the national. The government introduced in the Imperial Legislative Council two anti-sedition bills which were named after the judge Sidney Rowlatt, who had been the head of the committee that had recommended the bills. Once passed, the

Hind Swaraj

Pages from the original handwritten manuscript of the *Hind Swaraj* written by Gandhi in Gujarati. He is said to have written it using both his left and right hands, a technique he practised when his right hand was tired.

bills came to be known as the Rowlatt Act. From the time Gandhi heard about the Act, he decided to oppose it and began rallying support all over India. Gandhi gave a call for an India-wide hartal on 6 April 1919 to inaugurate satyagraha against the Rowlatt Act.

On 30 March, groups of young men went around the streets of Old Delhi raising slogans that condemned the Rowlatt Act and praised Gandhi. In the narrow and crowded streets of the walled city the protestors clashed with the police who used tear gas and rubber bullets to disperse them. They retaliated with sticks and stones. The

Sabarmati Ashram, Ahmedabad, Gujarat

To demonstrate his vision for India which was not based on Western norms of modernity, Gandhi founded the Satyagraha Ashram in 1915 near Ahmedabad on his return from South Africa. The ashram was shifted to the banks of the Sabarmati in 1917 and it was here in the newly named Sabarmati Ashram that Gandhi lived from 1917 to 1933. He lived in a small hut constructed with natural materials, similar to those found in rural India. The hut was named Hridaya Kunj, the 'heart' of the place, and it was here that Gandhiji lived and practised the principles of life so dear to him—being self-sufficient; learning to spin yarn on a charkha without a machine; to join others in cleaning the ashram; and doing manual labour that included cleaning the toilets.

police fired into the crowd, this time using live bullets, and killed at least eight people and injured many more. Gandhi's inauguration of the satyagraha against the Rowlatt Act with an all-India hartal on 6 April was preceded by this episode of violence. The hartal was a huge success across India and across different sections of the people. The satyagraha was poised to escalate. But the escalation happened along lines that Gandhi had neither planned nor expected.

Sevagram, interior of Gandhi's house, Wardha, Maharashtra

In the ashram, on land donated by Jamnalal Bajaj at Sevagram, Gandhi continued his effort to break centuries old artificial caste, occupational boundaries, and traditions. He welcomed members of all faiths and castes, including those considered 'untouchables', to play an equal role in his community project, by sharing work in their common kitchen—an idea that some upper-caste Hindu followers of Gandhi found difficult to accept. Gandhi strove hard to establish the idea that no one was the master, but everyone, like humble servants, worked in the service of others and for the common good of their community.

Sevagram Ashram, his model village community where he lived from 1933 onwards, became the venue for political discussions with other leaders of the independence movement. Gandhi gave public talks that drew crowds of common people and wrote extensively on non-violence and his search for Truth. Today the ashram is a museum, a place of historic value. Domestic and international visitors visit the ashram, and are able to appreciate the simplicity of his lifestyle, the magnitude and significance of his work and ideas, in a world still ruled by violence and ridden with inequality.

On 8 April, Gandhi travelled to Punjab, a province where opposition to the British was very intense. The government decided to stop him from visiting Punjab, and while Gandhi was on his way, he was served with orders prohibiting him from entering Delhi and Punjab. Gandhi's detention incited protests across India but in Ahmedabad these took a violent turn. On 11 April, there was a major disturbance with crowds of people resorting to direct action by attacking Europeans, burning government buildings, and looting the houses of officials. The violence continued into the next day when troops were called in to fire at the crowds—killing twenty-three and injuring more than 100—and the city had to be put under martial law. A non-violent movement called by a firm believer in ahimsa had morphed into its exact opposite. Gandhi returned to Ahmedabad on 13 April and broke down when he heard what had happened.

Further events overtook Gandhi's personal sorrow. On 13 April 1919, Punjab, though in political turmoil, was celebrating Baisakhi, the traditional New Year's Day. The day also marked the anniversary of the formation of the khalsa by Guru Gobind Singh in 1699. Baisakhi is thus a special and auspicious day in Punjab. As part of the celebrations, and also to make a political statement against British rule and its oppressive laws, a large number of people had gathered in an enclosed space called Jallianwala Bagh in Amritsar. The word bagh literally means a garden but in 1919 this space was no longer much of a garden. It was a place where the people of the neighbourhood gathered for fresh air and where children could play. It was a popular spot because of its proximity to the Golden Temple complex. Jallianwala Bagh measured approximately 2.5 hectares, about 200 metres long and was nearly a square; it was surrounded on all sides by high walls of houses and compounds. It had five small entrances, some of which had gates that led to narrow lanes. Within the compound, near its centre, was a large well about 6 metres in diameter and with water 6 metres below its parapet. There was also a small samadhi, a tomb or a memorial. Around the well and the samadhi were a few trees offering shade. Otherwise, the space was bare. The walls surrounding it were nearly 3 metres high. Entry and exit from Jallianwala Bagh were thus restricted and difficult at the best of times.

By the late afternoon on the fateful day, some 20,000 to 25,000 people had gathered in Jallianwala Bagh. But this was a quiet crowd, by no means an angry mob. In the crowd there were some women and children. A little after 4 p.m., the crowd noticed soldiers, Gurkhas and Baluchis, enter the Bagh and take up positions barely 100 metres away; the fringes of the crowd were perhaps only eight or nine metres away from the soldiers who were on a low rise at the western end. The crowd was quietly listening to a speaker, Pandit Durga Dass, the editor of *Waqt*. The platform on which the speaker stood was 45 or 54 metres from where the troops had taken up position. The presence of the troops naturally caused alarm, and many began to try and escape. At this point, the troops were ordered to open fire. The man who gave the order, a premeditated decision, was Brigadier-General Reginald Dyer, the commander of the troops at Amritsar. As whistles blew, the firing commenced.

The walled enclosure pitted with bullet marks and the names of the dead, 1919, Jallianwala Bagh, Amritsar, Punjab

It is not difficult to imagine the chaos that ensued but it is almost impossible to imagine the carnage that followed. There was a stampede towards the gates which became jammed with people. The soldiers were ordered to directly shoot at those trying to flee; many died in the firing and many others were trodden underfoot or crushed under a mountain of corpses, three or four metres high. Those trying to scale the walls were easy targets. People, facing the prospect of no escape, huddled in groups in corners, and they were shot down. Some lay down on the ground to avoid the bullets but they were shot where they lay.

One hundred years later bullet scars remain on the buildings surrounding Jallianwala Bagh, Amritsar, Punjab

Today, Jallianwala Bagh is open to the public, and commemorates this dastardly act of violence on innocent people that took place over a hundred years ago. The bullet wounds on buildings and walls of the enclosed space, the well where many jumped to their death, and a memorial, continue to remind visitors of the horror of the day. Soon after this event, Rabindranath Tagore sent a moving and powerful message of protest to the world by relinquishing his knighthood given by the British.

Occasionally, the firing stopped as soldiers reloaded their guns and the firing resumed. Dyer personally directed the firing, ordering his troops to fire where the crowd was thickest. Soldiers were either kneeling or lying down to pick off their targets. People, to save themselves, jumped into the well; many drowned or were crushed by the rush of people trying to jump in. Some hid behind the well and behind a peepul tree. Dyer directed the firing at them. Even onlookers from the surrounding houses were shot at and some were hit by ricocheting bullets. Maulavi Gholam Jilani, a survivor, recalled: 'I ran towards a wall and fell on a mass of dead and wounded persons. Many others fell on me. Many of those who fell on me were hit and died. There was a heap of the dead and wounded over me, under and all around me. I felt suffocated. I thought I was going to die.' The firing continued for ten to fifteen minutes. The sound of firing and of bullets ripping through human bodies was matched by the screams of people. It was hell on earth. Punjab was under martial law so news of the massacre at Jallianwala Bagh took time to trickle out to the rest of India. Gandhi when he got to know the details decided that the time was opportune to launch an all-India mass movement to oust the British from India.

In 1920, the first issue Gandhi chose to challenge the British empire with was the one concerning the Khilafat. By the harsh terms of the Treaty of Sevrès (14 May 1920), Turkey not only lost all her colonies and the Greek-majority areas but the Islamic holy sites and places of pilgrimage were placed under direct or indirect British control. Muslim opinion in India was outraged and in this anger, Gandhi saw an opportunity to bring together Hindus and Muslims in one colossal non-violent movement to throw out the British from India. The Central Khilafat Committee of India's Muslims embraced Gandhi's call for non-violent non-cooperation. To launch such a movement, Gandhi knew he needed a committed organization. To this end, he initiated the process of transforming the Congress into a mass political party that was present at every level—locality, province, and nation. Gandhi also launched the Tilak Swaraj Fund to raise ₹1 crore. Simultaneously, he emphasized the importance of spinning cotton thread on a charkha. The latter became the hallmark of Gandhi's movement. It was Gandhi's programme to have 20 lakh charkhas across India. On the basis of these organizational pillars of mass mobilization, Gandhi launched the Non-cooperation Movement in the winter of 1920–21.

He mobilized the Congress, the supporters of the Khilafat movement, and the people around three issues: 'the Punjab wrong', 'the Khilafat wrong', and swaraj. Gandhi defined non-cooperation as the boycott of titles, civil services, police and army, and, finally non-payment of taxes. As the movement unfolded, people began to surrender titles, boycott educational institutions, courts, councils, and foreign goods. The formal aim of the Congress was changed to read 'attainment of Swaraj by all legitimate and peaceful means'.

By the end of the year, the government's policy of arrests and suppression made many leaders put pressure on Gandhi to make the movement more radical and Gandhi decided to launch a no-revenue campaign in Bardoli in Gujarat in the second week of February 1921. But on 5 February a violent mob attacked a police station in Chauri Chaura in eastern Uttar Pradesh which resulted in twenty-two people being burnt alive. Hearing of this incident, Gandhi withdrew from the movement: he declared he would have nothing to do with a movement that had turned violent.

In the Congress session held at the end of 1929, it was resolved that Purna Swaraj (complete independence) would be the aim of the Congress. It was left to Gandhi to decide the precise form of the non-violent struggle through which Purna Swaraj would be attained. Gandhi launched the Civil Disobedience movement by manufacturing salt—a commodity over which the government had monopoly—after marching from Sabarmati to Dandi by the sea. The march lasted from 12 March to 6 April 1930 and was one of the most dramatic moments of the Indian national movement. Gandhi marched through the heart of Gujarat at the head of a team of seventy-one drawn from all parts of India. As Gandhi progressed towards Dandi, village officials along the route resigned from their posts. Gandhi announced after he had broken the salt law that others should follow and also boycott foreign cloth and liquor.

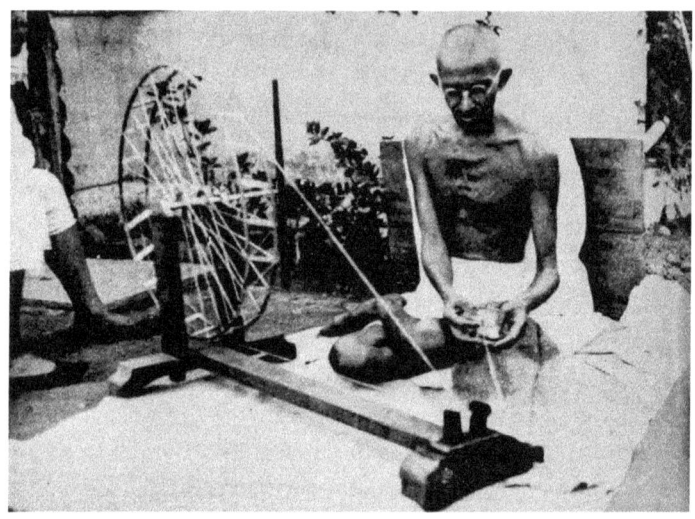

Gandhi spinning the charkha, Sabarmati Ashram, 1925

Joining the Civil Disobedience Movement meant facing government brutality; the government did not hesitate to attack peaceful demonstrations. A large number of women and teenagers joined the movement: on 15 November 1930, of the 29,054 persons arrested, 2,050 were below seventeen years of age and 359 were women. What was missing, in comparison to the Non-cooperation Movement, was Hindu–Muslim unity. Outside a few pockets, Muslim participation in the Civil Disobedience Movement remained low. The response from the peasantry and business groups was substantial. Businessmen like G. D. Birla and Jamnalal Bajaj supported and funded the movement. From around the end of 1930, there were signs of the enthusiasm tapering off and this was reflected in the Gandhi–Irwin Pact of February 1931 (Irwin was the then viceroy) which resulted in a kind of fragile truce. The movement resumed at the beginning of

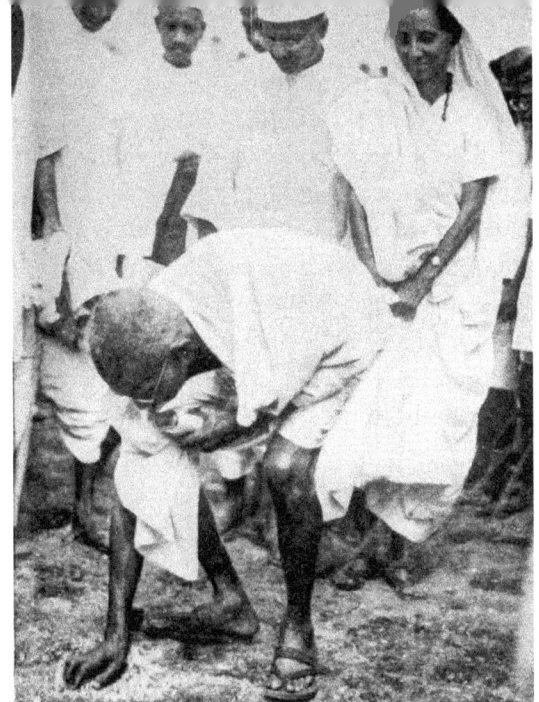

Iconic photo of Gandhi picking up the first handful of salt at 8.30 a.m. on 6 April 1930, Dandi, Gujarat

It is said the British did not understand the momentous meaning or the impact that the Salt March would have when Gandhi first put forward the idea. The purpose of the Dandi March was to adopt a cause that was profoundly significant for a majority of India's population, even the poorest village dweller, and to seek their cooperation in the Civil Disobedience Movement. The path from Ahmedabad to Dandi was over 300 kilometres and it took twenty-six days to complete the journey, and many feared that Gandhi would not survive the ordeal. It began with a group of around seventy people from Sabarmati Ashram trained in the discipline of passive, non-violent response to police brutality. Daily the group rested en route in villages where Gandhi talked and listened to the problems of the rural poor. As the march progressed, thousands of villagers followed him, and even after his arrest, the march continued. The international and Indian press were present to witness this momentous event at Dandi and the harsh police action on the crowds that followed. The news of the Dandi March spread, and captured the world's attention, and sympathy and gradually support grew for Indians suffering under colonial rule. With this simple and defiant act of making salt Gandhi made history.

1932 because the Congress leaders and supporters were convinced that in spite of promises, the attitudes and the policies of the British had not changed. The new viceroy, Lord Willingdon, pursued a policy of suppression of civil liberties. With so many things made illegal, law-breaking or civil disobedience became easier and between January 1932 and March 1933 the number of persons arrested was 120,000. The movement, faced as it was by massive repression, petered out by the beginning of 1933.

The road to Dandi, Gujarat

The road that Gandhi took to reach the sea to make salt has today become a commemorative route with leafy avenues for tourists and Gandhi's followers, inviting them to walk in his footsteps.

Immediately after the outbreak of World War II, there was great disquiet in India. All the provincial assemblies elected under the Government of India Act of 1935 were suspended and India and Indians were drawn into a war with which they had nothing to do, and they were not even consulted about whether they wanted to join the war. Sensing the mood of the people, Gandhi gave the call for a mass movement that would force the British to Quit India—thus the name of the movement. It was set to begin on 9 August 1942. Early that morning the entire Congress leadership was arrested. But this could not prevent a popular outburst the likes of which India had not witnessed since 1857. The first phase of the movement was largely urban and saw hartals, strikes, and clashes with the police in Bombay, Delhi, Calcutta, and Patna. From the middle of August, the protests spread to the countryside from centres like Patna, Cuttack, Banaras, and so on. Lines of communication were the main targets of attack in what is best described as peasant insurgency. The situation, from the point of view of the British administration, was so grave that fifty-seven army battalions had to be deployed to re-establish control. The repression was savage and from September the movement entered a long phase of guerrilla war and of young men attacking government institutions, installations, and officials. By the end of 1943, nearly 92,000 persons were behind bars; there had been 600 bomb explosions; 200 police outposts, 332 railway stations, and over 900 post offices had been destroyed. Anti-British feelings ran high.

The Quit India Movement did not win its immediate objective but it made it evident to the British rulers that they were on borrowed time in India. Clement Attlee, who was elected the prime minister of Britain after the end of the war, acknowledged this when he declared that Britain would pull out of India no later than June 1948. The months between 1946 and 1947 would see the unravelling of this process of withdrawal.

It is a common but mistaken belief that the Indian people's struggle for freedom from British rule happened only under the leadership of Gandhi and under the banner of the Indian National Congress. There were, in fact, movements that were outside the Gandhian fold, movements that differed from and questioned the ideas and practices of Gandhi, and movements that were openly hostile to Gandhi.

Quit India poster, 1942

A poster of Gandhi, by the artist Dayal, for National Art Studio.

One important articulation of non-Gandhian nationalism was the firm belief among sections of young men and women that British rule could only be overthrown through violence. The British ruled India through force and violence and could, therefore, be challenged and defeated through the same. Many young men and women sacrificed their lives or spent many years in jail (often in solitary confinement in terrible conditions in the Cellular Jail in the Andaman Islands) to achieve the violent overthrow of British rule. This project started during the Swadeshi Movement under two groups—the Anushilan Samiti and the Yugantar group. Members of these groups carried out daring dacoity and assassination attempts. In spite of Gandhi's charismatic mobilization, this emphasis on violence as a means to attain freedom remained a part of the Indian national movement.

Cellular Jail, Port Blair, the Andaman Islands

This prison was constructed around 1906, is three storeys high, and situated far from mainland India, in the Andaman Islands. The prison was used by the British colonial rulers to incarcerate freedom fighters. The jail acquired a horrific reputation as stories of the inhuman and brutal treatment of political prisoners spread to the mainland.

During the Civil Disobedience Movement, there were violent outbreaks in Peshawar, Sholapur, and Chittagong. In Chittagong, under the leadership of Surya Sen, a group of armed revolutionaries took over the local arsenal and issued an Independence Proclamation in the name of the Indian Republican Army on 18 April 1930. The revolutionaries fought a pitched battle against the British forces. What is worth noting is that even though the methods of the Chittagong revolutionaries were far from Gandhian, when the armoury was seized the cry that went up among the revolutionaries was 'Gandhiji's raj has come'. The Chittagong encounter led to a series of violent attacks on British institutions and individuals. In 1930 alone there were fifty-six such incidents whereas the decade between 1919 and 1929 had seen only forty-seven.

Gandhi with Khan Abdul Ghaffar Khan, October 1938, New Delhi

There was another popular uprising in Peshawar which was the direct fallout of the arrest of Khan Abdul Ghaffar Khan and other Pathan leaders on 23 April in the course of the Civil Disobedience Movement. Crowds confronted armoured vehicles and defied firing in which, according to official estimates, around thirty persons were killed. Unofficial estimates put the number between 230 and 250. A platoon of Hindu soldiers refused to fire at a Muslim crowd. It took the British ten days to quell the uprising and this was followed by brutal retaliations under martial law. In Sholapur, Maharashtra, there was a textile strike from 7 May soon after Gandhi's arrest.

Millhands joined by others attacked police outposts, law courts, the municipal building, and the railway station. The uprising lasted till 16 May and could only be put down with considerable violence.

The most dramatic opposition to British rule through violent means happened in the 1940s during World War II. This was the work of Subhas Chandra Bose who in Southeast Asia had formed the Indian National Army. Bose, since his return in 1921 from Cambridge where he had refused to join the Indian Civil Service despite qualifying for it, had been a loyal and prominent Congress worker. Within the Congress he, together with Jawaharlal Nehru, articulated radical views that brooked no compromise with the British. In the late 1930s, through a series of petty schemes in which even Gandhi was involved, he was outmanoeuvred in the party and he resigned. He set up his own political party, the Forward Bloc. In spite of police surveillance, Bose made a dramatic escape from his home (where he was under house arrest) in Calcutta and surfaced in Berlin just before Hitler's attack on Soviet Russia. His plan was to secure Germany's support to overthrow British rule in India. The Nazis treated him well but he received no encouragement from Hitler who arranged for Bose to travel by submarine to Southeast Asia where the Japanese appeared at that time to be triumphant. With Singapore as his headquarters, Bose formed the Indian National Army which joined the Japanese forces in attacking Imphal in Manipur in the summer of 1944. This campaign failed and the defeat of the Japanese in 1945 made Bose's position precarious and he became a fugitive from the Allied forces. It is believed that he died in a plane crash while trying to escape. There are many admirers of Bose who do not accept this account. The failure of the INA notwithstanding, Bose's campaign made him a hero and his courage captured the popular imagination. His military campaign and his popularity were grim reminders to the British that they could not take for granted their dominance over India and Indians.

A completely different kind of movement revolving around caste and untouchability emerged under the leadership of B. R. Ambedkar.

In the second half of the nineteenth century, in western India, Jotirao Phule had written and campaigned for the lower castes against the dominance of the Brahmins and the discrimination practised by them. He and his wife, Savitribai, were also pioneers in the sphere of education for women. Phule had argued that the removal of caste discrimination, which was at the heart of Brahmanical Hinduism, was far more important than freedom from British rule. In South India, under the Justice Party, similar anti-Brahmanical views were expressed in the early twentieth century. Ambedkar, the son of a low military official, was born into the untouchable caste. Through his sheer intellectual competence, he won scholarships that took him from Bombay University to Columbia University and to the London School of Economics. In the latter institution, he was awarded a doctorate. In the 1920s, he argued that the lower castes in India represented a distinct identity and interest group; they had their own history of suffering and had their own grievances and aspirations. He wanted the British in their policymaking to recognize the distinct identity and interests of the lower castes in the same way the Muslims were being treated as a separate interest group by the British. The British government acknowledged Ambedkar's position. The prime minister, Ramsay MacDonald, announced the creation of reserved constituencies for the untouchables in 1932. This led to a stand-off between Ambedkar and Gandhi. In protest against the government's decision, Gandhi began a 'fast unto death' on 20 September. With Gandhi's health deteriorating, Ambedkar had little choice but to agree to negotiations. The outcome of the negotiations was the Poona Pact by which MacDonald's award was modified. According to the pact, Hindu joint electorates were retained with reserved seats for untouchables who had larger representation than what was provided for in the framework of MacDonald's decision. Gandhi, it should be said emphatically, was not against the removal of untouchability which he considered to be evil and immoral. He campaigned in word and deed against it. But Gandhi was against the creation of further divisions within Indian society. He believed that untouchability could be removed through intense campaigning from within Hindu society. This was a position that Ambedkar could not accept. The issue of caste continued to haunt the Indian national movement and there was no resolution of it and there has not been a resolution of it. It should be noted that notwithstanding his differences with Gandhi and the Congress, in 1946 Ambedkar became the chairman of the committee that drafted the Constitution of India.

The primary claim of Indian nationalism was that India was one united country. On the basis of this, the Indian National Congress stated that it represented all Indians irrespective of caste, region, and religion. Even the INA based itself on the same premise. As a counterpoint to such claims was formed the Indian Muslim League which met for the first time in Dacca in December 1906. The leaders of the Muslim League argued that the Congress was a Hindu organization and represented only Hindus and articulated the interests of Hindus only. The Muslims, according to the League, were a separate community with their own history and own traditions. They pushed this point to say that Hindus and Muslims formed two separate and different nations within India. Such arguments were music to the ears of the British policymakers who found in them support for their divide and rule policies.

Statue of Subhas Chandra Bose, Moirang, Manipur

This Subhas Chandra Bose statue marks the site where the first Indian National Army flag was unfurled in the town of Moirang, Manipur, on 14 April 1944.

Memorial to B. R. Ambedkar, twentieth century, H. D. Kote, Karnataka

Statues of Ambedkar such as these were erected throughout India, especially in villages and towns in states like Andhra Pradesh and Karnataka, where Dalit communities lived in dense concentrations.

The Khilafat and the Non-cooperation movements had witnessed scenes and episodes of Hindu–Muslim unity. This atmosphere of harmony began to dissipate in the 1920s in the aftermath of the mass movements. Moreover, as education spread and employment opportunities did not, Hindus and Muslims found themselves competing for jobs. This facilitated the fanning of communal tensions. The Muslim League expanded to take over the space vacated by the various Khilafat bodies which had lost their relevance. Organization and propaganda began to spread and intensify. In 1924, the Muslim League met separately from the Congress—this was the first time it happened since 1918 and was the beginning of a persisting trend—and raised the demand for federation with full provincial autonomy to ensure that Muslim majority regions would be free from Hindu domination. This demand would continue till 1940 when the demand for Pakistan as a separate country for Muslims would become the most important demand of the League. Significantly, the Lahore session of the League (1940) was presided over by Mohammad Ali Jinnah who by the 1930s and 1940s had emerged as what the historian Ayesha Jalal has termed, 'the sole spokesman' of the Muslims in India.

By the time India had been unilaterally drawn into World War II, the Muslim League, under Jinnah, was strong enough to claim that it was the sole representative of the Indian Muslims and that the League should have a veto on all future constitutional changes. The British were not averse to these proposals.

A new and pivotal dimension was added to the ideology of the Muslim League by the adoption of the Pakistan resolution in March 1940. This idea of a separate state called Pakistan, which constituted the territories of Punjab, Afghanistan, Kashmir, Sind, and Baluchistan, has an interesting history. It was first put forward by a group of Punjabi Muslim students in Cambridge; at the forefront of this group was Choudhry Rahmat Ali. Ali, in two pamphlets written in 1933 and 1935, demanded a separate national status for a new entity called Pakistan, defined as above. In the early 1930s, no one took this very seriously even within the Muslim League As the League's fortunes began to revive post-1937, it needed a concrete programme and it toyed with various different schemes and in this it was encouraged by the British government. After much discussion, it settled on the idea of Pakistan and making it the plank of its future campaign. The resolution was drafted by Sikandar Hayat Khan and moved with many modifications by Fazlul Haque.

In this way, the shape of India's independence would be influenced by movements and ideas which would be far removed from the original vision of a united India and from Gandhi's dream that freedom would be inseparable from ahimsa. Political leaders who had been driven by idealism would be forced to yield to the compulsions of reality. The triumph of independence would be tempered by tragedy and disillusionment.

Rashtrapati Bhavan, New Delhi

While the national movement occupied the minds and actions of the people, enormous colonial structures were being constructed as symbols of the power and might of the British empire.

The making of the new capital in Delhi was a matter of intense debate—colonial rulers specified the buildings that they needed and dictated the style in which they were to be built. Payment for this expensive project came from taxes and earnings from the Indian colony and it was Indian craftsmen who laboured for nearly twenty years to build the new capital (1911–29).

Gateway of India, Mumbai

The gateway commemorates the visit of George V and Queen Mary to Bombay on 2 December 1911 when they laid the foundation stone for this structure. George Wittet was the architect who modelled this gateway like the triumphal arches of classical Rome and similar ones erected in England and France. The gateway is 26 metres high and made of yellow basalt stone, and faces Bombay harbour. It was through this gate that the last British troops made their departure from India in 1948.

Lord Hardinge was the viceroy of India, in charge of the administration of colonial India. He suggested to the architects that he wanted 'to see at Delhi a fine and broad style of architecture with Indian tradition and sentiment running throughout....' Lutyens and Baker formulated a design for the building shown above, referred to now as the Oriental Style that combined European imperial features, drawn from classical Greek and Roman architecture, with equally imperial Indian elements such as chhatris (domed kiosks/ cupolas), chajjas (overhanging eaves), jalis, and pillars. The dome over the building was inspired by the seventeenth century dome of Saint Paul's Cathedral in London, modified to look like the hemispherical shape of the third century stupa at Sanchi, Madhya Pradesh. The result was a cocktail of styles and motifs. The Viceroy's Residence covered an area of 154 hectares and was completed in 1929, with the Mughal Gardens at the back of the building. After Independence, the Viceroy's Residence became the official home of the president of India.

· CHAPTER 20 ·

INDEPENDENCE AND PARTITION

1945–1947

India became free of British rule on 15 August 1947. But this independence came with the terrible price of Partition. A new nation state called Pakistan was carved out of India. This division affected the lives of millions of people who, because of decisions made by political leaders, lost their homes, their properties, their jobs, and their sense of belonging. Partition also resulted in violence in which thousands were killed, injured, and raped. This chapter attempts to look at this process very briefly and consider how Independence came with Partition.

The Atlantic Charter of 1941, which the US president Franklin D. Roosevelt had insisted upon and which the British prime minister Winston Churchill had reluctantly agreed to sign, had put it down that once the World War II was over, and the Allied powers were victorious, Britain would pull back the frontiers of its empire and begin the process of decolonization. This process received a boost with the defeat of Churchill in the British elections of 1945. The new prime minister, Clement Attlee, belonged to the Labour Party; he, in 1947, announced that Britain would pull out of India by June 1948. This not only set a timetable but also introduced an urgency to the negotiations and decision-making. Within India, there were two factors which were important. One was that most of the Congress leaders had been in prison from August 1942 to June 1945. They emerged prison-weary but were forced to face a very volatile political situation (about which more later). And the second was the growing strength of the Muslim League. By 1943, League ministries were in place in Assam, Sind, Bengal, and the North-West Frontier Province. More significantly, the Pakistan demand was gaining in popularity among sections of Indian Muslims. There were reasons for this

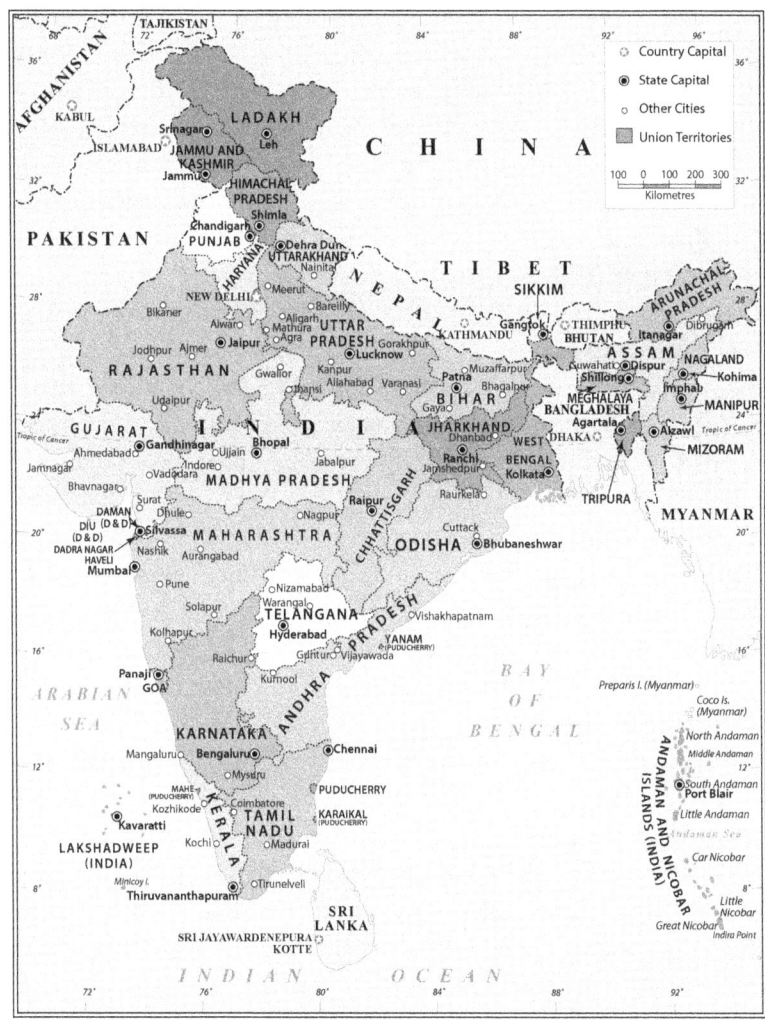

The Indian nation in the twenty-first century

Not to scale. This map has been prepared in adherence to the 'Guidelines for acquiring and producing Geospatial Data and Geospatial Data Services including Maps' published vide DST F.No.SM/25/02/2020 (Part-I) dated 15th February, 2021

growing popularity. Pakistan was being presented to the peasants of Bengal and Punjab as the end of the domination and exploitation of Hindu landlords and moneylenders. Pakistan also meant an area where there would be no or less competition from Hindu business groups and professional classes. These factors made the League a force to reckon with in the negotiations regarding the transfer of power.

Immediately after the end of the war, parts of India witnessed militant popular movements that were completely outside the Gandhian fold and the control of the Congress. These movements were so powerful that the autumn and the winter of 1945–46 pushed British rule, in the words of one British official turned historian, to 'the edge of a volcano'. One such movement was the protest that followed the government's decision to hold public trials of the INA prisoners. In an incredibly stupid move, the British decided to hold the first of these trials at the Red Fort where they put in the dock a Hindu (P. K. Sehgal), a Muslim (Shah Nawaz), and a Sikh (Gurbaksh Singh Dhillon). The accused were defended by Tej Bahadur Sapru, Bhulabhai Desai, and Jawaharlal Nehru. For this momentous trial, Nehru donned his silk gown after twenty-five years. Even the Muslim League joined the protests. The protests clearly went beyond any kind of communal divide and aroused widespread public sympathy. The magnitude of the protests made the British fear that there could be another uprising like the one witnessed in August 1942. Calcutta, over two days, 21 to 23 November, saw an upheaval in support of the INA prisoners in which supporters of the Forward Bloc, the Communist Party, and Muslims participated. The protestors were fired at by the police, killing two students, a Hindu and a Muslim. This led to strikes and large-scale violence. What surprised the police—and this was noted by officials—was that firing in no way dissuaded the crowds; in fact, the people stood their ground. What is equally significant is that episodes of this kind of popular militancy were frowned upon by the Congress leadership. Calcutta witnessed another such upheaval in February 1946 against the seven years' rigorous imprisonment sentence passed on Abdul Rashid of the INA.

These protests again saw remarkable shows of unity between students and workers and Hindus and Muslims. Such protests were by no means futile. The British were forced to make concessions which included the reduction of imprisonment sentences passed on the first batch of accused in the INA trials.

INA trials in the Red Fort, 1945, Delhi

Photograph of the courtroom with Tej Bahadur Sapru, Jawaharlal Nehru, and others during the INA trials held at the Red Fort, Delhi.

In Bombay, around the same time as the protests in Calcutta against the prison sentence on Abdul Rashid, a different and a more radical protest occurred. On 18 February 1946, ratings (low-ranking sailors) of the Royal Indian Navy, on the signals training ship *Talwar*, went on hunger strike against the bad food offered to them and the racial discrimination they suffered. The strikes spread on shore and on twenty-two ships moored in the Bombay harbour. The ships put up the tricolour, the hammer and sickle flag, and the green crescent flag on their masts. The ratings formed a Naval Central Strike

Committee and put forward their demands—better food, equal pay for white and Indian sailors, release of INA and other political prisoners, and withdrawal of Indian soldiers from Indonesia. Violent encounters with the army ensued. The ratings received support from the common people of Bombay—crowds brought food for them and shopkeepers invited them to take whatever they needed. By 22 February, the strike had spread—all the naval bases in India went on strike as did some of the ships out in the ocean. The numbers at the height of this protest were huge—seventy-eight ships, twenty establishments on shore, and 20,000 ratings. In Karachi there was a gun battle, and Hindu and Muslim students and workers displayed their solidarity through violent clashes with the police and the army. While the Communist Party of India called for a general strike in Bombay, the Congress leadership remained indifferent to the movement. The general strike was successful with 300,000 workers refusing to work on 22 February; all mills remained closed and there were violent encounters between the people and the police on the streets. Two army battalions had to be deployed to restore normalcy in Bombay. An official estimate said that 228 civilians were killed and over 1,000 injured. Sardar Patel and Jinnah worked overtime to persuade the ratings to surrender. The ratings were assured that the national parties would ensure there would be no victimization. The promise was never kept. The ratings were betrayed by the elite national leadership but their uprising deserves the epithet, 'the last war of independence'.

A few months after the heroic rising of the ratings, in September 1946, a series of peasant uprisings occurred, with the largest number taking place in Bengal. The demand was that sharecroppers should be given two-thirds of the crop instead of half or even less. The movement thus came to be called the Tebhaga Movement. The movement peaked during November, the time of the harvest, with sharecroppers taking the harvest to their own threshing floors (instead of to the houses of the landlords) to ensure that they could keep two-thirds of the crop. The struggle was most intense in North Bengal. Police violence sponsored by landlords tried to suppress the movement. The peasants resisted and put up a fight with their traditional weapons like lathis; the fight was thus unequal and destined to fail. A full-scale armed struggle was not possible as the peasants did not have access to arms.

Men of the Royal Indian Navy marching to a meeting in Bombay, 1946

From July 1946, Telangana (then in the princely state of Hyderabad) saw the beginnings of a sustained peasant guerrilla war that lasted till October 1951. At the height of the war, it covered 3,000 villages, 41,000 square kilometres, and involved 3 million people. The war was waged against various forms of extortion practised by upper-caste landlords on lower-caste and tribal peasants and debt slaves, and against the nizam of Hyderabad. Once the Indian Army entered Hyderabad in September 1948 to force the nizam to join the Indian union, the guerrilla war turned against the new Indian state. The guerrilla war, even though it was eventually suppressed, was not without its moments of glory. In the villages that were under the control of the peasant guerrilla bands, forced and bonded labour was abolished, there was a rise in agricultural wages, lands that had been unjustly seized were returned to their previous peasant owners, waste land was redistributed as well as land above 40 hectares of dry land and 4 hectares of wet land. Some of these gains remained even after the movement had been quelled.

While these movements—all outside of Congress control—were on, the elite politicians belonging to the Congress, the League, the princes, and British officials negotiated across tables to decide the future of India—how power was to be transferred and to whom.

Aftermath of communal riots, 1946, Karachi

In Karachi pitched battles took place between police and rioters. Remains of the violence can be seen on the street that is left littered with rocks and bricks as the crowds dispersed.

An added dimension to the negotiations was the spread of

communal rioting across India, especially North India. It started in Calcutta on 16 August 1946 with Jinnah's call for Direct Action for Pakistan. It spread to Bombay in early September, to Noakhali in East Bengal in early October, to Bihar in late October, to Garhmukteshwar (in UP) in November, and to large parts of Punjab from March 1947. The scale of this communal violence can be gauged by the figures from Calcutta where in three days from 16 to 19 August at least 4,000 people were killed and 10,000 injured.

Growing popular militancy and communal violence were increasingly closing the options of the negotiators. Moreover, the negotiations and the various proposals that were put forward were going nowhere. In February 1947, the League refused to join the Constituent Assembly and cooperate in the functioning of the cabinet. In retaliation, the Congress demanded that the League ministers resign from the Interim government. Things seemed to be leading to an impasse especially with Attlee's announcement that come what may, the British would pull out of India by June 1948.

One of the proposals that the British were seriously considering was to break up India. Though this was firmly rejected by the Congress, it was becoming evident that some sort of partition would have to be accepted. The Congress was eager to avoid more communal violence and popular militancy outside its control. Under the Mountbatten Plan, hurriedly worked out, after what was code-named Plan Balkan (a plan to transfer power to separate provinces or confederations) was rejected, it was decided that power would be transferred to two central governments—India and Pakistan. This was accepted by the Congress, the League, and the Sikh leaders on 2 June 1947 and announced the next day. This led to the enactment of the India Independence Act which was presented to and passed by the British parliament and the Crown on 18 July. And on the basis of this India became independent on 15 August 1947; a day before that a new nation state called Pakistan was also born.

Refugees arriving by train from West Pakistan to India, 1947

The Partition of India led to the largest mass migration known to human history. An estimated 14 million people were displaced from their homes and land. More than a million Hindus, Sikhs, and Muslims lost their lives, as trains and groups of travellers on the road were killed, raped, decapitated, and robbed.

This narrative would be incomplete without the mention of the one man who stood apart from the negotiations and refused to be part of any discussion that had the division of India on the agenda. This was Mohandas Karamchand Gandhi. As soon as he realized that his hand-picked men, Vallabhbhai Patel, Jawaharlal Nehru, Rajendra Prasad, and so on were disregarding the people to retain political power, and when he saw the country being engulfed by communal violence, Gandhi withdrew from Delhi to go and work among the victims of communal violence—in Noakhali, Bihar, and Calcutta. He wanted the British to leave India and let the Indians decide their own future. Thus, when India erupted in jubilation on the midnight of 14–15 August,

Gandhi was not in Delhi and he was in no mood to celebrate. He was in a very poor part of eastern Calcutta working among those who had been scarred by communal violence. When asked on the morning of 15 August for his reaction, he said, 'Today is a day for fasting and prayer.' The person called the Father of the Nation was not present at the birth of the nation.

Jawaharlal Nehru, the first prime minister of India, at the Indian Constituent Assembly, New Delhi, 14 August 1947

Nehru delivered a now famous speech to the Indian Constituent Assembly on the eve of Indian Independence, at midnight on 14 August 1947. He began by saying: 'Long years ago, we made a tryst with destiny; and now the time comes when we shall redeem our pledge, not wholly or in full measure, but very substantially. At the stroke of the midnight hour, when the world sleeps, India will awake to life and freedom.... A moment comes, which comes but rarely in history, when we step out from the old to the new—when an age ends, and when the soul of a nation, long suppressed, finds utterance. It is fitting that at this solemn moment we take the pledge of dedication to the service of India, and her people, and to the still larger cause of humanity.'

Independence Day, 1947, Calcutta

Gandhi plugging his ears against the deafening din of demonstrators outside his Beliaghata residence in Calcutta, 15 August 1947.

· CHAPTER 21 ·

INDEPENDENT INDIA

1947–2025

In his very first speech as prime minister of India, Jawaharlal Nehru had coined a phrase that became an integral part of India's national vocabulary: 'Years ago we made a tryst with destiny.' The use of that pronoun 'we' would come to haunt him at least in the very first few months of his premiership. Who had he spoken for? He had certainly not spoken for Gandhi who, as we saw, refused to be part of any tryst that involved the partition of India. Did the 'we' include the betrayed ratings of the Royal Indian Navy Uprising, did it include the peasant guerrillas of Telangana and the sharecroppers of the Tebhaga Movement? Equally importantly, it did not include the tens of thousands of people in the divided provinces of Punjab and Bengal who were uprooted by Partition. Nehru seriously underestimated the emotional upheaval that Partition had brought to the lives of people. Ignoring the trauma, he saw the violence that ensued in terms of groups of individuals who had lost their reason: 'There is madness about in its worst form,' he wrote to Lady Ismay, the wife of a senior British official, a fortnight or so after 15 August. But he was honest enough to admit, at least privately, that all his calculations when he had agreed to Partition as a way of ending communal violence had proved to be utterly misplaced. He was also aware that he had a responsibility to his countrymen in spite of his growing sense of helplessness. He had to begin the process of building anew from the remains of devastation.

In the early years of the Indian republic, the political leadership, especially Nehru was driven by the commitment to build a democratic polity and society in India. Nehru saw this as his most important responsibility. It was to this end that, contrary to all expectations and the surprise of many, he was an unswerving advocate of universal

Republic Day parade, New Delhi

adult franchise (the right of all adults to vote). The first general elections of the republic of India were held under these conditions—all adults had an equal voice in the building of India's future. His commitment to democracy was evident in the importance he gave to parliament and its procedures; he led by present in parliament as prime minister whenever parliament was in session and he was in the capital. He took steps to establish the rule of law and the cabinet form of government in which the prime minister was primus inter pares (first among equals). He anchored democracy in India on religious tolerance and secularism and ensured that India belonged to all Indians irrespective of their religious beliefs.

Gandhi's last footsteps, Gandhi Smriti, Tees January Marg, New Delhi

On 30 January 1948, Gandhi emerged from his room at Birla House, the home of a prominent industrial family, and walked toward the garden where a crowd had assembled for his daily evening prayer meeting. While he was walking there, at sunset, at 5.30 p.m., he was shot dead by Nathuram Vinayak Godse, at point-blank range.

Godse was tried in court and sentenced to death in November 1949. The path of Gandhi's last footsteps has been preserved and Birla House has been turned into a museum to commemorate Gandhi's life and record this violent event. The museum is visited every day by thousands of people from around the world. They come to pay their respects to Gandhi—a messenger of peace and follower of the ancient principle of ahimsa.

The building of a new republic was made possible by three institutional structures that were inherited from the British Raj. The first of these was the bureaucracy that had served as 'the steel frame' of the British Raj. The British had formed the bureaucracy by building up the Indian Civil Service. This was an elite service whose members were selected by an examination. The Nehruvian administration began the process of Indianizing this service and by splitting it up into separate units like the Indian Foreign Service, which formed the diplomatic corps, and a cluster of services that managed the internal administration—the Indian Administrative Service, the Indian Police Service, the Indian Revenue Service, and so on. The elected politicians within the chambers of national and provincial legislative bodies enacted laws and ordinances which members of the bureaucracy at different levels implemented. The relationship between the politicians who made the laws and the bureaucrats was problematic. In the initial years of the republic, both the legislators and the bureaucrats worked together in the spirit of service to the nation. From the 1970s, however, there was a noticeable erosion in the relationship. Self-interest and vested interest corroded the spirit of service and corruption among politicians and bureaucrats became the rule rather than the exception. This experience seemed to confirm the oft-quoted observation of the historian Lord Acton that power corrupts.

The second inherited institution was the elaborate military apparatus that the British had created in India to protect themselves. Indian soldiers had fought with great bravery and heroism in both World War I and World War II. There were two problems concerning the military that faced the government of independent India. One was the fact that the army, by far the largest of the armed forces, had been recruited by the British on the policy of divide and rule. The colonial policymakers described sections of the Indian people as 'martial races' and confined the recruitment of the army to such groups. Nehru argued that the entire background of the Indian army had to be transformed if democracy had to be maintained.

Old Parliament House or Sansad Bhavan, New Delhi

This circular colonnaded building, resembling a wheel, was designed by Edwin Lutyens and Herbert Baker and was opened in 1927 as the Imperial Legislative Council. Today, it is no longer used for its original purpose, and a new parliament building has been constructed. Since 1951, after the Constitution of India was adopted, parliament conducts all legislative functions for the country and its people. It houses the Lok Sabha (lower house or Council of the People) and Rajya Sabha (upper house or Council of the States). The Lok Sabha is the house of representatives elected by the people from the twenty-eight states and eight union territories of India for a term of five years. The Rajya Sabha has members that are indirectly elected to represent all the states and territories of the country.

The parliament and the legislative assemblies in the states serve as one of the basic pillars of democracy. In the chambers of the legislature, laws are enacted after debate and discussion. The assumption was that these debates would be serious and substantive. This unfortunately has sometimes not been the case. Often parliament has been disrupted by unruly behaviour and laws have been passed without the presence of the Opposition during the Emergency. In spite of these lapses, parliament remains the most important forum for discussion and debate. The challenge before parliament and the state level legislative bodies has been, since their inception, to overcome and re-enact some of the laws that the colonial state created and implemented. The importance of parliament is indicated by the fact that even during the Emergency, when every democratic institution fell under the hammer of Indira Gandhi, she never formally shut down parliament.

The government then pursued the policy of reforming the Indian army by ensuring the higher ranks were manned by Indians thereby making the army more representative of the Indian people. The second problem was to make the armed forces subordinate to the civil–administrative apparatus—the army would be loyal to the Indian republic, not to any political party and least of all to any individual. This was to serve as the backbone of the Indian forces and it is to the credit of the Indian armed forces that it has remained steadfastly loyal to the republic. It is true that the Indian armed forces, fortunately, have not faced a prolonged war but they have always made India proud whenever they have been called upon to defend India's borders and security. They have performed their role with extraordinary courage at times against severe odds.

The third institution that the new republic inherited was the education system that the British Raj had created to serve the needs of the empire. The three universities of Calcutta, Bombay, and Madras created in 1857 were at the heart of the system. These universities were entirely state-funded while school education was by and large left to private or Christian missionary initiatives. The government of India sadly neglected primary education which continues to languish. State-funded or public universities mushroomed and, till very recently, private universities were not allowed to be established. But as noted in the next paragraph a new dimension was added to the realm of education by the setting up of institutes that would produce scientists, engineers, and managers. Education, especially primary education, does not receive the attention and resources it deserves. This is perhaps one of the more important problems and liabilities of independent India. Education is yet to be an integral part of India's growth story.

As the prime minister of a country in which the incidence of illiteracy was high and the penetration of education shallow, Nehru thought that the state should be an active player in the society and the economy. He initiated, despite hostility and controversy, reforms to change some aspects of traditional Hindu society. It was in the economic sphere that Nehru made the state a key actor: introducing

The Supreme Court of India, New Delhi

This building in the Lutyens style of central Delhi, with its play of red and yellow stone, colonnades, and domes was opened in 1958. It serves as the apex court of the republic. Each state of the Indian republic has its own high and lower courts. It goes without saying that it is the responsibility of the Supreme Court to uphold the laws of the land and the Constitution without being influenced by any kind of pressure. The Supreme Court thus serves as the conscience keeper of the republic and has been the site for many major legal battles and debates regarding the protection of the environment, freedom of expression, the rights of women, minorities, and LGBT communities, the right to property, and other fundamental human rights. These battles and debates have produced many landmark judgments. The functioning of the Supreme Court is by definition a work in progress. This progress is often slowed down by the backlog of cases and also by meaningless and trivial matters that are brought before the court and are often heard.

planning where the state became the principal allocator of economic resources; the state became owner of important manufacturing units to control the commanding heights of the economy; and the state was also in charge of all major projects relating to the building of infrastructure. Nehru was conscious that India's path to economic self-sufficiency and modernity would not be viable without Indian scientists, engineers, and managers. To this end, he made the state invest in building institutes of technology and management modelled on international norms and standards.

The death of Nehru in May 1964 saw his close colleague Lal Bahadur Shastri become prime minister. His tenure was brief because of his untimely death but it was marked by India's victory in a short war with Pakistan in 1965. He was followed by Indira Gandhi as prime minister. She came to power in a very difficult situation with acute food shortages, spiralling inflation, and growing unemployment. There was also the grim reality that in many parts of India the popularity of the Congress was plummeting, and this was reflected in the election results of 1966–67. Indira Gandhi had to secure her position within the Congress and to impose her own control as prime minister. She proceeded to do this through a series of measures. Her rise to the prime ministership had been sponsored by a group of powerful regional governors who had thought that she would be their puppet. They could not have been more wrong. She politically eliminated each one of them and began the process of personalizing all decision-making. She was aided in this by P. N. Haksar, her principal secretary and till 1975 her key adviser. Neither Indira Gandhi nor Haksar had any qualms about undermining democratic institutions (the judiciary, the executive), manipulating the institutions of civil society (the media, educational institutions), and fostering nepotism. It was not only the political institutions that were the victims of this drive but also the Congress party was made to work at the bidding of the prime minister and her handpicked supporters like Haksar. Indira Gandhi encouraged the culture of flattery, hero-worship, and bhakti—these were stepping stones, as Ambedkar had said, prophetically in his closing speech to the Constituent Assembly, to a 'road to degradation and to eventual dictatorship'. The manifestation of this dictatorship was the declaration of the Emergency at the end of June 1975 of which more later.

While Indira Gandhi's popularity was on a spectacular high,

objective conditions in India were changing rapidly. Food prices were rising, there were severe shortages, unemployment was growing, and there were growing criticisms of the corruption of Congress leaders. These became the focus of what is known as the JP movement—named after Jayaprakash Narayan—which grew out of popular protests against Indira Gandhi and the Congress first in Gujarat and then in Bihar. In Bihar—JP's home state—which was backward and poor, students and youth took to the streets against inflation, growing unemployment, corruption, and a repressive state administration. JP emerged from his self-imposed political retirement to lead the movement. The movement, comprising various discontented sections of society, moved from strength to strength during 1973–74: it formed Janata sarkars that took over power grids, ration shops, collected funds, created local bureaucracies, courts, and even armies. It appealed to the citizens to withhold taxes and resign from public sector jobs. JP aimed at what he termed a 'total revolution'. The movement withstood severe state repression. The JP movement enjoyed an almost natural synergy with the Rashtriya Swayamsevak Sangh (RSS) and the Sangh Parivar (family of Hindu right-wing organizations). It grew out of a deep socio-economic crisis that Indira Gandhi had failed to resolve. Its popularity was based on the Congress's alienation from four sections of society—the smaller gentry, students, farmers, and the working class. The threat of being unseated became real for the prime minister with the judgment of the Allahabad High Court on 12 June 1974 which debarred her from contesting elections for six years. Indira Gandhi retaliated by imposing an internal emergency over and above the external emergency that was already in place since 1971. By the imposition of the Emergency in June 1975, democracy was suspended in India. It was independent India's first encounter with dictatorship.

There is a tendency, especially within the Congress party, to underestimate the immediate impact of the Emergency. The numbers are actually staggering: 11 million Indians were forcibly sterilized and 110,000 locked up. In Delhi alone, of the city's 5 million citizens, 700,000 were displaced and 161,000 sterilized; 20 per cent of Opposition MPs were imprisoned and the rest silenced; and the media was put under strict censorship which did not allow it to report dissenting speeches. Congress parliamentarians of the Lower House, kowtowing to the prime minister, passed law after law sanctioning and widening the scope of emergency powers. Judicial independence was similarly compromised. Through these steps and measures aptly termed 'institutional violence' by scholars, the Emergency ripped apart the fabric of Indian democracy. The impact of the Emergency was, however, not uniform across India. The focus of the tyranny was Delhi: it was from there that power radiated, affecting first Haryana and then Uttar Pradesh. From these areas the tyranny spread into other parts of North India. The great divide in the impact was between the North and the South. Beyond the Vindhyas, the tyranny lost much of its voltage. Also, in states that were not run by Congress ministries, the authority of Indira Gandhi faced 'considerable resistance'.

The Emergency lasted for eighteen months. No one has quite been able to explain why in 1977 Indira Gandhi withdrew the Emergency and decided to call an election, which she lost. Perhaps she did not imagine that the people of India would reject her. Her first two terms as prime minister were followed by the Janata government, a coalition of parties who had opposed Indira Gandhi and the Emergency. The Janata government collapsed under the weight of its own contradictions and Indira Gandhi returned to power in 1980. This second phase of Indira Gandhi's prime ministership was marked by three interrelated violent episodes. First was the rise of a very militant Sikh insurgency demanding a separate Sikh state called Khalistan. This movement made the Golden Temple in Amritsar its headquarters. To suppress the movement, the Indian Army was deployed and, in a massive operation in June 1984, the Golden Temple complex was bombarded and nearly destroyed. To avenge this attack, the Sikh bodyguards of Indira Gandhi assassinated her on 31 October 1984. This train of violence did not end with the death of Indira Gandhi. In the aftermath of her murder, a pogrom was unleashed against the Sikhs in Delhi and its surrounding areas. Many important Congress leaders were involved in this pogrom.

Indira Gandhi was succeeded by her eldest son, Rajiv Gandhi, who was murdered by Tamil militants in 1991. This was a critical point for India as the Congress only had a slender majority in parliament but was leaderless; more importantly the country was bankrupt. In June 1991, India's foreign exchange reserves had fallen so low that it could pay for just two weeks of imports. It was also evident that India was at the edge of defaulting on its external debt obligations. The International Monetary Fund (IMF) did not believe that India was in a position to repay any loans it could provide. The IMF thus refused to provide a loan. As a guarantee India pledged its gold reserves which were lodged in the vaults of the Bank of England. This decision was taken by the new prime minister, P. V. Narasimha Rao, whose government did not command a full majority in the Lok Sabha. The first problem that faced Rao was the economy.

Rao appointed as his finance minister Manmohan Singh, a well-known economist who had held every single important economic post in the government and had worked in global financial institutions. The Rao–Singh duo undertook a series of bold and pathbreaking economic reforms. The first step in these reforms was the devaluation of the rupee; next was the dismantling of the state's control on the economy. These were the first momentous steps towards liberalizing the economy. A looming crisis had led to the reforms which changed the face and the future of the Indian economy. By the middle of 1992, foreign exchange reserves were inching towards normalcy, the stock market was booming, and the signs of rapid economic growth were also evident.

The demolition of the Babri Masjid, December 1992, Ayodhya, Uttar Pradesh

If rescuing the economy was a golden moment when Rao held the top job, another episode was like a black blotch. This was the demolition of the Babri Masjid on 6 December 1992. The Babri Masjid had been built in 1528 in Ayodhya by a courtier of the first Mughal emperor, Babur. There was a belief, dating back to the late nineteenth century, that the mosque had been built on the remains of a Hindu temple. Organizations who upheld Hindutva—an ideology that believes that India is a land that belongs only to the Hindus and that all Muslims are outsiders and should therefore live in India on terms set by the Hindu majority—had claimed that the Babri Masjid symbolized the humiliation of the Hindus and should be demolished. On 6 December 1992, this demolition was carried out in the presence of certain prominent Hindutva leaders. Rao, as prime minister, was fully aware that thousands of Hindutva volunteers had come to Ayodhya but he took no steps to prevent the demolition.

CHALLENGES AHEAD FOR CONTEMPORARY INDIA

India's wealth of languages, cultures, and people
The loss of language results in the loss of cultural identity and an understanding of the community's heritage. India is a multilingual nation and had over 19,500 languages and dialects till the twenty-first century. The richness and wealth of this linguistic and literary heritage was not appreciated in the early years of Independence.

The Constitution of India suggested that Hindi was the official national language, however, this was unacceptable to the majority of non-Hindi speakers. The division of the country into states based on language proved to be a disaster. From the 1950s riots, strikes, and violent expressions of frustration on the streets of India continue to express a collective passion to preserve unique cultural and regional identities.

The New Educational Policy, 2020, adopted a three-language formula to enable students to learn their mother tongue in the primary stages and in later years to learn two 'link' languages—Hindi and English. The language policy today recognizes only twenty-two official languages. These policies have resulted in the gradual erosion of a myriad languages, dialects, and cultures of India.

Ingenuity and hard work of the unorganized sector sustain cities
Every sixth person in the world is an Indian. The population of India was 361.1 million in 1951 and rose to 1.36 billion by 2021. The rising literacy rates amongst girls had a profound effect on lowering the fertility rate. Yet, after seventy-eight years of Independence, every fifth person is still economically disadvantaged.

Poor people with little education are forced to migrate within the country to work for meagre daily wages.

For labourers (in construction and similar occupations) neighbouring countries like the UAE offer attractive but insecure employment while privileged, educated Indians migrate to other countries for monetary advantage. The urban poor are mainly employed in the unorganized sector. Nearly 15 per cent of the entire work force earns less than ₹5,000 per month. During the Covid-19 pandemic, the harsh lockdown measures imposed by the central government resulted in 60 per cent of the migrant population fleeing cities to return to their villages. By 2050 more than 50 per cent of India's population will have moved to cities, mainly in the unorganized sector, without any social security and protection in times of crisis.

Mounting urban waste

Fallout of rapid industrial growth and unplanned development

India's economic progress is evident. One significant indicator is that 1.2 billion mobile phone subscribers were recorded in 2021. A large percentage of mobile users are from rural areas, and are projected to rise. With progress and growth over the last seventy-eight years, India now faces the enormous task of mitigating the harmful effects of uncontrolled, unregulated development and a magnitude of waste.

At COP26 India committed to 'phase down' its dependence on coal and fossil fuel by 2050, though it continues to build new coal-fired power stations. As a result, rising temperatures are causing glaciers to melt, 30 per cent of India's geographical area is degraded, and there has been significant decline in the productivity of land and forests. The 7,500-kilometre coast that frames the subcontinent, where millions of people live, is threatened by rising seawater.

Since Independence the focus on rapid industrialization and urbanization, the clearing of forests, and extensive use of chemical fertilizers has led to the severe loss of biodiversity—rare wildlife and plant species—fertility of the soil, air quality, and natural water resources. This is already having an evident impact on the economy, the climate, and India's ability to feed its people.

Growth and the way forward

The first underground rapid transport system was developed in Kolkata in 1984, and other cities followed suit. This system enables the daily movement of millions of people from underdeveloped suburbs. Despite these advances there is enormous social and economic disparity.

In 2023, India overtook China to become the country with the largest population in the world. This is creating still more challenges. To echo the Indian Constitution and policies of the past—to secure a democratic, culturally diverse, equitable, and sustainable future several issues have to be addressed: elimination of poverty, universal education and health care, caste inequalities, divisions based on religion and language, gender-based violence, threats to minority communities and dissenters, degradation of land and water resources, and production of green energy and practices.

Delhi Metro station

These critical matters have not been adequately resolved in the last seventy-eight years. If they are not addressed, they will pose a threat to India's democracy, economic growth, and sovereignty and this will in turn impact its people and their aspirations for a better tomorrow.

The years following Rao saw Atal Bihari Vajpayee of the Bharatiya Janata Party as the prime minister, and the return of the Congress with Manmohan Singh as the prime minister. The defeat of the Congress in 2014 was a turning point in the politics of independent India. Narendra Modi, a highly successful chief minister of Gujarat and a loyal worker of the BJP, emerged as the leader of the party and became the prime minister. Modi's massive victory in the elections in 2014, for a second term in 2019, and again for a third term in 2024 was based on promises of hope to the people of India, especially the young. The promise was that of clean and open government, of the creation of jobs, of a favourable ambience for investment and, most importantly, of making India into a strong and powerful nation. He enjoys, in spite of the calamity of the Covid-19 pandemic, a popularity that can only be compared to what Indira Gandhi enjoyed in the heady days of 1971.

While Narendra Modi has not yet delivered on all his promises, especially in the sphere of the economy, it cannot be denied that among large sections of the population, he has brought in a new confidence and buoyancy. Without denying any of this, it should be noted that under Modi there is a pronounced intolerance towards minorities and dissent, and this majoritarian turn is serving to divide society along communal lines. All these suggest that deep and fundamental currents of change are pulling India towards a new tryst with destiny in which, one hopes, all Indians, irrespective of their caste and creed, will be involved.

Acknowledgements

Non-implicatory thanks are due to Pradip Krishen, Shireen Jejeebhoy, Mahesh Rangarajan, and Zainab Wani for valuable comments and suggestions. At Aleph, Aienla Ozukum and Bena Sareen worked to edit and design the manuscript. No words are enough to express our gratitude.

We are indebted to the following photographers, museums, and organizations for allowing us to use their spectacular pictures. Any error in attribution or omission is deeply regretted and will be amended in future reprints of the book.

Archaeological Survey of India: pp. 23, 24 top and bottom, 40, 41 top and bottom, 42, 77, 99, 108.

Alamy: p. 284.

Indira Gandhi National Centre for the Arts: pp. 48.

Mehrangarh Museum Trust, Jodhpur (Neil Greentree): p. 162.

iStock: (Mrinal Pal) p. 277; (TkKurikawa) p. 279.

National Museum, New Delhi: pp. 38 top and bottom, 83, 90 top and bottom, 112, 144, 153.

The Prime Ministers Museum and Library: pp. 222, 223, 236, 244, 249, 252 (Acquired by Sh. J. S. Nahal), 254, 265, 270, 267, 268, 271.

Parzor Foundation: p. 106.

Raoul Amaar Abbas: p. 160.

Sabarmati Ashram Preservation and Memorial Trust, Ahmedabad: pp. 232, 240, 248, 250, 272.

Uma Bhattacharya: maps on pp. 1, 26, 32, 50, 64, 78, 88, 101, 114, 129, 143, 164, 175, 187, 198, 208, 218, 263.

Wikimedia Commons: pp. 219, 225, 237.

All other photographs are by Toby Sinclair.

Index

Abdali, Ahmad Shah, 168, 183
ahimsa, principle of, 71, 275
Ahom dynasty, 197, 199, 200, 201, 203
Aibak, Qutb-ud-din, 115, 116
Ajanta Caves, 93, 95
Akbar, Emperor, 146–150, 154
Alberuni, 192-194,
Alexander of Macedon, 65
algebra, mathematical system of, 189
Ali, Haider, 169, 171, 180, 181, 182
'Amar Sonar Bangla' (My Golden Bengal) national anthem (Bangladesh), 235
amazonite, 29
Ambedkar, B. R., **255,** 256, 257, 258, 280,
ammonite fossil, 7,
Arab astronomers and mathematicians, 98
Archaeological Survey of India (ASI), 23, 32, 39, 66, 73
Arthashastra (Kautilya/Chanakya), 66
Aryabhata, 97, 98, 189
Aryans, 43, 45-46
Ashoka, 57, 65-77
Ashokan Lion Capital, 75
Ashoka's inscriptions and edicts:
Asiatic Society, Mumbai, 209
astronomy, advances in, 97
Auliya, Nizam al-din, 136
Aurangzeb, 155-158, 163, 167-168, 172

Babri Masjid, Ayodhya, 284,
Babur (Zahir-ud-din Muhammad):
Battle of Baksar (1764), 180
Battle of Chausa (1539), 145
Battle of Kohima War Cemetery, Kohima, 204
Battle of Plassey (1757), 185
Bengal, partition of, 238
Bentinck, William, 213, 220
Bharatiya Janata Party (BJP), 288
Bhimbetka Caves, Madhya Pradesh, 17, 18

Bodhi Tree, Bodh Gaya, Bihar:
Bodhisattvas, 95
Bombay, 209, 212, 216, 217, 230, 231, 232, 238, 251, 256, 261, 265, 266, 267, 269, 278
Bose, Subhas Chandra, 255, 257
Brahmanical Hinduism, 256
British conquest of India, 173
British rule, in India: divide and rule, 228, 233, 276
Buddha, 48, 53, 54, 55, 57, 58, 59, 60, 61, 62, 63, 72, 76, 77, 82, 85, 95, 99, 189, 192
Buddhism 10, 53, 54, 62, 70, 71, 72, 73, 81, 82, 99, 194
Buddhist monasteries 66, 85, 97
Burmese invasion (1817–24) of Manipur, Assam, and the Cachar plains, 202

caste system, 52, 112, 159
Chandragupta, 65, 66, 69, 89
Chauhan, Prithviraj, 115, 116
Chauri Chaura incident, 247
Chittagong revolutionaries, 253
Chola dynasty, 109
Chola, Rajendra (Chola king), 109
Christian missionaries, 278
Civil Disobedience Movement, 248, 249, 253, 254
Clive, Robert, 178
communal divide, 264
Constituent Assembly, 269, 271, 280
Constitution of India, 257, 277, 285
Covid-19 pandemic, 286, 289
Cunningham, Alexander, 66

decimal system, 98, 189
decolonization, process of, 262
Delhi Sultanate, 113
Dravidian languages, 67
Dutch trade, in India, 176

Dyer, Reginald 244, 246
Eastern Ghats, 10
elections in India, 274

Emergency, declaration of (1975), 280, 281
English East India Company (EIC), 166, 171, 177, 178, 179, 181, 184, 185, 207, 209, 230

Farrukhsiyar (Mughal emperor), 177
Faxian, 57, 194
fire, discovery of, 15
First Indians, 232, 257
French, entry into Indian trade: Compagnie Française des Indes Orientales, 176
fundamental rights, debates regarding, 279

Gandhi, Indira, 277, 280, 281, 282, 283, 289, 291
Gandhi, Mohandas Karamchand, 238-243, 246-257, 260, 270, 272
Gandhi–Irwin Pact (1931), 248
Ganga River, 105, 109
Ghalib, Mirza, 193
Gupta empire: Chandragupta, 65
Guru Amardas, 251
Guru Gobind Singh, 172, 243
Guru Granth Sahib, 251, 252
Guru Nanak Dev, 121

Harappan Culture, 8, 25-42, 186; *see also* Indus Valley Civilization
Harshavardhana, King (Harsha), 92, 104
Himalaya, 6-10, 12, 163,
Hind Swaraj, 238, 239, 240
Hindu–Muslim unity, 227-228, 248, 258
Homo erectus, 14, 15
Homo sapiens, 14
human development, stages of, 15
Humayun, 142, 145-147, 149, 150, 152, 154, 160, 169
Huns (Hunas), 91-92

Iltutmish, Sultan, 116-118, 128
Indian mathematicians and astronomers, 98
Indian Muslim League, 257
Indian National Army (INA), 255, 257, 264, 265, 266

Indian National Congress (INC), 232, 238, 257
Indian national movement, 247, 252, 257
Indian nationalism, 229, 238, 257
Indo-Pakistan War of 1965, 280
Islam, 10, 53, 113, 117, 120, 121, 123, 138, 158-162, 192

Jahan, Nur (Mehr un-Nisa), 154, 155
Jahangir, Emperor, 151, 154,
Jainism, 53, 62, 73, 98, 99
Jallianwala Bagh massacre (1919), 244-246
jati (caste) system: differences with varna system, 52

Khalistan, 282
Khalji, Ala-ud-din, 115, 118
Khilafat movement, 247
Khusrau, Amir, 193
King George V, 237, 238
Koh-i-noor diamond, 140
Lothal, Gujarat, 31, 186
Lutyens, Edwin, 237, 277

Magadha, 49, 51, 65, 79, 80, 89, 92
Mahavira, Lord, 49, 53-55,
Marathas: Anglo-Maratha War
Mauryan empire
mlechchha, 91, 94, 120,
Modi, Narendra, 288, 289
Mohenjo-daro, Pakistan, 25, 28, 38
Mount Everest, 6
Mughal empire: **emperors of**, 143, 150, 154, 156, 163, 164, 172, 173

Naoroji, Dadabhai, 231
Nehru, Jawaharlal, 255, 264, 265, 270, 271, 273, 276, 278-280,
Nizam of Hyderabad, 167, 267
non-Gandhian nationalism, 252

Pakistan, formation of, 269
Pala dynasty, 128
Pali language, 53
Pallavas of Kanchipuram, 102
Panchatantra, 98
Pangaea, 1, 3
Panipat, Battle of:

partition of India, 273
Patel, Vallabhbhai, 266, 270

Rajya Sabha, 277
rakhi, practice of, 235
Rakhigarhi, exploration of, 39-41
Ramanuja, 162
Revolt of 1857, 220, 229
Rig Veda, 43, 44, 48
Rowlatt Act, 240, 241
Roy, Rammohun, 217, 219-220

Savarkar, V. D., 375
Shah II, Bahadur, 222, 223
Shah Jahan, Emperor, 151, 152, 153, 156-158, 160
Shah, Muhammad, 169
Shah, Nadir, 172, 173
Shastri, Lal Bahadur, 280
Shivaji (Maratha leader), 167
Shukoh, Dara, 147, 153, 155, 156, 158-159
Sikh Gurus, 121
Silk route, 9
Singh, Guru Gobind, 172, 243
Singh, Manmohan, 283, 288
Singh, Ranjit, 184
Sino-India War (1962), 411
Siraj-ud-daulah (nawab of Awadh), 165, 178, 179
Sultan, Tipu, 169, 170, 171, 180-182, 214,

Tagore, Rabindranath, 235, 236, 245
Taj Mahal, Agra, 4, 147, 150, 152, 157
Taxila, 49, 65, 66, 69, 70, 84
Tethys Sea, 5, 7
Thar Desert, 3, 9
Tibetan Plateau, 6, 12,
Tilak, Bal Gangadhar, 348
Timur: as founder of the Timurid empire, 142
Tughluq, Muhammad bin, Sultan, 118-119, 123, 128, 130

Upanishads, 44, 48, 188

Vajpayee, Atal Bihari, 288
varna system, 51-52, 60, 86

World War II: opposition to British rule through violent means during, 255

www.ingramcontent.com/pod-product-compliance
Lightning Source LLC
Chambersburg PA
CBHW031421150426
43191CB00006B/347